The Czech and Slovak
Legion in Siberia,
1917–1922

The Czech and Slovak Legion in Siberia, 1917–1922

JOAN MCGUIRE MOHR

McFarland & Company, Inc., Publishers
Jefferson, North Carolina, and London

LIBRARY OF CONGRESS CATALOGUING-IN-PUBLICATION DATA

Mohr, Joan McGuire, 1949–
    The Czech and Slovak Legion in Siberia, 1917–1922 /
Joan McGuire Mohr.
        p.   cm.
    Includes bibliographical references and index.

    ISBN 978-0-7864-6571-2
    softcover : acid free paper ∞

    1. Legie ruská.   2. Siberia (Russia)— History — Revolution,
1917–1921— Participation, Czech.   3. Siberia (Russia)— History —
Revolution, 1917–1921— Participation, Slovak.   4. Soviet Union —
History — Allied intervention, 1918–1920.   5. Czechs — Russia
(Federation)— Siberia.   6. Slovaks — Russia (Federation)— Siberia.
7. World War, 1914–1918 — Czechoslovkia.   8. World War, 1914–
1918 — Russia — Prisoners and prisons.   9. Prisoners of war —
Czechoslovakia.   10. Prisoners of war — Russia (Federation)—
Siberia.   I. Title.

DK265.9.F52C834 2012
947.084'1— dc23   2012003913

BRITISH LIBRARY CATALOGUING DATA ARE AVAILABLE

Front cover: Legionnaires in Kirgis dress guarding locomotives in
40-degrees-below-zero weather; cover design by David K. Landis
(Shake It Loose Graphics)

Manufactured in the United States of America

McFarland & Company, Inc., Publishers
    Box 611, Jefferson, North Carolina 28640
    www.mcfarlandpub.com

Table of Contents

When we were just little kids, my father used to grab onto us, try to get us to listen to him in that thick accent of his. But we were all ashamed, just kids trying to be real Americans, so we ran away. And he finally quit trying. Later, when he was an old man, I would see him sitting there quietly remembering. We never knew what it was that happened to him out there. He never said and I never asked. Now all these years later, I wonder. I really wonder. — Stephanie Majaers, 1999

Acknowledgments

This work would not have been realized without the support and encouragement of many individuals. Over the past two and a half decades of research on this subject, I have received an incredible amount of guidance from far too many sources the world over to give justice here. For those whom I do not explicitly acknowledge, my apologies and my gratitude; I could never have accomplished this research without all of your help.

This work began with the generosity of the Czech-American and Slovak-American communities of Cedar Rapids, Chicago, Pittsburgh, New York, Washington, D.C., San Diego, San Francisco, St. Paul and Minneapolis, to name but a few. I especially thank the families of Bohemia Hill and Spring Garden in Pittsburgh, Pennsylvania, and members of the Czech and Slovak Cottage in Balboa Park, San Diego, California — many who are no longer with us, for opening up their family histories to a total stranger. They generously allowed me to share in their recollections and questions concerning relatives who suffered as legionnaires. In particular Mary Andrejka, Stephanie Sjolem Majaer, Joseph Mesterhausen, and Bill and Billie Vlastnik all helped to provide a human face for this project.

I wish to express my deepest appreciation for the friendship and advice of scholars and civic leaders in libraries and universities from Vienna to St. Paul, Budapest to New York, Prague to San Francisco, Pilsen to San Diego. Information garnered in archives in Austin, Bratislava, Budapest, Cedar Rapids, Chicago, Lincoln, Minneapolis, New York, Paris, Prague, San Diego, San Francisco, St. Paul, Vienna, and Washington, D.C., all added to the story told here.

Thanks also to David Muhlena and Carmen Langel of the National Czech and Slovak Museum and Library; Dr. Carol Hochman, Joseph Bielecki, and Dr. Martin Votruba of the University of Pittsburgh. Acknowledgments to the staff of the Immigration History Research Center in Minneapolis, Minnesota, and to Paní Zuzana Pivcová of the Military History Institute in Prague for expert advice and encouragement.

Legion records were uncovered over 25 years of investigative work, sifting through dust and cobwebs in basements, and in the bowels of archives both abroad and in the United States. The journey I made brought me into contact with many people, and each one contributed in a substantial way toward the end result. What eventually became revealed would prove worth every moment of my discomfort and emotional strain through the last days of the Soviet era and on into the present. In the end each contribution helped to build a clearer story of what the Legion went through as it struggled across western Russia and Siberia with the only goal of trying to reach home.

During the writing phase of this book, I garnered collegial support, encouragement, and feedback from many friends. In particular deep appreciation goes to Karen Belgard, Robert Fanella, Michael Kravcar, Dr. Bernadette Harris Lambert, Tim Lambert, and Robert Sweetland, who each provided invaluable encouragement and feedback. Thank you to Michael Bagstad for his expert knowledge concerning the preparation of photographs and to Rodney Lee Volkmar for graphic design. I am especially grateful to David Berg for his remarkable creative and editorial expertise and Ashley Cooper, who both painstakingly read and reread this manuscript and provided expert stylistic advice for the final product. Thank you as well to Steven Potach who offered legal suggestions and to Mrs. Sophia Pischtek for her help with linguistic and technical matters.

Finally I would like to convey my deepest love and regards to my sons, Matthew and Benjamin, and to Jeffery P. Mohr for their sense of humor, love and perseverance — a special thank you to Matt for all the hours of sharing ideas. To each and every person mentioned here and to all the others, especially the soldiers of the Czech and Slovak Legion and their families, I dedicate this work.

Preface

There was nothing special looking about the man, only that he was wearing a peculiar uniform and that his face appeared terribly weathered. He squinted while staring vacantly into the camera lens with a smile playing on his lips. The rim of his rumpled cap covering his hair cast a shadow onto his forehead. He looked tired. It took a couple of seconds to note the little puppy held in one arm. I lifted the photograph from the small box and stuffed it into my book bag. After class, I asked Professor Gilbert if I could borrow it for a while.

Funny how one steps through a doorway, or into a stairwell, or sits in a certain seat next to a certain stranger and life is changed forever in an instant. When I first became interested in a history degree, it was to follow the trail of Nazism in Germany. I could never fathom how a nation that gave us Beethoven could become enraptured with the Brownshirts. As my studies in German history developed, my interest was pulled eastward into Russia, and if one develops an interest in the Germans and the Russians, it's not long before central Europe beckons. It was through the homeland of the central European peoples that so many others marched, century after century, arriving from both east and west. I began to wonder about the character of these people — to marvel at their resiliency. How did the Slavs withstand wave after wave of conquering armies and still remain true to their heritage? In the end, my interest in the Germans and the Russians merged into a focus on the peoples in between.

Dr. Gilbert was teaching a course in Russian history when he brought in a cache of historical items he had collected over the years — bits of writing, photographs, and artifacts that he had never been able to identify. The box passed around the room and I dove in to sift through its contents like everyone else. When I pulled out the glossy photo of the odd-looking soldier with the puppy over his arm, I was overwhelmed with emotion.

I took the photograph with me to the San Diego Historical Society photo archive that weekend, where I placed it on the counter in the photographic collections department. The curator, Mr. Larry Booth, glanced down at it,

Legionnaire with puppy, San Diego Harbor, July 4, 1919 (credit San Diego Historical Society).

saying, "We have ten others sitting on a filing cabinet in the corner collecting dust and cobwebs." He disappeared through a doorway only to return a moment later. Mr. Booth placed two neat rows of photographs in front of me along the counter and there in the middle was the same image of the soldier with the dog tucked over his arm.

The only thing Larry Booth could tell me for sure was that the photos had been taken by someone who knew the camera well. They were mostly group shots of columns of tired-looking soldiers in the same odd-looking uniforms. Several photos included views of San Diego Harbor. In one, a little man in a pin-striped suit stood on a box with people gathered in a tight circle around him. They looked like a group of dignitaries: next to them stood rows of soldiers at attention. Neither of us recognized the uniforms they wore. Another photograph revealed the side of a ship with the name *Nanking* clearly visible. Soldiers walked down the gangway, some obviously wounded, and carried bundles over their shoulders while overhead on deck sailors leaned over the railing to watch. Of special interest were the women crowded around the harbor wearing long dresses topped off with wide-brimmed hats. Many of the dresses were light in color and I knew that this was our next clue. It must have been summertime. The plethora of American flags flying from street lights and poles might have meant the Fourth of July. Alongside the

American flags were odd tricolored flags, not as many but still a good number.

Larry Booth and I decided that it might be World War I, and if it was, then perhaps the photo was taken on July the Fourth. So we went to the microfilm machine, shoved in a reel from the *San Diego Union* newspaper from July 1919, a date toward the end of America's involvement in the aftermath of the war, and pushed the button. The microfilm stopped at page 1, July 4, 1919. At the center of the page was a photograph of the *Nanking* docked in San Diego Harbor with a story about visiting troops who had come all the way from Siberia to Camp Kearney. We read the column, then turned the knob to the inside pages. On page 5 different photographs accompanied the text; this time there was the man with the puppy — the same photograph I had retrieved from Professor Gilbert's box of tidbits.

When I returned home after that visit to the San Diego Historical Society, I had the subject for my master's thesis, but somehow it had become so much more than that. I began to call and write Slavic studies departments and libraries at universities around the country. I began to research who these soldiers were only to find little to nothing written about them. For most historians, these troops apparently had never existed.

This was the first in a series of steps that took me on an odyssey around the world, through personal histories and political intrigue. I ended up assisting families in the United States to reconnect with relatives inside the Eastern Bloc. All the while my true intent had been to restore an incident to its rightful place in history. From studying its beginning during the Bolshevik Revolution, I became part of the unfolding story of the demise of the Soviet Union.

Finally, I reached a noted professor who had worked in Prague during the Communist era. He answered my phone call, listened to my questions and informed me that "no housewife from San Diego could ever tackle THAT story." His words stung. So I entered a Ph.D. program and began to travel and to research — began to get the credentials I thought I needed to write about the incident.

In time I began to receive tidbits from families all over the United States who heard I was researching the "Lost Legion." Czech-Americans and Slovak-Americans sent me photos and letters, postcards and paraphernalia from "out there." In every case, a soldier relative had headed to the Eastern Front only to disappear for years. Many never returned. The ones who did often refused to talk about what happened to them. Descendants had no idea where "out there" was or why grampa, granduncle, papa, uncle, father or brother never talked about where he had been during the Great War.

I began to piece together footnotes in other histories of the Eastern Front until I finally found the names of Carl Ackerman and Herman Bernstein, two reporters from New York. Each had traveled with the Legion, sending weekly reports and photographs back to their respective newspapers. The story had made a big splash in the media of the day. It had been called "the miracle of the summer of 1918" and there were even suggestions that the Legion had caused the murder of the tsar and his family in Ekaterinburg, one of the best known and most intriguing stories of the twentieth century.

In October of 1918 the new nation of Czechoslovakia was born. A short time later World War I ended. Thomas Masaryk, the first president of the fledgling nation, wrote his constitution with support and advice from U.S. president Woodrow Wilson. This document was later used as a template by other new countries of Central Europe for their own constitutions. As World War I ended, few references remained of the small contingent of Czech and Slovak soldiers who had passed through my hometown on their way to meet the American president.

I became astounded and then irritated that an army so well known and so widely heralded for its accomplishments during World War I had so quickly disappeared from public view. I found that under the Nazi Regime many of these men had been rounded up and sent to camps. Monuments erected to them by the Masaryk and Beneš governments were later removed by the Gottwald and Novotný administrations after the Communist Party took power in 1948. Later, I was to learn that the Legion had been expunged from history through rewriting efforts by party historians in both Eastern Europe and the Soviet Union. Nonetheless, what about the West? Why had these soldiers so seldom been mentioned in the histories of World War I by American, British, Canadian, French, or Japanese historians? Even their numbers didn't compute. There seemed to have been as many as half a million "out there" to as few as 40,000.

I felt compelled to tell the story that follows. Others had tried and sometimes succeeded, but there was so much more that had not yet been revealed. I became overwhelmed with personal stories as well as government documents gleaned from newly declassified collections. I traveled, interviewed, researched yellowing documents in archival collections, and poked through dusty cellars abroad and at home, making contacts and friends who helped and whose knowledge of the incident changed along with mine. I found a wealth of information and a treasure trove of photographic evidence. I began to talk to groups who would listen.

The first time I lectured to a large group was in a hall filled with wide-eyed Czech- and Slovak-Americans in Chicago. I spoke in the dark with slides showing overhead. As I listened to my own voice, the stillness of the participants made me question myself. Possibly no one cared about this subject. Maybe it was ridiculous to expect Americans to be interested in what happened to these men so long ago and so far away? Perhaps I was just a housewife from San Diego after all. I wondered whether the audience had fallen asleep, but when the lights came up, I saw faces wet with tears. And when Bill Vlastnik stepped forward to tell us of his personal search for "Uncle František," I joined the others by tearing up. It turned out that the room was filled with people like Bill Vlastnik who had been searching for lost legionnaires — people who had promises to keep and answers to find.

A couple of years later I was invited by the National Czech and Slovak Museum and Library in Cedar Rapids, Iowa, to organize an exhibit documenting the plight of the Legion. At a banquet on the night before my lecture, a tall handsome man with silver hair asked me to dance. He was quite the dapper guy. I knew who he was but he had no idea who I was. Later the next day, during my talk, he stood up in the middle of the lecture hall and interrupted me. He asked me about my research. Had I read this document — that history? I replied "yes" to him over and over but he continued to interrupt my lecture. I had asked the attendees to hold their questions until the end. At this pace, I would not be able to finish the presentation. Finally, in front of the entire group of people listening, I asked him if he remembered me? He looked startled. Was I really going to tell these people that he had groped me while dancing the night before?

I asked him if he remembered that I had called him years ago for help and advice only to be told, quote, "No housewife from San Diego could ever handle the story of the Legion." There was a shudder and then quiet across the hall. The elderly man sitting next to the dapper professor tugged at his sleeve and said loudly, "Sit down!" Fate has a funny way of coming full circle.

This story is still unfolding, being studied here and abroad as homeland countries now revisit family histories and legionnaire memoirs. Lectures to scholars who have never heard of this incident continue. After one such talk I presented, a well-known Czech-American educator took me aside to tell me a rumor he had heard. His father had been "out there." Had I been aware that these soldiers had reportedly been rounded up during the Stalinist era and returned to Siberia where they ended their lives in Gulags? The suggestion made my stomach ache.

I am continually stunned, and I still don't have all the answers. Did some of these men finally make it all the way back to Czechoslovakia in their youth only to die as old men right back where this all started? How could any of this be true without traces of arrest and imprisonment left behind? History has always been and always will be the constructing of narrative. What follows was once one of the most important human interest stories of World War I, covered by both the *New York Times* and the *New York Herald* on a weekly basis with photographs and field reports. Through collusion and embarrassment on the part of all countries involved, much of the odyssey of the Czech and Slovak Legion became buried or expunged for purposes of political expedience. When it occurred, however, this incident was of worldwide importance. The story that follows describes what is still considered to be the largest mass migration of human beings in the history of mankind since Hannibal and before Cambodia.

Prologue

After the popping noise, Sophie's gaze paused. Suddenly there was a flush of shock and then composure. Still playing the part, she sat upright and regal. And then Sophie saw the blood spurting from Franz's mouth. Screaming, the Archduchess slumped down in the seat next to her husband. Franz knew he was dying, but never realized his wife had gone before him, a victim of the same assassin.[1] Until the end, thinking that his darling Sophie had only fainted, Franz Ferdinand kept muttering, "It's nothing, it's nothing...."[2]

With the deaths of Franz Ferdinand, heir apparent to the Austrian throne and inspector general of all the Hapsburg armed forces, and his wife Sophie, Countess Chotek von Chotkowa und Wognin, all of the Austro-Hungarian provinces became mobilized.[3] Like many moments in history, this one would remain pure and lucid — frozen forever with the passing of time. Across Europe, published photographs of the Archduke and Archduchess slumped over in their carriage seats startled a viewing public. In a few short months, the polished sabers and cavalry charges of a bygone era had given way to the mud and desperation of trench warfare.

The war that exploded throughout the Continent beckoned the ethnic minorities of Central Europe. By 1914, Bohemia, the land of Sophie's ancestors, was only one of many Hapsburg provinces on the verge of revolt.[4] For three hundred years, the Czechs and their southern cousins, the Slovaks, had cursed the gentry. Instead of fighting for their liberation, however, Bohemians, Moravians, and Slovaks were forced to join other Slavs from across Central Europe to fight on the Eastern Front for the very ruling elite they resented.

Lying across the center of Europe, with a population of more than ten million, the Czech lands encompassed over 30,000 square miles. Rimmed by high mountain peaks and valleys, rich in minerals, thick forests, and fertile black soil, the Czech lands had always been a region well worth conquering.[5] Equidistant from the Baltic, North Sea, and the Adriatic, Bohemia and Moravia contained many of Europe's greatest rivers. The Morava, Elbe, and Danube all flowed through its countryside, and along these currents cut the paths that conquering armies had taken since before the Middle Ages.

The mighty Gauls and Celts first settled the area, but by the fifth and sixth centuries, endless waves of Asiatic warriors invaded from the east along with Germanic tribes from the west. In the tenth century, Prince Václav, the good King Wenceslas of Christmas carol fame, turned his kingdom forever west, tying it to the Christian church of the Holy Roman Empire.[6] As a result, Czech culture melded with the educational efforts of German monks, Italian artisans, and French musicians sent by Rome. The Czech lands later shared in the flowering of the Renaissance, with Prague as their urban center.

In 1526, with the election of Ferdinand Hapsburg as King of Bohemia, all the Christian nations of Central Europe pulled together to force back the Turks along the southern borders.[7] Christianity had been saved, but Czech and Slovak self-determination was sacrificed in the process. For 300 years, the Hapsburg monarchy ruled over the Slavs of Central Europe in the name of the Church of Rome.[8] After the Renaissance came the Reformation and all of Central Europe shared in its upheaval. Catholic turned against Protestant, Protestant against Catholic, and everyone against Jew. Martin Luther so inspired the Czechs and Slovaks that they were the first to revolt against Rome and thus the first sacrificed to the cause. With the Thirty Years War came the fury of a total Austrian victory. Czech language and culture were held in contempt as Vienna demanded that every trace of them be wiped away. The Czechs were now mere vassals in an empire too large for them to fight.

The Czechs in the north and the Slovaks to the south banded together in resentment over the Hapsburg elite who settled into the region for good in 1527, taking large family holdings and dictating policy. Slovakia to the east was colder, less hospitable and ringed in by craggy mountains. In this region, over five million Slovaks nurtured their fiercely held traditions. The Czechs, many of whom were urban and middle-class, had the highest literacy rates in the empire. From their cities, the Czechs, Bohemians and Moravians looked westward toward industrializing Europe.

Bitterness had been building, not just in Bohemia, Moravia, and Slovakia, but all across Central Europe. The assassination of the Hapsburg heir apparent would finally signal the time for revolt.[9] To the conquering gentry, the Czechs and Slovaks cloaked their faces in resignation, yet beneath this mask a belief in tradition and history kept Czech and Slovak culture alive. The desire for freedom gnawed at them from one generation to the next. Laborers in the cities and families on the farms taught their children the cultural heritage of their ancestors. In time, Slavs across Central Europe watched the Austro-Hungarian Empire grow fat and complacent.

The heir to the Austro-Hungarian throne, accompanied by his lovely wife, Sophie, rode to a luncheon engagement with their royal entourage. They would never arrive. Along the route six members of the revolutionary Serbian Black Hand waited for them. Emperor Franz Joseph's closest living relative, a man he disliked intensely, had been targeted for assassination. For decades, Emperor Franz Joseph answered Slavic minority demands first by ignoring them and then with force. Ironically, the emperor and his nephew, the heir to the throne, never got along because they disagreed over the status of the empire's Slavic minorities.

In private, Franz Ferdinand championed minority rights, arguing with his uncle to establish a series of independent provinces under a federated umbrella much like the one existing in the United States. Each region would elect its own leaders, a right the emperor doggedly refused. In a tragic turn of events, the heir to the throne who privately espoused the cause of the empire's minority peoples would be the one targeted for assassination by them.

Franz Ferdinand and Sophie would become instantly famous throughout the world. Their names, little recognized outside of the empire before their deaths, soon elicited emotion, be it fury or sorrow. Through their murders, Sophie and Franz became catalysts for a world war that was likewise a catalyst for yet another — ushering in the most violent century in the history of mankind. This was a relatively new century and a new style of warfare — fought with weapons previously unimaginable on the field of battle. Machinery, not the gallant horse, dictated maneuvers, and the first army to learn this lesson would surely gain the advantage.

Chapter One

Thomas Masaryk, a coachman's son from Hodonín, spent his childhood living on various Austrian-owned estates in southern Moravia.[1] His life should have mirrored that of his father's, except that Thomas was born into a world chaffing under the yoke of a faded aristocracy.

By the late nineteenth century, the Slavic minorities of Central Europe living under Hapsburg rule began to press hard for equal rights. Father Patora, the village priest of Hodonín, persuaded the elder Masaryk to allow his son Thomas to enroll in a grammar school in a neighboring village. The boy's quick mind soon outgrew even this small town and within a few years Thomas was sent farther away to Brno in the heart of Moravia to continue his education.

By 1876 Thomas Masaryk had worked all the way through doctoral programs in both philosophy and the new science of sociology. His insights into both disciplines placed him in the top echelon of internationally known social scientists.[2] Yet everything Professor Masaryk knew had been fostered in the Hapsburg institutions of Austrians and Germans. Though securing a professorship in Vienna had been Masaryk's original intention, when the new Czech University of Prague offered a post as lecturer in philosophy, he accepted. Masaryk had spent years learning only facts the ruling Austrians sanctioned, but in Prague he discovered truths that set his able mind reeling.

Masaryk soon learned that the usual explanations and interpretations he held were no longer sufficient. Instead, he found himself the pupil of students who hungered for information concerning their Czech and Slovak heritage. Masaryk soon joined the Young Czech Party of Prague with several of his colleagues. He then surprised them when he ran for and won the only Reichstag seat ever held by the Young Czech Party. After educating himself in the culture of his ancestors, Masaryk found this small association far too confining. As yet, there was no party available for Czech national interests; consequently, Masaryk established one. He so impressed associates with this ambition that they willingly helped to organize the New Realist Party. Again Masaryk ran for office and again he was elected. This time he gained a seat in Parliament.

11

Dr. Thomas Garrigue Masaryk, first president, Republic of Czechoslovakia, not dated (courtesy Military Historical Archive, Prague).

It seemed to New Realist Party members that under Masaryk's tutelage anything was possible.[3] Members of the New Realist Party demanded substantial changes in the structure of the monarchy — beginning with broader rights and self-government for all minorities.

Though more than 28 million people of the Hapsburg population were considered minorities, authority rested in the hands of the 22 million Austrian, German and Hungarian gentry. Nowhere was this discrepancy in population size versus power more evident than in the Czech lands, where the original Czech aristocracy had been either executed or exiled.[4] After 1620 a majority of the larger estates had been given to German or Austrian nobility. Later, the elite demanded that German become the official government language. Only peasants spoke Czech and even in outlying areas that custom had begun to wane.

Beginning with Czech intellectuals like František Palacký and philologists like Karel Havlíček, Czechs and Slovaks began to restore the national history and language of their people. The Pan-Slav Congress of 1868 also linked itself to Slavic interests by emphasizing the role Russia would play.[5]

Building upon what they had learned, Thomas Masaryk made a name for the New Realist Party through its vision of a newly organized Central Europe that would restore Slavic languages and rights within a federated state.[6] Masaryk began to travel and to lecture; in doing so, he passed along the central tenets of Czech reformers and called for an end to Germanization efforts occurring within the Austro-Hungarian-held provinces. When he was invited to speak in Russia, Masaryk's popularity caught the attention of authorities at home who warned the imperial court in Vienna that this soft-spoken father figure had become a threat to the crown. Masaryk was not alone, however. On the day of the assassination of the heir apparent Franz Ferdinand and his wife Sophie, Masaryk, his family and followers joined a list of provincial leaders under the careful scrutiny of the Austro-Hungarian foreign ministry.

In the summer of 1914, Masaryk turned 66 years old, an age at which most men considered themselves ready for retirement. His career had already been a full one when the war began. Beyond his standing as a world-renowned social scientist, Masaryk's lectures had garnered a vocal following in Czech reform movements blossoming throughout the Hapsburg provinces and inside Russia. Friends admonished Masaryk to stand aside and allow younger men to take the helm. They advised him to settle down with a good book in front of a warm fireplace.

Despite threats to his safety, Masaryk continued to speak out for Slavic rights. Although he might have earned a rest, the assassination that occurred in Sarajevo changed Masaryk's future plans. When war came to Europe, Masaryk's sympathy for the Allies, especially those espousing democratic ideals, led him on a path in direct conflict with the imperial government in Vienna. This was partly due to his national beliefs but also to the influence of his American-born wife.

Charlotte Garrigue met Thomas Masaryk while attending Leipzig University in 1876. The possibility that Germany could defeat the forces of republicanism frightened Charlotte and she offered full support to her husband's revolutionary lecture tours.[7] Masaryk's voice stirred the hearts of Czechs and Slovaks alike, whose determination to free themselves from Hapsburg rule began to surface openly before the war began.

As the westernmost of all the Slavic peoples, the Czechs had no geographic borders with Russia. Instead, they neighbored Germany, Austria, and Poland. Yet, Czechs historically looked to the Russian people for friendship and support; many Slavs believed that Russia longed to see Central Europe freed from Hapsburg control. Even though the tsarist regime in Russia was the very antithesis of Czech and Slovak democratic values, the Pan-Slavic ideal connected many of the Hapsburg minorities to this easternmost neighbor. Internal clashes between Nationalist, Agrarian, and Monarchist parties had never fostered radicalism in the Czech or Slovak lands as they had in Russia. Instead, the political culture of Bohemia, Moravia, and Slovakia developed a steady enthusiasm for multiparty constitutional reform.[8]

At the same time, Milan Rastislav Štefánik had also become an ardent supporter of the New Realist Party. Štefánik, the sixth child of a Slovak Lutheran minister, was born in the village of Košariská in Nitra County, Slovakia, on July 21, 1880. In 1898, according to his father's wishes, Štefánik attended Charles University in Prague to pursue a career in civil engineering. While in the Czech lands he read the student activist newspaper *Hlas* (*Voice*). *Hlas* inflamed Štefánik's anger at the Magyarization policies of the Hungarian half of the Austro-Hungarian Dual Monarchy — policies which adversely affected the Slovak people living under the Hungarians' rule.[9] Štefánik did not yet know how, but he became determined to fight against these repressive laws.

After two years as a student at Charles University, Štefánik changed his major from engineering to astronomy. Even so, upon graduating he found it impossible to secure a position in Slovakia, where the professions were all but impossible to occupy for a Slovak under Hungarian (Magyar) rule. Štefánik moved on to Paris where he accepted unpaid work with famous astronomer J. Janssen at the Meudon Observatory. While at Meudon, Štefánik proved capable enough to join the ranks of world-class astronomers. He was soon traveling to Turkestan, Algeria, Brazil, and many other destinations.

By 1910, Štefánik had settled in Tahiti where he constructed an observa-

Dr. Milan Rastislav Štefánik, first minister of war, Republic of Czechoslovakia, not dated.

tory for the French government.[10] (Rumor has it that much of his time in the Pacific was actually spent spying on German positions throughout the region.) He observed eclipses of the sun and Halley's Comet while in Ecuador, and later constructed a wireless station in competition with five other scientific teams.[11] Later, Štefánik was also accepted into the French Air Corps — one of only six Slovaks to be admitted at the time.

After marrying, he returned to Paris — where his reputation had flowered. The French accepted him as a gentleman explorer and a consummate intellectual whose circle of friends included some of the world's most accomplished politicians and scientists. In the salons of the wealthy and famous, Štefánik met the elite of Europe and began to educate them on the growing discontent of Central European Slavic minorities. It inevitably followed that he introduced these influential men and women to his mentor, Thomas Masaryk. As a result when war threatened in 1914, the name of Thomas Masaryk was fresh in the minds of the French leadership.

By 1915, Štefánik regularly attended salon functions at the Paris apartments of Louise Weiss and Claire Bois de Jouvenel, self-proclaimed "French Slovaks" in his honor. Štefánik continued to speak out for the rights of his Slovakian kin even after he attained naturalized French citizenship.[12]

As a member of the French Air Corps, Štefánik flew MF 54s for the 10th Army in the Artois. Later, he was stationed with the MFS 99 Squadron on the Serbian front.[13] There Štefánik was quoted as saying, "I am carrying out long flights above the enemy lines, they shoot at me from cannon all the time but I have not yet been injured. I will fulfill my duty in order to do honor to the Slovak nation and to prove my sincere love of France...."[14]

Conditions in the early months of the war, both in the army and throughout the homeland, were well known to Thomas Masaryk and his colleagues. In a terrible twist of fate, young Czech and Slovak men found themselves fighting for the aged Austrian emperor Franz Joseph, who had staunchly refused them autonomy over their own land. Early in the war, Franz Joseph's power began to diminish under the influence of an efficient German war machine.

Russian reports paid homage to the Czechs and Slovaks who fought valiantly against their line in Krašnik and Komárnow. Czech and Slovak leaders began to smuggle detailed reports out to the West to expose to the world the repressive acts the Austrian and Hungarian officers were committing against their own troops during the month of August.[15] The following month, German press blamed unruly Czech and Slovak behavior for losses at Lwow that in fact occurred due to panic in the Hungarian line. Czech and Slovak troops' morale slipped drastically as they combated abuse from within and heavy losses at the front.[16]

Another pivotal player in the future of the Czech and Slovak people was Dr. Eduard Beneš, also a student of Thomas Masaryk. During the earliest part of his career, Beneš frequently traveled to the West, and, like Štefánik, maintained close ties to many important intellectuals in both Western Europe and the United States. Once Masaryk came under surveillance by the imperial authorities in Prague, the connections of his pupils became of central importance to his nationalist agenda.

Due to Russia's earlier promises to aid its Slavic brethren to the west, Austrian authorities accused anyone having contacts in Russia of being "Pan-Slav conspirators"—a crime considered tantamount to collaborating with the enemy. As a result known minority party leaders in the Czech lands and Slovakia began to disappear behind imperial prison walls — their voices silenced. Orders were issued that "all pro–Russian propaganda" be punishable by death.[17] Sokol leader Dr. Scheiner, for example, was convicted of treason. Even Dr. Karel Kramář, the first premier, and his close associates, Stránský and Stančík, were implicated in antiimperial efforts.

In this climate of terror, Masaryk decided to flee his homeland for abroad. He intended to meet with Štefánik to begin work to further the rights of the Slavic minorities of the Hapsburg Empire by tying Czech and Slovak aspirations to the outcome of the Allied war effort. Beneš's and Štefánik's crucial Western contacts offered both awareness and essential funding for their cause.[18] Masaryk continued providing speaking tours across Western Europe, advocating a federated system under the auspices of Austria for the Slavic minorities currently living within the Hapsburg Empire. However, none of these revolutionaries imagined what lay ahead.

Masaryk had picked his friends well. The foundations of a new state would one day rely upon the skill of these three men. Not only were Beneš and Štefánik intelligent and well informed, they also proved themselves equally as brave and cunning.[19] Masaryk, Beneš, and Štefánik held

Dr. Eduard Beneš, first minister of foreign affairs, Republic of Czechoslovakia, second president of Czechoslovakia, not dated.

great hopes for a freer people to emerge once again along the banks of the Vltava and Danube rivers. Even so, none could be sure they would survive to ever see their homeland again.[20]

By 1915, Štefánik had become a fellow conspirator with Masaryk and Beneš, dedicating himself to the Czecho-Slovak National Council and the resistance movement. Masaryk was named chairman with Beneš as the Secretary General. Beneš called Štefánik "the first and best diplomat."[21] Working from different offices in the Entente nations (Canada, France, Great Britain, Japan, and later the United States), Štefánik, Beneš and Masaryk, ambassadors of democratic freedoms for all Slavs, negotiated for Czech and Slovak autonomy to become a condition of Allied victory over the Central Powers. Štefánik concentrated his efforts on diplomacy by opening the way for the concept of united states within Austria-Hungary. Later, as the war deepened and German influence over Austria increased, all three men began to argue for an alternative notion to the Hapsburg concept of empire.

In Russia, various ideas concerning the war reflected international political confusion. While Czech and Slovak émigré communities throughout Russia maintained views that the aristocracy was repressive, Pan-Slav sentiments heightened feelings of brotherhood with the Russian people. Much of the information these communities relied upon came to them through the publication *Čechoslovan*, a Czech-language paper published in Kiev. To ensure that they would not be detained by the tsar as wartime enemy aliens when Russia mobilized, émigré communities worked as *Krajanské spolky* (societies of compatriots).

Tsar Nicholas II also attributed the trial confronting his people to the daily struggle between the forces of Pan-Slavism and Germanism. Despite several partial mobilizations issued by Tsar Nicholas since 1912, the war surprised both the Russian court and its people. In the summer of 1914, full-scale world warfare seemed an impossible notion to all of the nations involved.

Grand Duke Nicholas Nikolayevich, commander in chief of the Russian forces, seconded Tsar Nicholas II's promises, and Sergei Sazonov, minister of foreign affairs under the Grand Duke, repeated, "It makes no difference whether the war lasts one year or fifty, their [Germans] psychology is out of tune with civilization and I think it is now realized that they cannot win against world public opinion."[22] These inflammatory statements brought a ray of hope to Slavs everywhere — and a new wave of police brutality in the Hapsburg provinces.

Pronouncements such as these sent a ripple through Prague where Mayor Dr. Grosz reversed his original antiwar stance. By August of 1914, the First, Third, and Fourth armies were already fighting courageously on the Eastern Front against Russia even though sentiment in the Czech and Slovak ranks

Prague children in soup line, not dated.

ran counter to the imperial stance.[23] Prague became yet another center for mounting oppression against many former Czech and Slovak leaders. Even Masaryk's daughter, Alice, languished in prison under a death sentence after charges of conspiracy had been brought against her.

Measures of oppression were undoubtedly felt most strongly within the Hapsburg provinces. From the start, Austro-Hungarian leaders outlawed political meetings. Strangely, one of the few arenas for successful political propaganda proved to be puppetry. Local Austrian administrators failed to realize that this children's art form was actually a literal stage for the propaganda of the Czech and Slovak underground. Puppets encouraged insurrection or explained the political struggle occurring within the provinces to large audiences of adults as well as children.[24]

In the trenches, Czech and Slovak soldiers found themselves fighting against Russia — ironically, the same nation they looked to for salvation. Slav units, deliberately kept smaller than other Austrian and Hungarian regiments, had been placed under the command of German and Austrian career officers. For the most part, Austrians, Germans, and Hungarians, the self proclaimed "master races," believed Slavic troops, the "minority races," to be inferior to themselves.[25]

Over a quarter of a million Czechs, Slovaks, Romanians, Poles and other Hapsburg minorities fought and killed for their Austro-Hungarian and German masters.[26] Trained Slavs were sacrificed by the tens of thousands wearing their hated imperial uniforms. They fought in the heaviest battles under the most precarious of circumstances.

Discontent spread wildly among these troops, especially those in forward positions. Companies of Czechs and Slovaks were said to be drunk and disorderly, and complained of being only minimally equipped. Throughout 1914 and 1915, hostile to their officers, Slavic units sang folk songs while refusing to leave their barracks. News of executions in the imperial army filtered back to families waiting in provincial areas of the homeland.

Throughout 1915, desertions plagued the Hapsburg ranks, especially in the First and Ninth army corps.[27] At every turn, Slavic troops escaped over enemy lines or permitted their own capture. In doing so, thousands of Czech and Slovak recruits risked torture and execution at the hands of their own Austrian and Hungarian officers. Horrified by the number of runaways, Hapsburg officials rounded up minority units for the Italian front, but desertions soon increased there too.[28]

As fighting along the Eastern Front became intolerable, Czech and Slovak regiments hoped for capture or a quick end to the war. Neither came. Execution was immediate for any Slavic soldier in the Hapsburg ranks caught conversing over enemy lines.

With oppressive conditions escalating, the leaders of the Czech and Slovak national movement, who had formerly called for a federal system within the Hapsburg Empire, began to demand separate autonomous nation-states.

Bolsheviks execute Czechs, Slovaks and others who opposed them, summer 1918.

Thomas Masaryk began to champion the belief that any future cooperation with the Hapsburg monarchy would be completely untenable.[29] German influence over the Central Powers, especially over the Austrian emperor, had become suffocating. A different means for securing minority rights would have to be negotiated at war's end. Thomas Masaryk began to look to the Western Allies for answers. First, however, Masaryk and his two cohorts hoped to offer the Allies regiments of Czech and Slovak volunteers to join their effort along the Western Front. Few young Czech and Slovak men lived in the British Isles but thousands had settled within Russia, the United States, and Canada.[30]

Milan Štefánik became a tireless recruiter, pulling together three armies of Czech and Slovak volunteers: one in France, one in Italy, and one in Russia. Masaryk settled in Geneva, where he initiated a series of diplomatic efforts to gain recognition for the establishment of a free Czech and Slovak government.

Though Czech- and Slovak-Americans had been poorly organized when war broke out, lodges and sokols shared information. Throughout 1915, organizations developed which represented a broader liberation-oriented national outlook.[31] First generation immigrants were often well versed in the political situation developing throughout their homelands. Their sons, who were volunteering for service in higher percentages than any other ethnic group in the United States, demonstrated the same interest as their parents. As a result, Masaryk looked to the United States for large numbers of Czech- and Slovak-American volunteers.[32]

Campaigns to induct Czechs and Slovaks living abroad produced buttons, pins, flags, posters, and badges — all calling for volunteers to serve the homeland by fighting for the Allies and against the Hapsburg Empire. This effort resulted in over 140,000 men of Czech and Slovak heritage volunteering for combat years before the United States entered the war. Some 41,000 alone were of Slovak background.[33]

In Pittsburgh, Pennsylvania, recruits moved to transport areas each Wednesday en route to a training camp in Stamford, Connecticut. They were then dispatched from neutral America to enlist in French, Belgian, and Italian units fighting the Hapsburgs on the Western Front. Often these troops contributed most of their daily 15 cent salary to the liberation movement.[34]

French children came to welcome new arrivals by yelling out the familiar Czech greeting *Nazdar*, "welcome." French president Poincare was so impressed by volunteers arriving from the Slavic organizations overseas that he appointed General Maurice Janin the head of these Czecho-Slovak units.

Czech and Slovak immigrant communities throughout the United States and Canada started raising funds and awareness for Masaryk's call to establish a government in exile. These communities exposed the international public to the brutal conditions occurring within their homeland.[35] Contributions at town meetings across the United States and Canada made their way to fund Masaryk's effort.[36] Shipments of medical supplies and financial assistance were prepared by organizations such as Klub Slavia in Pittsburgh, the Red Cross, and the District of Columbia Relief agencies. Supplies sent each week aided the efforts of General Maurice Janin and his volunteer troops.

In October of 1915 an important conference held in Cleveland, Ohio, cemented the relationship between Czechs and Slovaks by defining common goals of the Slavic minorities in the Austro-Hungarian Empire. As a result, the National Czech Alliance, founded in September 1915, settled into offices in Chicago. Catholic Czechs, however, shunned this organization, thinking that it would be led by anticlerical free-thinkers.[37] The Catholics instead formed the National Alliance of Catholic Czechs and Slovaks to cooperate in the war effort. Masaryk continued to call for a free Central Europe, working to establish Slavic self-determination as a cornerstone to be addressed in future peace negotiations in the case of an Allied victory.

Within the Russian cities of Petrograd, Moscow, Warsaw, Odessa, Charkov, Ekaterinodar, and Rostov-on-Don, Czechs and Slovaks living in the Ukraine, Russia and Siberia petitioned the Russian Army to establish a Czech and Slovak regiment. The Russian provinces of Volhynia and Kiev contained sizable Czech and Slovak immigrant communities that had contributed to Russia's social and economic climate for decades. Over 120,000 of these prewar émigrés believed in the close association of Slavs that called for Russia to lead their fraternal brothers.

Because of the growing influence of Czech and Slovak organizations overseas, hundreds of Czechs and Slovaks were placed under arrest by the secret police in the homeland. In addition, executions of Poles, Czechs, Slovaks, and many other minorities increased along the Eastern Front. For the Slavs of Central Europe, there was no place to run, no place to hide as national fervor convulsed with spasms of ever rising terror and violence. News of this harsh and arbitrary treatment found its way into the western press where it was reported in lurid detail.

The Allies soon learned from captured German spies of efforts to foment strikes, arson, and assassination throughout the United States. To help capture instigators, Allied nations began to rely upon Slavic informants within the Hapsburg Empire. The most reliable of these were agents scattered throughout Bohemia, Moravia and Slovakia who smuggled information out for Thomas Masaryk's *Mafie*.[38] Americans, not yet in the war, continued to travel freely abroad, visiting both Entente nations as well as the Central Powers. Some of these "neutral" visitors were Czech- or Slovak-Americans who alerted Masaryk's network to changes within the Hapsburg army. Others informed Štefánik and Beneš of strategic developments along the Eastern Front.

Masaryk organized an underground network of eyes and ears based upon the structure of the Italian Mafia. Individuals in the Prague Mafie were only known by the next member in the line of command. As a result, when a Mafie member fell into police hands, the majority of members remained safe. Though the Italian Mafia developed into a highly criminal association, the Czech Mafie proved a technically skilled espionage network that lasted throughout the war.[39]

Allied Command soon began to rely upon Mafie insights into Austrian or Hungarian military maneuvers. Members of the Mafie would remain in Prague feeding information to Masaryk and his associates living in exile.[40] One of the most significant channels for information sprung directly from the household of the Austrian minister of the interior.[41] A Mafie spy using the name Kovanda became a trusted servant to the Austrian minister of state secret police. Kovanda's information not only saved untold numbers of Czechs and Slovaks, but earned Masaryk's group a sterling reputation for information gathering.

Against the wishes of a neutral American government, a few American citizens of Czech and Slovak descent continued to engage in espionage, passing messages through belligerent lines to Masaryk, Beneš, and Štefánik. Their information sometimes shed an unfortunate light on friend as well as foe. News from Russia regularly fell into this latter category. Early in the war, bombastic statements made by Russian grand duke Nicholas Nikolayevich predicted the war would end within a few months.[42] Masaryk considered such remarks unwarranted. Though no real friend to Lord Kitchener, Masaryk had always agreed with this British statesman's estimate that the war effort would last well over three years.

When Turkey joined the Central Powers with Austria and Germany, the Balkans acquired immense importance in Allied strategy. Britain's declaration to protect Egypt from Turkey enlarged the scope of the war, turning it into a worldwide conflagration. The war that would to be over by Christmas had grown with each passing season like an amoeba feeding upon itself.[43] By the end of the second year, the Eastern Front became highly crucial for the success of Allied forces fighting in the West. A two-front war effort placed the tsarist regime under Tsar Nicholas II in a pivotal role within the Allied effort. At the same time, Allied Command had long acknowledged rumors of a decidedly Germanophile clique within the tsarist family circle.

Austria's initial reverses, especially her resounding defeat in Serbia, were applauded by Italy, France, and Britain; unfortunately, a series of German successes under the leadership of General Hindenburg soon ushered in a period of humiliating Entente defeats.[44] Hindenburg's strategy in East Prussia and at Tannenberg revealed serious flaws within the Russian officer corps.

While maintaining relations with Czech and Slovak contacts inside Russia and the Romanov court, Masaryk continued publishing the newspaper *Čas* (*Time*). *Čas* had a large readership in Slavic communities throughout Western Europe and North America.[45] Masaryk tempered many of his editorial remarks concerning the Romanov war effort, however, due to growing concerns about the attitude of the Russian court toward Slavic desertions along the eastern trenches. Masaryk and his followers believed that the Allied Command was naive, never fully understanding the hazardous conditions these Czech and Slovak troops faced. He later wrote, "What I knew filled me with apprehension...."[46]

Slavic soldiers implored the Romanov Court to permit them to join the Russian army on the front. Masaryk, Beneš, and Štefánik also prompted Tsar Nicholas II to organize a Czech and Slovak regiment within the Russian army. The court in St. Petersburg ignored these petitions, however, and began instead to relocate German, Austrian, and Hungarian prisoners of war (POWs) eastward to camps in the Siberian interior. Making no concessions for the Slavic soldiers who deserted into their armies, whole Hapsburg units were stripped of their belongings and shepherded together. Czech and Slovak deserters suffered brutally under the command of captured Austrian, German, and Hungarian officers.

Deeply troubled by the complex problems facing the Russian soldiers in the field, Masaryk held hopes that Czech and Slovak troops would be allowed to fight alongside them. If so, this might enhance democratic tendencies in the Russian army. Masaryk and the Mafie were not alone in their concerns over conditions faced by Russia's noncommissioned officers.

In 1905, Russia had suffered a morale-shattering defeat at the hands of the Japanese. A deep sense of shame and humiliation over losing a war against an emerging world power became the Russian military's legacy. By 1906, the *Duma*, the first Russian parliament, requested that the tsar reorganize the general staff and modernize the navy.

The life of Aleksandr Kolchak would be especially influenced by this change. Born in 1874, Kolchak grew up in a middle-class St. Petersburg family that believed that the future of Mother Russia and her role in the twentieth century had arrived at a turning point. Aleksandr's father, Vasili, a retired major general, had been an artillery officer during the Crimean War. He married into landed gentry from the Ukraine. Despite their Turkish roots, Vasili Kolchak ingrained in his son the Russian esprit de corps. Vasili's ancestor, Bosnian Kolchak-Pashah, a prisoner of war captured in 1739 during one of the many wars fought between Russia and Turkey, had stayed in Russia after his release from prison to establish a long line of talented military men.[47]

The Naval School at St. Petersburg, authorized by Peter the Great in

1699, was the oldest in all of Russia. Aleksandr Kolchak enrolled and showed signs of brilliance from the very beginning. Young Kolchak encouraged other students through his own example of courage, patriotism, and humility. Even though he was of foreign descent and not a Russian noble, Kolchak quickly rose to the head of his class.

In 1899, his studies in St. Petersburg completed, Kolchak turned an eager mind to life as a naval officer. His efforts in the field of oceanography quickly brought the scientific world to his door. Thin and austere, Kolchak cut a dashing figure in uniform, resembling more a matinee idol than an explorer. He set off to the Arctic Sea, north of the New Siberian Islands, satisfying a boyhood quest for adventure.[48] Once there, Kolchak joined a mission of dogsleds crossing the coast of northern Siberia, Novaya Zemlya, the Taimyr Peninsula, and the New Siberian Islands.[49]

The world press marveled at this dynamic effort, spotlighting the young Russian officer who helped to lead it. Kolchak's mastery of the unknown made him an instant hero back home where the Sword of Honor of St. George was bestowed upon him.[50] Tsar Nicholas II counted himself among Kolchak's newest admirers. In Kolchak, Nicholas II found the kind of young forward-thinking officer a newly reorganizing navy could use. On Kolchak's return from the exploration of the Siberian Islands, the tsar awarded him a position coordinating the reorganization of the Russian Admiralty's general staff. Kolchak accepted this new challenge with relish.

During the summer of 1914 Russia entered the war on the side of Serbia with a smaller but more efficient naval fleet. Kolchak worked closely with another famous Russian naval officer, Admiral Essen, to estimate German naval capacity and then to mine Russian port approaches. This mining effort and a renewed esprit

Admiral Alexandr Kolchak, supreme ruler, Omsk, November, 1918.

de corps established professionalism within the Russian navy while effectively rerouting iron ore shipments away from the Baltic and German hands. The mining of the Gulf of Riga, thanks to Kolchak's early planning, saved Russian supply routes from German minesweepers. Too dangerous for German naval operations to handle, both waterways remained free of German and Austrian intrusion throughout the war effort. In addition to these successes, Kolchak revealed an understanding for the need for naval air power ahead of his time by incorporating capacity on gunships to accommodate airplanes.

Kolchak once again received the Sword and Cross of St. George for a depth of strategic planning that many felt bordered on genius. At the age of 32, he was promoted to rear admiral, the youngest in all of Russia. Wise and confident, Kolchak announced to friends and family that this promotion, the triumph of his middle-class background, was an omen of the bright future that lay ahead for the Russian people.

Kolchak planned to rebuild the national armed forces into a position of preeminence above all of the world's great powers.[51] He faced the coming months with an unshakable patriotism impressive to all who knew him. Kolchak's determination was compounded by that of many in Russia's young officer class who tied destiny to the fortunes of their country — an entire generation of young officers like himself who believed they would right the mistakes of the past. From his destroyer in the Black Sea, Admiral Kolchak worked to strengthen Russia's military might and ensure a resounding victory for Mother Russia at the end of the war.[52]

At the same time, Thomas Masaryk — aging statesman, philosopher, and father to a reawakening people — faced the fortunes of war from his cramped headquarters in Geneva. Unlike young Admiral Kolchak, decades of dealing with both the tsar and the Russian aristocracy had left the elder Czech and Slovak statesman believing that Mother Russia had grown too top-heavy and corrupt to help foster an atmosphere of self-determination for the Slavic peoples of Central Europe.

Masaryk's faith in a leadership role for Russia within a Pan-Slav movement had been dashed so often that he could no longer bring himself to believe as Kolchak did that Russia could turn her military and social ills around. Instead, Masaryk observed the Romanov court falling further and further into chaos and under the spell of men like Rasputin.

Neither Kolchak nor Masaryk had ever heard of Vladimír Ilych Ulyanov Lenin or of his able compatriot Lev Davidovich Bronstein. One day, however, Lenin and Bronstein would alter the future of both Aleksandr Kolchak and Thomas Masaryk, as well as the entire map of Central Europe and Russia.

Lenin had been sitting out the war in self-imposed exile in the West. Lenin's middle-class background in Simbirsk, where his father was a school administrator, had been shattered at the age of seven when his beloved elder brother had been arrested and subsequently executed for a failed attempt on the life of Tsar Nicholas II's father.[53] Lenin's youth became defined by petty acts of retribution and bitterness as nothing, not even later success in studies at the university or fame as a Marxist intellectual, could undo the impact of his brother's loss.[54]

Regardless, by 1903 Lenin emerged as a noted Marxist theorist — a role earning him an invitation to London's Second Congress. Yet of all the noted Russian thinkers, it was not Lenin who captivated the admiration and notoriety of the Congress attendees; Lev Davidovich Bronstein possessed considerably more talent as both a writer and theorist.

Though born the son of a lowly Jewish peasant on November 7, 1879, Bronstein's brilliance in mathematics quickly won him an invitation to schools far from his home village, Yanovka, in the province of Kherson.[55] Later, at university, Bronstein's discovery of philosophy and economics lured him away from life as a student.

Bronstein soon traded purely intellectual pursuits for the life of a populist radical. By 1902 he had changed his name to Trotsky, a nickname given to him by a jailer during one of many stints in Russian prisons.[56] After his escape, Trotsky spent the following decade traveling the world as a journalist and political reporter, even covering the Balkan War. With each passing endeavor, Trotsky impressed those he encountered with his insight and compassion for the human condition. Trotsky's growing reputation gained him the admiration of attendees to the Second Congress in London.[57] There Trotsky befriended Lenin and together they began reshaping the world according to a shared vision.

Predictions of a quick knockout blow to Austria, Germany, and Hungary by enthusiastic military leaders in Russia were soon made ridiculous by setbacks in Poland and the Carpathian Mountains. The disastrous Tarnov and Galician fronts foreshadowed a different future for the Russian troops. General Mackensen's advances along the Eastern Front frustrated and angered the Russian people. Casualty figures from the East seemed to grow uncontrollably as Russian soldiers and their families at home became increasingly troubled by the appearance of a bloated and corrupt government under the Romanovs.

Throughout 1914 and 1915, word spread that the tsarina, preoccupied with her son and court involvements, neglected her subjects in favor of past German connections. The royal family rarely appeared in public, seeming far removed from the war effort. Apprehension over the royal court was not eased by the apparition hovering behind it. The monk Rasputin, dark and foreboding with a ferocious appetite for power, maintained an influence over the Romanov family that stretched beyond the bounds of rationality.

Like a speeding train, Russia seemed propelled toward calamity. The masses bore with them a cargo of growing resentment from centuries of deprivation and insult. While Russia simmered, Kolchak was at sea and Masaryk in exile, both far removed from the battlefield. Masaryk would later find it ironic that as he worked to harness the revolutionary zeal of Bohemians, Moravians, and Slovaks, only a few miles away, also living in exile in Geneva, Vladimír Ilych Lenin plotted a revolution of his own. All four men — Masaryk, Kolchak, Lenin and Trotsky — felt sure they knew what the future promised for Russia, with no two predictions alike.

Shoulder to shoulder and ankle deep in mud, common recruits on the Eastern Front tried to remain calm, to adjust to the sickening disparity between boredom and fears of impending death. The war had not turned out to be what their officers had expected. As children, they had listened to tales of cavalry charges, brightly polished boots, and the shimmer of steel sabers in the heat of battle. Instead, troops hid behind a bank of eroding dirt and peered across a flat and barren landscape only paces from their fallen comrades.

By and large, the troops found the enemy completely wanting, ignorant of the art of warfare, with no experience, no chivalry — in fact, much like themselves. The sons of common laborers waited for the sons of common farmers, wondering why they would soon shoot at one another. Stories passed

Dr. Thomas Masaryk arriving to speak to Czech-American community, Chicago, Illinois, May 5, 1918.

from soldier to soldier: rumors of men carrying dummy rifles, of entire regiments on both sides driven into battle at pistol point by brutal officers. Unlike Masaryk, Kolchak, Trotsky, or Lenin, these soldiers found no interest or solace in their future.

The war was not winding down and not moving forward; instead, it was at a standstill. The allied troops grew more desperate as the German war machine delivered inconceivable terror on a daily basis. The politicians promised freedom to a public eagerly devouring news of the triumphant battles of brave men. The soldiers, however, could see their future: it was lying out in no man's land, a rotting, worm-infested horror that used to be one of them.

Chapter Two

On August 15, 1914, Tsar Nicholas II turned the old Michailov Monastery over to volunteers from Czech and Slovak communities in Russia.[1] Touched by the large numbers of Bohemians, Moravians, and Slovaks volunteering to join Russia's effort on the Eastern Front, the Romanov court had given permission for a *Družina* (brigade) of over 1,000 sharpshooters to be trained on the monastery grounds. Hearing this news, Czechs and Slovaks flocked to Kiev to enlist in the brigade.[2] It was not the tsar or his court, however, that motivated these young men to volunteer — it had been the call for independence which Thomas Masaryk sounded. Despite his unpopularity with the tsar, Masaryk maintained a strong relationship with members of the Duma and Russia's ambassadors in London and Paris.[3]

These original Družina volunteers lived inside Russia and Ukraine, working in professional capacities in industry. Others learned about the Družina unit through a vast network of Czech and Slovak sokols in both countries. Sokol societies, similar to their cousin, the German gymnasium movement, had become an integral part of Czech and Slovak culture. Sokols, built around sports and cultural activities, acted as a conduit for Czech and Slovak education. Since the mid–1800s the nationalist spirit of the Czech and Slovak renaissance coalesced around the sokol. This local ideal played a unifying part around which Czechs and Slovaks voiced their concerns for autonomy and the rebirth of Czech and Slovak culture. In addition, Masaryk and his associates began to use sokol associations for military recruitment.

During the first months in the field, the Družina sharpshooters faced internal squabbles between Russian troops and the Russian officer corps. Lieutenant Colonel Lotocký, the first commander of the Družina, lacked organization and training skills and was quickly replaced by Lieutenant Colonel Sozentevic. The Družina consisted of educated men recruited to work in Russia prior to the war.[4] They had little patience with inept officials. Nevertheless, living conditions at the monastery grew worse as Sozentevic proved even less capable than his predecessor. Under Sozentevic, the Družina received inadequate food and supplies for the field.

In the first weeks of the brigade, a committee comprised of Družina members had been selected to voice the concerns of Czechs and Slovaks from every major city in Russia. Delegates to the Central Council communicated directly with the Russian Duma, petitioning for improved living conditions and for the release of all Czech and Slovak prisoners from Russian prisoner of war camps. The Družina Central Committee requested that able-bodied volunteers be assigned to the Czech and Slovak Družina at Michailov.

Before the establishment of the brigade's Central Committee, the only additional unifying link between various Czech and Slovak communities inside Russia and Ukraine had been the *Čechoslovák*, a newspaper published in Kiev. The *Čechoslovák* soon reported a second Družina election. This election concerned the four major Czech settlements in European Russia and Ukraine: Warsaw, Kiev, Moscow, and Petrograd. A new committee of Družina delegates, the Provisional Preparatory Committee, met to draft a memorandum to present to Tsar Nicholas II at Tsarskoye Selo on September 17, 1914. The *Dokladnaya Zapiska*, as this memorandum became known, presented a program for the unification of Czechs and Slovaks, calling for immediate anti–Hapsburg activities to occur within the Hapsburg Empire. Members of the Russian cabinet saw the *Dokladnaya Zapiska* as a dangerous precedent — the sanctioning of revolutionary tendencies of subjects against their ruler. Surprisingly, Tsar Nicholas II and a majority of his ministers accepted the *Dokladnaya Zapiska* memorandum, publicly backing this crusade. Despite the tsar's reassurance, however, the Russian High Command became disturbed when discovering that only three percent of the Družina had sworn allegiance to Russia.

In reply to the *Dokladnaya Zapiska* memorandum, Austria-Hungary and Germany announced that Družina sharpshooters captured in the field would be executed immediately. In answer the Družina boldly proclaimed that its men would never be taken alive. If Družina soldiers became incapacitated in the field, compatriots would end their lives rather than leave them to face the enemy alone.[5]

In addition, the Družina established a system of honor rather than adopting Russian military discipline. Czech and Slovak troops voted to use the traditional Bohemian second person "brother" instead of "sir."[1] The absence of a highly regimented structure within the Družina scandalized the Russian officer corps. Tsarist officers believed that the Družina's unprofessional manner would surely translate into chaos on the battlefield. In time, however, Czech and Slovak troops proved sincerely motivated and disciplined, dying for "brother" soldiers in a manner unimagined by Russian troops.

In the first few weeks of Russian command, the Družina created four complete companies uniting under a banner designed to signify ties between Russia and Slavic independence. The Russian staff named Lieutenants Čeček and Fierlinger to lead the First Company, Lieutenants Švec and Klecanda the Second Company, Husák and Voženílek the Third, and Syrový the Fourth. Each man had reported to Kiev to join the Družina and each had the prewar experience and educational background highly valued by Russian industry. Voženílek, a former brewer, later became a general, as did Čeček, who previously represented a Czech motor car firm in Russia; Colonel Varnach had managed a Petrograd restaurant.

On October 9, 1914, the Czech Družina left Kiev for the southwest corner of the Eastern Front. It crossed the Austrian border under the leadership of Russian officers with most of the brigade made up of Czechs and Slovaks below the rank of major. At Lemberg, it was reviewed by the commander of the Third Army, General Dieterichs. Touched by the palpable spirit and dedication of these men, General Dieterichs, a Russian, quickly took command of the small but fierce Družina. The soldiers treatment improved immediately. Dieterichs recognized how important they could be in reconnaissance at the front; after all, Družina members were fluent in the language of the enemy: German.[2]

Night after night, the Czech and Slovak brigade spread out between the lines, collecting vital information on enemy positions and relaying it back to Russian Command. Though manned by expert shots, when behind enemy lines the Družina refrained from firing its rifles for fear of giving away its own position. Among the most important of its orders was to capture and question prisoners.

After December 1914, when deserters crossed enemy lines from their Hapsburg units, they ran into the arms of the waiting Družina.[3] Družina soldiers often sang Czech and Slovak folksongs to alert anyone who might be thinking of escaping. Night raids collected thousands of former Hapsburg soldiers — all men eager to fight in the Družina alongside their Russian compatriots.

Ignoring the pleas of Masaryk, his cohorts, and those deserting, local Russian officials scrutinized Czech and Slovak deserters. The enthusiasm the Družina exhibited for newly captured Slavic prisoners at first alarmed the Russians.[4] They could not comprehend why the Družina embraced soldiers wearing the enemy uniform.

Deserters regarded Russia as their nationalist hope and applied tenaciously to join the fight at the front. A melding of Slavic prisoners of war into the Družina ranks guaranteed tens of thousands of talented and well-trained reinforcements. Foolishly, the Romanov Court treated prisoner of war recruitment into the Družina with disdain, shuffling Czechs, Slovaks, Poles and others deserting along the Eastern Front to camps further east alongside German, Austrian, and Hungarian captives.

The initial reservations the Russian troops harbored were soon alleviated, however, as deserting Hapsburg Slavs impressed the Russians and appealed to their shared Pan-Slav sympathy. This newfound confidence mobilized

Russian officers to petition the tsar to allow Czechs and Slovaks in prison camps the opportunity to fight at the front. They reasoned that if these foreign troops fought for Russia, they could do no damage and perhaps provide help.

Again the tsar denied the entreaties. Consequently, ablebodied soldiers needed at the front rotted away in POW camps. True to the suspicions of Masaryk and many others, the court mandated that all prisoners of the same uniform be placed under the command of former officers. Despite their reliance on one another, thousands of Slavic deserters starved to death or were murdered by the Hapsburg officers they were interned with.[1]

Gustav Bečář had been attending college in Brno, Moravia, when the war broke out. Mere hours before his scheduled hanging for an unspecified offense at the front, Bečvář ran to freedom across the eastern trenches to escape his Austrian commander.[2] Bečvář's hopes to battle alongside the Czech and Slovak Družina became dashed when he was sent to a camp in Lublin, where he shared facilities with the very officer who had earlier conspired to have him hung. Eager to help with the Allied war effort, some of Bečvář's comrades found their way to a Jugo-Slav division fighting in Dobrudja. During this famous retreat, nearly half committed suicide rather than fall into Austrian hands.

Russian successes during the first year of the war helped prevent Germany from exacting a quick knockout blow to Western Europe. The second front fought by Russian troops kept the Central Powers tied down in the east. Early on, however, news from the front underscored serious flaws in the tsar's war effort.

The Družina Rifle Brigade consistently beat back heavy odds in battle. The highly decorated brigade remained uniquely successful when compared to Russian troops fighting alongside it — often remaining in battle long after tsarist units had fallen back in retreat. Ignoring the lack of supervision and confusion in Russian ranks, the Družina overran Austrian positions, capturing thousands of prisoners and huge quantities of arms.

Nevertheless, by 1915 the need for reinforcements became crucial. Germany's efforts at the Battle of the Marne had bogged down the Western Front. Russia's allies demanded pressure be applied in the East.[1] In order to enact this effort, the Družina, now under General Dieterichs, once again petitioned for reinforcements from the thousands volunteering within POW camps across Russia.

Officers with exceptional skills languished in camps, literally dying to fight in the Družina Rifle Brigade at the front. Major Hajda, a highly decorated Hapsburg aviator, deserted the elite flying corps in the desire to turn his skills against the Austro-Hungarian Empire that ruled his homeland. The talent of Hajda and many others wasted away month after month, neglected by the powers they wished to serve.[1]

In early April of 1915, Gustav Bečvář, the prisoner of war and ex-Brno college student who had once been faced with certain execution by his Hungarian officer, heard astonishing news. An entire regiment of Hapsburg soldiers, the 28th from Prague, had deserted en masse while on patrol in the Carpathian Mountains. High casualties in the 28th found the "Prague Children," as the regiment became known, temporarily lacking Austrian or Hungarian officers. Members of this unit made initial contact across the front with care, having heard of deserters being fired upon by confused Russian troops. They asked their future Russian captors' permission to march across the front lines in formation as the unit band played to the slogan "*Ted'anebo Nikdy*" "Now or Never." For months afterward, Czech and Slovak POWs swelled with great pride over news of this astonishing escapade.

Tsar Nicholas II eventually granted Slavic prisoners one concession as a result. As the scope of the war widened, the tsar's courts ordered Austrians, Germans, and Hungarians to be sent to labor camps deep within Siberia. Deserting troops would be allowed to volunteer to relocate to work in areas where they could live without harassment in self-contained communities. These new facilities, although overcrowded, underventilated, and generally understaffed, were better than living among former Austrian, German, and Hungarian officers. To win favor with the tsar, more than 25,000 Slavic prisoners petitioned the government to work in Russia's war industries. If the deserting troops could not fight, then they would help to ensure an Allied victory by contributing building materials and equipment for the men at the front. Gathered together in labor camps, Slavic prisoners pooled their meager resources and freely discussed nationalist aims while befriending Russian workers and guards.

It was from these new contacts that many Czechs and Slovaks first learned of the growing hostility in the countryside against the tsar and tsarina. Russians talked openly of incompetence and corruption in the Romanov court. Political news concerning the Czechs and Slovaks' own fate and that of their homeland also filtered into the work camps. Prisoners rejoiced at Thomas Masaryk's call for the establishment of free and autonomous states in the Hapsburg lands. In addition, news of Milan Štefánik's efforts to transfer all Czech and Slovak POWs inside Russia to Canadian, English, French, and Italian units on the Western Front also met with their approval.

Czechs and Slovaks wallowing in Russian labor camps discovered their crusade was not finished after all. Prisoners also heard of the Mafie's work and its declaration of war on the Hapsburg Empire. Throughout the remaining months of 1915, Czech and Slovak desertions in the Hapsburg Army rose to alarming levels — unfortunately, so did executions of those caught trying to flee.

Within the homeland, secret societies flourished while the number of arrests and executions increased. The Czech and Slovak lands suffered as huge numbers of professionals and workers — engineers, farmers, machinists, physicians, and teachers — were either forced to fight in the loathsome Hapsburg army or to be confined in prison. Relatives of deserting troops in Russian POW camps stoked their faith in the hopes that Russia would exonerate their men; instead news from the tsarist regime grew more alarming. An astounding two million POWs, a quarter of a million of whom belonged to Czech and Slovak families in Bohemia, Moravia and Slovakia, continued to languish in the tsar's camps with no foreseeable relief.[2]

Though Družina soldiers did not tell captives of the fate awaiting them in Russian camps, they discussed among themselves their own distress over faltering conditions on the Russian front. The Družina continued to press for deserters to cross over to join them even as the *Stavka*, the Russian High Command under the leadership of Grand Duke Nicholas, rejected the use of deserters as reinforcements at the front.[3]

As the debate over the fate of the deserters raged, Allied ships delivered war materiel to the docks in Archangelsk, Murmansk, and Vladivostok. Deliveries included everything from canned goods to airplanes for use by Russian troops. Concurrently, tsarist troops fighting along the eastern trenches began to suffer from a continual lack of supplies. While Družina officers' suspicions about dwindling supplies grew, the sinking morale of the Russian units at the front further enflamed distrust of the Russian High Command. Rumors of black market profiteering and incompetence in the Romanov court appeared to be true. Complaining to Gustav Bečvář, a fellow brigade soldier confided:

> Think of the bravery of the Russian soldiers who captured all Galicia as far as Karkov, penetrated the terrible Carpathian Mountains into Hungary, with the bayonet as their chief weapon, for munitions of all kinds were deplorably short. Today, these men are being sold, cheated by corruption in high places at the rear. In the front lines, they are short of even primary necessities, while here in Karkov anything from caviar to champagne may be bought in the restaurants. One day, the soldiers will find out. When they do, it will be the end of Russia as we know her now.[4]

Making matters worse, the tsar dismissed his uncle, Grand Duke Nicholai Nicholayevitch as commander in chief of the Russian High Command in the autumn of 1915. Despite frequent disagreements with the Czechs and Slovaks, the Grand Duke remained avidly pro-Slav. His dismissal angered and astounded not only the Russian troops but the Družina, which worried that a pro-German clique in the court of St. Petersburg had been behind his dismissal.

The tsar's wife, a common topic of discussion among Russian units, was now assumed to be pro-German, siding with her ancestors and against Mother Russia. Allegations even circulated in the Duma that the empress was a German spy.[5] On the front, soldiers accused the tsarina and Rasputin of conspiring to ship mismatched grenades and weapons to the front in order to sabotage them in battle. Throughout 1916, rumors grew that a pro-German element within the Romanov court openly petitioned the Central Powers for an end to the war. Adding to the public's trepidation over a seeming lack of Romanov dedication to troops at the front were rumors that many newly promoted Russian generals came from Baltic provinces, areas largely settled by Germans who openly sided with Germany.

Reports like these reached Thomas Masaryk by way of his Mafie. For the most part, they were viewed with cynicism by a war-weary Russian public. Even so, Masaryk began conducting negotiations with a progressive bloc inside the Russian Duma in hopes that liberal statesmen could reach the tsar and beg him to rethink the "Družina Question."[6]

With reversals on the Eastern Front throughout 1916 resulting in huge numbers of casualties, Russian foreign minister Sasonov became convinced of the need to recruit Slavic POWs. The previous winter, on December 13, 1915, the Družina — 1,600 troops comprising eight companies — merged with a trench mortar company. Russian Command had already renamed them the Czech Rifle Brigade. Taking into consideration the decorations of valor that Tsar Nicholas II had bestowed upon members of the Družina Rifle Brigade and the waning strength at the front, it was a shock when Sasonov's plan was immediately tabled by the court.

As a result, the POW camps in European Russia once again settled into a dreary malaise. The camps were filthy, overcrowded, and disease ridden; living conditions caused many internee deaths from lack of food and poor sanitation. Masaryk, Beneš, and Štefánik attempted to apply focused pressure in Kiev, site of a particularly large prison population, but to no avail. It soon became clear to Štefánik that the Russian armament dealers were manipulating the tsar to keep prison laborers in manufacturing and away from the battlefield.

By the summer of 1916, Czech and Slovak war laborers noted drastic changes in their Russian guards. It became apparent to the Czechs and Slovaks that the Russians not only finally recognized but also empathized with the intense hatred felt by various minority groups towards their former Hapsburg oppressors. Guards reported to superiors that Slavic internees maintained a fervent desire to switch uniforms and to fight against the enemy: their own emperor, Franz Joseph.

Astonishingly, the reports of Russian guards were taken seriously by those in power. In an attempt to utilize their skills, thousands of Czech and Slovak prisoners with engineering and railway expertise were sent southward to Bukhara and Mariinsk to complete a section of railroad line. Unfortunately, conditions in the Uzbek hills were even worse than those at the camps. Workmen lived in the very locomotives they repaired, often dying from malaria and exposure before shelter could be completed. As they toiled, information concerning Masaryk's efforts on their behalf reached them through both the Čechoslovák and the Čechoslovan journals. Both newspapers included news of the Russian war effort and kept Czech and Slovak internees better informed than many of their guards.

Although highly decorated, throughout 1916 the Družina still only numbered 6,000 men. It had been used in the most brutal fighting, under the worst conditions, month after month, and still the Družina outfought its enemy. Newspapers continued to lavish praise on the brigade for its accomplishments under the leadership of Generals Brusilov and Dieterichs. And while the Družina was grateful to fight rather than sit out the war in camps, the soldiers exhaustion and frustration could not help but lead them to wonder how much longer they could maintain their pace of engagement without a fresh infusion of recruits. By the summer of 1916, their hopes had soured.

In August, Lieutenant Milan Štefánik visited Russia and was introduced to General Maurice Janin, acting emissary of the French government. Štefánik, already a naturalized French citizen, conferred with Janin about the chaotic conditions in which the Czech and Slovak internees were living and of the disheartening situation for the Družina at the front. Initially, Janin was wary of the intentions of the young Slovak officer, about which he had heard so much. Within one month, however, General Janin sent reports to the Ministry of Defense in Paris recommending that Štefánik be placed in charge of recruitment for the "Czecho-Slovak Army."[1] Janin's push for a "Czecho-Slovak Army" helped to expedite the fate of the POWs by gaining the attention of the Allies.[2]

Meanwhile, the number of Slavic POWs had swollen to over 300,000, with more than half on a waiting list to be sent to fight at the Russian front. As they waited for news, many continued to die from dysentery and other epidemics common in the camps. Joseph Skelnička was just one of tens of thousands of Czech soldiers suffering.[3] Red Cross workers came to visit Skelnička one day as he lay near death on his cot. They could not speak Czech and Skelnička was unable to understand either English or Russian; nonetheless, both sides mimed their way through his evaluation. Red Cross representatives decided that Skelnička's case was fatal unless he could be moved immediately to Kazan by train for further help.

Through a series of incredible events, a young soldier also from Prague took it upon himself to befriend and nurse Skelnička on the trip. The young soldier shared food and encouragement, and by the time the two reached Kazan, Skelnička had begun to rally. It came as a shock to learn later that his young friend, a man he would always see as his savior, died from the very same illness before ever reaching the hospital in Kazan.[4]

Estimates of the numbers of Slavic men dying from epidemic and disease in labor camps and POW camps were known to Masaryk, Beneš, and Štefánik, who grew increasingly more frantic as the months wore on. Worse still, huge numbers of soldiers died in transit centers before ever making it to camps. In Murmansk, where officials had transferred Czech and Slovak academics, nearly half succumbed to scurvy. In Semibratovo and Samara, thousands of others died from a typhoid epidemic.[5]

The problems of Russian society soon mirrored the situation in the labor camps. Through it all, the Russian monarchy appeared unable or unwilling to help ease the suffering.[6] As rich Russians continued to squander their resources, the poor slipped closer and closer toward famine. In the cities of western Russia, the laboring poor turned from feelings of estrangement to those of fury against the aristocracy. War casualties continued to soar as war supplies grew scarce. By the beginning of 1917, Russia had suffered one-third of all war fatalities and was well on her way to increasing that percentage.

While Czechs and Slovaks died in labor camps across European Russia, boxcars filled with Austrian, German, and Hungarian prisoners continued on schedule into the interior of Siberia. The newly built Trans-Siberian Railway brought thousands to live in camps deep within the wilderness. Many of these soldiers had grown up in the world's most sophisticated cities — Berlin, Bratislava, Budapest, Frankfurt, Munich, Prague, Vienna, Warsaw, among many others. Moving eastward into the interior, prisoners watched fearfully as traces of European influence disappeared. Russia, an ancient nation of Slavonic influence, had been familiar but much of Siberia resembled nothing these prisoners of war had ever experienced.

Though rich in geology and natural resources, Siberia had remained relatively unexplored only a few decades earlier. Few places on earth were as desolate as this. Few had been allowed to stand the passing of time without the encroachment of civilized man.[7] But the track that sliced its way across this quiet landscape now brought settlers who broke open the land and thinned out forests in order to build shelter.[8] As the animals of Siberia caught the interest of the fur markets of the West, these settlers began to unearth the wealth that lay dormant here.

There were others, however, under whose care the land had prospered over centuries of use. The Siberian wilderness, like her sister frontier in America, had been peacefully inhabited by indigenous tribes who arrived at least 500 years before any white man. In the Russian Far East provinces there were over 40 different native groups, all in a state of decline by the twentieth century. The rails presently cutting through these plains had been built on their ancestral land.

The *Buriates,* relatives of the *Khalkas* of eastern Mongolia and the *Barga* of northwest Manuchuria, were the most vocal and powerful of the Siberian native peoples. The Buriates settled the Siberian steppes after fleeing from Genghis Khan in Mongolia during the thirteenth century. Attracted by the spectacular mountains of the Lake Baikal region, they put down roots and vigorously opposed all incursions into the area by the Russian tsars.

As far back as 1659, the Buriate leadership tried to integrate itself with the Russians but efforts always failed. For centuries, the tsars used Siberia as a dumping ground for malcontents, housing political prisoners and criminal exiles in vast colonies of labor camps throughout the interior. The Buriates tried to protect themselves from Russia's push eastward by combining their strength with the indigenous *Tiurk* and *Tungus* peoples but to no avail.

The sight of chain gangs working the land of their ancestors became familiar to these herdsmen. In time, they befriended the oppressed outcasts, teaching them how to grow crops in order to feed themselves. Exiles learned of the mink and silver fox from nearby tribes, and how to breed the large-horned cattle and small sturdy ponies that thrived in the region's intensely cold winters.[9]

Everything from crop rotation to construction techniques combined into an authentic Siberian lifestyle. Many of the original political prisoners grew to love this place. They often stayed on and intermarried with the tribes in the region. The very prison system to which many Central Powers soldiers were being sent owed its small comforts to a legacy started by the tens of thousands of political exiles who had come before. The Buriate herdsmen witnessed these camps filling again and again with human cargo and knew that each surge of newcomers could only survive the long savage winters with their help.

The *Raskolniks*, members of a religious sect of the early eighteenth century, were some of the first sent into Siberia to die. To the Raskolniks, the "old believers," the tsar's decision to alter both "Mother Russia" and "Holy Mother Church" had become sacrilegious.[10] Through the intervention of the indigenous tribes and their own heartiness, the Raskolniks not only survived but prospered. Exile gave them a chance to live freely, keeping their religious tradition pure. Priests, compelled to marry the daughters of other priests, gave their firstborn sons to the priesthood. This tradition kept the church healthy and church doctrine at the center of village life. Under the tutelage of the priest class and the *mir* (world) council, Raskolnik heritage flourished from one generation to the next.[11] Presently Raskolniks found it hard to understand how one of their own, a man named Rasputin, could so easily leave the mir to live among the imperial court that his people despised.

Wave upon wave of exiles followed the "old believers." Those persecuted for political, social, or religious crimes arrived in greater numbers and with more frequency after 1800. Court officials who attempted to halt the accession of Nicholas I in 1825, for example, were either executed or deported to Siberia. From 1831 until the end of the nineteenth century, the Romanovs sent multitudes of Poles and other ethnics eastward to join "criminals" in labor camps dotting the Siberian interior.

Exile became a preferred punishment by the tsarist courts in Russia. Of the later arrivals, the Ukrainians and Cossacks flourished, most especially in the Amur region. And with their military flair and a special skill at intimidation, the Cossacks quickly subdued other groups who had arrived earlier. But their newfound status as large landowners brought the Cossacks resentment from their neighbors on whose land they had settled.

The entire area of Siberia had been barely touched, factories rare and natural reserves beckoning. On order from the minister of the interior, chain gangs worked the mountain mines. By and large, these men were derelicts or petty criminals, unwanted in more sophisticated communities to the west.[12] Only hardened criminals lived in the labor camps under lock and key. Instead, most political exiles were outcasts allowed to bring their families with them into the frontier. The majority of these were family men who stayed on after their prison terms ended, preferring the freedom available in Siberia over living under the watchful eyes of tsarist police back home in Russia.

Life in the wilderness was hard, but sharing hardships made it bearable. A large number of outcasts were educated men who now turned their innate curiosity toward exploration. These undesirables proved highly resilient, learning to love the land as the Buriates and the Raskolniks had before them. It offered something unfathomable in western Russia: a tradition of free thinking and individualism.

The lead, silver, and gold mines of the Altai Mountains, the forests and animals of Transbaikalia, and the oil fields of Suchan had all been discovered in the spirit of exploration. Siberia could yield riches, could provide for her people but, as often is the case, these riches had to be earned. Siberia was neither barren nor flat as many visitors believed. The high terrain combined each spring with the melt of heavy snowfall to cause treacherous rapids and heavy flooding in the majority of river valleys. Villages built upon these high plateaus could easily be swept away. Three to four thousand free settlers chose to return to the cities to the west each year rather than brave this harsh existence any longer. For those who stayed, a communal lifestyle proved most advantageous, suiting the rigors of the wilderness.

A vast majority of pioneers settled into small agricultural hamlets. Most towns were built around one central road lined with drab cottages. Every home fronted the main street, snugly wedged beside its neighbor to keep the Siberian winds at bay. Only the windows, traditionally bright with family souvenirs or flowers, showed any inclination toward individual expression. Usually each cottage consisted of one room of hewn logs with a gigantic fireplace as the centerpiece; consequently, fire posed a major hazard in these predominantly wood-constructed towns.

Like the American West, population expanded from west to east and east inward. After traveling from Odessa through the Black, Aeogean, and Mediterranean Seas to the Suez Canal, most settlers entered through the port of Vladivostok on the Pacific coast. Steam travel had been introduced on the Ob' River by 1846, and by 1898 more than 270 steamers transported newcomers inland. Cities in the interior soon developed around these travel routes.[13] The city of Chelyabinsk, with a population of 70,000 by the turn of the century, became an important junction despite its position alongside flat swampland and shallow lakes. The direct route from Moscow to Omsk dissected the line from Petrograd to Ekaterinburg, and another from Kustanai and Troitsk in the southeast at Chelyabinsk.[14]

Chelyabinsk became the largest and richest province in Orenburg because of the railroad. In the city of Chelyabinsk wooden sidewalks lined broad unpaved boulevards. Omsk, built upon an old Cossack fortress, also became a premier Siberian center. At 2,199 miles in altitude, Omsk appeared completely flat even though one and one-half miles from the depot the railway descended into the steep Irtysh Valley. A high steel bridge more than 2,000 feet across spanned the river into birch woods that surrounded the city.[15] Omsk's packing plants supplied Russia with much of her needed beef. The entire area surrounding Omsk, known for a series of Cossack settlements that extended out along the mail route, would later become known as the "bitter-line," nicknamed by prisoners for the horrors that occurred there.

If one was not on a prison train, Vladivostok remained the first stop on the way to a new life in the interior. The port city's population soared to over 85,000 by 1912, making it the most sophisticated and the largest city in all of Siberia. Thousands of settlers arrived annually through Vladivostok Harbor in the hopes of discovering either a new beginning or easy riches. In reality, they discovered that nothing came easily here. The city looked eastward as a door to the Orient and led the area as a shipping hub. This promising location would also become the source of the city's corruption. Vladivostok soon became the espionage, prostitution, and black market center of the Russian Far East — servicing numbers of grim characters who populated the harbor area. Yet the city also boasted institutions of higher learning, theaters, an opera house and paved streets — the only ones in all of Siberia.

Vladivostok's moderate coastal temperatures, a sophisticated lifestyle, and burgeoning society became the last sight of civilization before heading inland. By 1890, a bureau had been established to advise settlers new to the region. But newcomers heading into the hinterland often left Vladivostok with a false sense of security — a feeling that could easily prove deadly once in the wilds of the interior.

After 1890, serious plans to build the Trans-Siberian Railway were developed. It would branch inland from Vladivostok Harbor to redirect growth westward. Planned to accommodate several branch lines as well as the main track, the railway would proceed through the heart of Siberia to the outskirts of St. Petersburg (Petrograd) — a distance of over 5,800 miles.

Building began on May 31, 1891. The project would pass through every conceivable type of climate, over terrain unimaginable to Western Europeans, from the Gobi Desert in the south to the frozen ports of Archangelsk and Murmansk in the north. The westernmost route would connect Chelyabinsk to Novonikolaevsk and pass on to Innokentevsk into a third branch from the Transbaikalia to Sretensk. Its tracks would run through the wild steppe, changing forever everything in its path.

The scope of this project proved monumental and captured the imagination of the world's greatest engineers.[16] Decades of planning included industrialists from countries the world over.[17] Designers and workers flocked to help. The Transcontinental Railroad of the United States had been completed only a few years earlier, freeing up skilled workmen who traveled across the Pacific Ocean to Siberia, where their expertise became indispensable. They labored alongside adventurers, explorers, and criminals on chain gangs. For years these crews toiled in the summer humidity and the ferocious winter permafrost until the land slowly gave up its secrets.

By 1903, only a very dangerous section of black undulating rock that ran through the Lake Baikal region and into the mountains behind remained untamed. It included 39 tunnels blasted through the mountain range to connect St. Petersburg with Vladivostok nearly a continent away.

After operations became established along the Trans-Siberian Railway, a secondary link to the Chinese Eastern Railway united both into one operational unit. Japan became interested in the Chinese Eastern line since it was a major trade route for northern Manchuria extending into the heart of Siberia.[18]

The world applauded such persistence, marveling at the skill required to complete such a miraculous piece of workmanship. By 1915, the last section punched a hole through the mountains, connecting the entire length of track. Similar in monumental scale to the newly completed Panama Canal, it became an example to the age of man's superior mastery over the elements, a miracle of structural design and human effort.

There had been many interruptions and many mistakes, but the result made it possible for the Russian tsar to look eastward for expansion. It had been impossible for exiles and settlers to travel directly eastward overland

ARCTIC OCEAN
PACIFIC OCEAN
BERING SEA
SEA OF OKHOTSK
SEA OF JAPAN
BALTIC SEA
BLACK SEA
CASPIAN SEA
FINLAND
POLAND
BYELORUSSIA
UKRAINE
GEORGIA
KAZAKHSTAN
MONGOLIA
CHINA
RUSSIA
SIBERIA
URAL MOUNTAINS
Murmansk
Petrograd
Archangelsk
Kiev
Bakhmach
Billopillia
Kursk
Moscow
Yaroslavl'
Vetluzhskiy
Kotelnich
Kirovo-Chepetsk
Nizhny Novgorod
Tambov
Penza
Kazan
Glazov
Perm'
Kungur
Ekaterinburg
Volgograd
Volga
Samara
Ufa
Tumen'
Tobol'sk
Chelyabinsk
Zlatoust
Petropavlovsk
Irtush
Omsk
Ob'
Tayga
Tomsk
Novo-Sibirsk
Ermolaevka
Achinsk
Mariinsk
Krasnoyarsk
Yenisey
Angara
Kansk
Tayshet
Tulun
Cheremkhovosk
Angarsk
Irkutsk
Khilok
Verchne-Udinsk
Lake Baikal
Vilim
Lena
Chita
Chernyshevsk
Magdagachi
Belogorsk
Arkhara
Birobidzhan
Khabarovsk
Vayazemsky
Dalnerechensk
Ussuriysk
Vladivostok

until the Trans-Siberian Railway became a reality. Earlier travel had been ship to ship and then wagon to steamer, a process that often took years.[19]

Services along the Trans-Siberian existed in a variety of levels of sophistication. For example, the Petrograd Express had become notorious as a luxury train running twice weekly from Vladivostok to Petrograd.[20] It carried first-class cars unrivaled anywhere, with black walnut paneling and red velvet sleeper compartments that housed four comfortably.

The world had little time to applaud these great feats, however, and there were many who did not approve of the railroad. To some, it meant growth and potential riches; to others, it scarred the land. For the Buriates and other indigenous tribes, the growth of settlements along the railway line forced them farther into the mountains and away from European intrusion. As new hamlets appeared, deforestation followed. Village councils restricted the use of trees along the tracks and in areas surrounding their newer settlements. Generations of Buriate villagers witnessed encroachment onto their ancestral lands with growing resentment.

Because of the war in the West and the fact that Siberian money had become practically worthless by 1914, the region became a veritable dead zone. When the war effort began, valleys crisscrossed by rails continued to remain relatively deserted except for an odd train passing through on its way to somewhere else. Interior provinces in the Russian Far East remained little more than Russian colonies, a situation that galled political groups organizing from sites across Siberia. Concerns focused upon the thin silver ribbon of track that cut through the wilderness.

For a time, Siberia remained relatively free from the war effort, but presently the Austrian, German, and Hungarian POWs who arrived on each new train reminded all that violence continued to grow and spread over the western horizon. Even free settlers who had remained to develop Siberian resources hoped the European conflict could be contained far away. Though the conflagration between Russia and her neighbors across the eastern trenches made the Trans-Siberian distribution system ever more crucial, these efforts had been hampered from the start.

Vladivostok became a pivotal port in the Russian war effort. The Pacific coast harbor was occupied by Allied shipping that filled warehouses and barges with armaments, foodstuffs, and materiel meant for the Russian war effort far to the west. Imperceptibly at first, Siberia became a staging area in someone else's war. Soon residents began to wonder if the war they heard about so far way would one day find its way to their doorstep.

*Opposite: **Trans-Siberian Railroad through Russia and Siberia, 1919.***

Chapter Three

A death rate of over 70 percent throughout 1915 and 1916 along the Eastern Front exhausted the cadre of highly trained Russian officers.[1] As a result, men of little experience and even less character became increasingly common in the Russian officer corps. To make matters worse, soldiers under the leadership of newer officers suffered from a lack of supplies of war materiel and rations.

Thomas Masaryk and his staff regularly toured Russia and Ukraine — most often Kiev, the largest Czech settlement and site of heavy Družina combat. Trips to the Eastern Front were initially scheduled to raise morale and negotiate the status of POWs, yet more and more time was being devoted to securing food and supplies for Russian troops fighting alongside the Družina.[2] While doing so, Masaryk, well aware of corruption throughout the Russian officer corps, anticipated dire consequences. Before long, news of food riots in the cities of European Russia reached the trenches, inciting rioting and desertions amongst the troops.

By early 1917 the entire Trans-Siberian Railway system became littered with boxcars shunted onto sidings. Huge stacks of abandoned materiel sat alongside railroad branch lines and in the harbors of Archangelsk, Murmansk, and Vladivostok. Supplies desperately needed by both the men at the front and the cities of western Russia remained unopened or stolen to be sold on the black market. The entire distribution system in Siberia, both on the Trans-Siberian and in the farmlands, needed a swift and thorough overhaul to improve the war effort and save Russian cities from the immediate threat of famine.

Transporting foodstuffs to areas of need had once been the Romanov court's priority, even eclipsing the need for war materiel at the front. Now throughout the countryside, crops rotted while hunger spread. Machinery for cultivation and distribution lay broken along the roadbeds, ignored by the court's autocratic bureaucracy. By early 1917, Russia, a land immeasurably rich in grain, dairy products, and livestock, stood at the brink of disaster.

Tsar Nicholas II was evidently utterly incapable of saving his nation. As a child Nicholas lived in constant terror that fate might conspire to make him tsar even though his older brother, Alexander, was being groomed for the role.

In 1894, at the age of twenty-six, Nicholas was confronted with his worst fear: his older brother, and current Tsar Alexander III, was assassinated. A few hours after being crowned Nicholas Romanov II, he wrote a brother-in-law, "What am I going to do? What is going to happen to me — to all of Russia? I am not prepared to be Tsar. I never wanted to become one."[3]

By 1917 Nicholas II placed blame on what he believed to be a liberal Duma for a series of violent riots that spread throughout western Russia. Nicholas believed the end of the Duma would bring an end to the violence plaguing Russia.[4] Members of the Duma felt otherwise, however. They also intended to end mob violence and desertions at the front, but the Duma's solution targeted something quite different altogether — the Romanov court. Under pressure from tsarist officials, the Duma disbanded.

On March 10, 1917, the army in Petrograd mutinied. What started as another food riot quickly escalated into a full-fledged revolt. Two days later, a provisional government formed under the leadership of the former Duma's most vocal member, Alexander Kerensky. Like Lenin's elder brother, in his youth Kerensky had flirted with assassinating one of the Romanovs. Instead, Kerensky, the son of a Simbirsk school administrator, studied law. As a college student in Petrograd, he gravitated towards socialist circles that challenged middle-class complacency. Kerensky found himself becoming a voice for Russia's laboring poor. Because of his fiery rhetoric, he gained international notoriety but also became identified as an enemy of the imperial court, a distinction he welcomed. The same day the Provisional Government reorganized under Kerensky, an astounded Tsar Nicholas Romanov II abdicated his throne.

Through the act of abdication, Tsar Nicholas II effectively destroyed any future possibility of Romanov rule in Russia. In his last speech to the Russian army on March 8, 1917, Nicholas II announced to the world, "For the last time I address myself to you, my much beloved troops!"[5] The voice of the Russian people was finally being heard, and the imperial court feared its call. The tsar's autocratic style no longer fit efforts to modernize. In his last message to the Russian people, Nicholas II maintained that he was stepping down to help the war effort at the request of the former disbanded State Duma. Nicholas Romanov II ended his last public speech by whispering, "May the Lord God help Russia."[6]

Kerensky intended to retire the tsar and his family comfortably on a Romanov estate in the Crimea, where they would slowly disappear from public memory. Instead, fear of counterrevolution forced the Provisional Government to send Nicholas, his wife and children under guard to the palace at Tsarskoye Selo, where for the present news of their situation suddenly ceased.

A change in government may have been supported by many but Admiral Kolchak was not one of them. He believed Provisional Government policies would lead Russia into a dire future. For the young admiral who believed that Germany stood in Russia's way, the year 1917 had started out propitiously. In the first weeks of January, Russian destroyers swept mines and destroyed 39 Turkish sailing vessels.[7] By the spring of 1917, Kolchak had already become a highly decorated war hero who deeply believed in the Allied cause. In March, General Alexeev had asked his senior naval commanders whether Tsar Nicholas II should abdicate. Though the majority answered in the affirmative, Admiral Kolchak fervently disagreed with them.[8]

Russian troops and their families at home had suffered immeasurably throughout the waning months of Romanov rule. Former promises made to the Allies by the tsar carried little importance to his sailors, who were distracted by the threat of a famine constantly haunting their families back home. Riots in the city streets of western Russia erupted once again, this time with more virulence. Kerensky agreed with Kolchak that the war must continue, but the needs of frontline troops had been ignored for far too long. The Provisional Government scurried to secure provisions for soldiers along the eastern trenches, but lacked resources to transport supplies stranded throughout Siberia.

The Chinese Eastern Railway and the Trans-Siberian Railway had already been allowed to deteriorate immeasurably from lack of attention. Additional initiatives to supply Vladivostok had become critical. Recognizing Russia's predicament, United States senator Elihu Root reported that "the Germans had spent forty million rubles since the abdication of the Czar to undermine Russia and to misinterpret America's entrance into the conflict."[9] With the State Duma's approval, the United States stepped in to help. The head of the American Railway Advisory Commission, John F. Stevens, traveled from the United States to personally oversee the transport of war materiel and supplies from the docks in Archangelsk, Murmansk, and Vladivostok. Stevens had the expertise and the desire to turn the situation around.[10]

The Advisory Commission of Railway Experts under John F. Stevens docked in Vladivostok on June 1, 1917. An organization of engineers and technicians known as the Russian Railway Service Corps — under the leadership of Colonel George Emerson — soon combined with John Steven's group. More than 300 engineers and mechanics in the United States Army began a restoration effort on locomotives, tracks, and boxcars at the request of the Provisional Government. They immediately began to move stockpiled weapons and foodstuffs sitting idle in coastal ports into the interior.

To end Allied shipping to these ports and to stop a stringent British blockade, German submarines sunk six U.S. merchant ships in March 1917. The British notified Woodrow Wilson shortly thereafter that the Zimmerman telegram, a secret communiqué from Germany to Mexico, had been intercepted. In it, Germany proposed an alliance with Mexico to act against the United States. These incidents finally inflamed the American public. On April 6, 1917, America declared war on Germany and her allies.

Witnessing these events, Trotsky believed the capitalist world had begun to implode. While visiting New York City, word of the March Revolution and the events thereafter pulled Trotsky's focus back to Europe, where he joined Lenin in Geneva. Lenin convinced Trotsky that the time for a Marxist revolution was at hand; for Lenin, Kerensky's success at toppling the Romanov court was merely the predecessor of a much greater movement.

In April 1917, a "sealed" train passed through the Russian border without undergoing the usual search procedures. The railroad staff steered clear of the boxcars which had been labeled "Tainted with Infectious Disease." Inside one of the boxcars a small contingent of men sat in hiding — men who would change the face of Europe, men later rumored to be in the pay of the German government. Already in St. Petersburg an elite circle of friends had begun to organize a welcome committee for their Bolshevik leader, Vladimír Ilych Lenin, and his entourage.

By the summer of 1917, Alexander Kerensky visited Russian troops at the front to pledge the Provisional Government's undying commitment to them. The head of the Duma announced one more decisive offensive. All of Russia placed hope in a quick yet massive strike against the Central Powers along the Eastern Front. Russian troops, who had felt disconnected from the war effort after years of bungling, corruption, and disinterest, picked up their weapons and pledged to fight on.[11]

Although Alexander Kerensky had assumed power at an inopportune time, he had always been an able leader respected by the Allied Command. Military supplies once again began to arrive in the field from Archangelsk, Murmansk, and Vladivostok. Unfortunately, these ports were far from the war effort, with Archangelsk and Murmansk over eight hundred miles north and Vladivostok thousands of miles away.

Ironically, by the time these improvements had been enacted, the Provisional Government informed Thomas Masaryk that POWs would be allowed to enlist in the Russian army.[12] Kerensky fully backed the formation of a Czecho-Slovak Army Corps made up of prisoners sitting idle in Russian camps. The Provisional Government also threw its support behind federalization of the Hapsburg system, promising to work for an independent Polish state, among others, controlled by the Polish people. Polish affairs remained confused, however, and by the summer of 1917 as the Polish Legion fought beside the Austrians under Pilsudski, the French formed a Polish Corps with the help of the Supreme Polish Army Committee, mimicking what had already occurred in the Czech and Slovak ranks.[13]

Thomas Masaryk witnessed the untenable position of Kerensky's Provisional Government throughout western Russia. While visiting with Družina troops, Masaryk learned that "soviets" under the supervision of a Moscow group had begun to organize peasants in rural towns and hamlets across Ukraine. Caught in the middle, the Družina tried to keep peace. For the most part, Czechs and Slovaks understood and empathized with their frustrated Russian counterparts but they did not sympathize with Bolshevik ideas about the war.[14]

Even so, Czech Colonel Švec and other Družina commanders came under orders by ex-tsarist officers to fight and shoot any Bolshevik sympathizers in the field. Professor Procop Maxa, commissar of the Czecho-Slovak Army Corps, worked from Kiev trying to clarify Czech and Slovak status within the Russian war effort. Maxa protested the use of Družina troops as executioners and informed the Russian Command that the Družina would fight against the enemy, not against Russians.

At half strength, the First, Second, and Third Družina regiments occupied a four-mile section on the front west of the village of Zborov. When the main Russian assault turned sour, they continued forward to breach over four miles into the Austrian position, capturing 3,000 prisoners and huge quantities of armaments. These victories were nearly nullified, however, because of utter confusion in the field experienced by the Russian army. In the midst of chaos, one army corps continued to fight, to gain ground, to rout the enemy and take prisoners. Despite heavy casualties, the Czecho-Slovak Rifle Brigade held while Russian units fell back along the front. Many Czechs in Hapsburg uniform were also taken prisoner and incorporated into Russian POW camps only to join the Rifle Brigade in little time.

The Czech and Slovak rank and file knew that it was misguided to place the blame for failure solely on the Russian officer corps, especially since so many of Russia's best-trained officers had already fallen bravely in battle. The Czecho-Slovak Rifle Brigade cautioned fellow Russian soldiers not to overreact. Remaining in the trenches along the Eastern Front, legionnaires witnessed a Russian retreat as Russian units floundering behind the lines became confused and angry.

Over eight million men had died on the battlefield and more were now deserting at the front.[15] Thousands of troops merely turned, laid down their weapons and walked away. Others remained rooted where they sat, waiting for orders that never came. These troops were not incapable of courageous combat, they were instead exhausted and numb from years of loss and inattention. The heavy toll of millions year after year and the unrelenting demand for further sacrifice from their politicians had drained Russian troops of the desire to fight.

The sons of peasants had too often been forced into battle armed with sticks instead of rifles. Demoralized, isolated, and feeling betrayed, Russian conscripts found themselves fighting for liberal middle-class values they could not understand. The average Russian soldier no longer believed what his government promised.[16] He decided to reclaim his future. Under Lenin and Trotsky's tutelage, a new wave of political ideology based upon the theories of Marx geared up to confront the Provisional Government. Bolshevik recruiters encouraged crestfallen Russian units to turn against their officers in the field.

Ferenc Imrey, a Hungarian calvary officer, remembered fighting against such units. During one battle he observed a fellow cavalry commander who felt empathy for the undersupplied and demoralized Russian troops. The Hungarian offered the Russians opposing him a chance to leave the battlefield but Russian officers refused.

> He [the Hungarian officer] collected all our hussars and other mounted men at headquarters and galloped out to battle as in some medieval day ... [The Russians] awaited the oncoming hussars, their heads sunk between their shoulders and their weight thrown forward into their long, slender weapons. They outnumbered us four hundred troopers, three to one.... Our charging horsemen parted in the middle and, with a swiftness that threw the Russians into blank amazement and confusion, swung through sharp curves around either flank.... Some bodies fell cut in twain."[17]

Despite witnessing Russian comrades retreating, the Legion, as the Družina became referred to, surged into battle with the zeal of an inspired army. The elite rifle unit had been comprised solely of Czech and Slovak volunteers. The Austrian, German, and Hungarian troops facing them looked upon them as deserters to be shot on the spot. Like the Russian nation, the Czech and Slovak units were not quite in the war and not quite out of it. Poised to advance west, the Czecho-Slovak Army Corps also prepared to retreat eastward.

In the past, the railroads of Siberia were maintained as property of the tsar and their employees were paid through government funds. But the tsarist government that had once paid the bills no longer existed. Payment, distribution, and leadership ended, along with a system of generational employment for railroad families.[18] When the Romanovs disengaged from these efforts, *Semztoves* (city councils) took control. Stationmasters had authority up the line to the next depot as each branch became only as good as the city council that ruled over it. In many cases during the war these councils had been taken over by bandits and warlords who refused to pay anyone.

For some time, an Allied commission persistently warned Kerensky of Russia's impending collapse.[19] And while interest in the Russian war effort faltered, Kerensky single-mindedly pursued the Allied effort against Austria-Hungary,

Germany, and Turkey. Kerensky was viewed as impossibly optimistic and the Russian people once again began to cast about for an alternative. With American troops prepared for full all-out warfare, Kerensky's Provisional Government desperately tried to buy time. It didn't seem to matter that the infamous Rasputin had finally been murdered or that the tsar and his tsarina had been replaced. The Russian people no longer believed their leaders, no matter who they might be.

Kerensky dealt with troop frustration as best he could, but the main assault of the Great Kerensky Offensive had already turned into a rout.[20] The failure of the Russian forces along the Eastern Front — a strategic war effort that proved an elusive dream of a doomed government — signaled the need for change. Kerensky might have been the right man in the right job, but he had come too late to help the war effort or the Russian people.

On November 6 (October 24 in the western calendar), 1917, Lenin and Trotsky led a revolt against the Provisional Government. Members of the Russian armed forces who had mutinied warned Kerensky's Mensheviks to either flee the capital or be placed under arrest. On the following day, the Council of People's Commissars under the leadership of Lenin, Trotsky and their new colleague, Stalin, replaced Kerensky's recast Duma. Yet another government would rule Mother Russia. This time it would fall to the Bolsheviks to sort out the chaotic mess left behind by the Romanovs.

As early as the fall of 1917, American secretary of state Robert Lansing began to voice serious concerns over Russia's participation in the war. After Lenin gained power, Lansing again expressed concern that Bolshevik Russia would have no interest in remaining part of the war effort.[21] He was correct. The Bolsheviks announced their belief that the current world conflict had been an affair between decrepit and discredited imperialist nations, never a concern of the Russian people.

The first weeks of transition from a socialist state to Bolshevism proved highly frustrating for the Allies. The incoming Bolshevik leadership, disinterested in anything even slightly connected to the Allied war effort, refused to meet emissaries from Russia's former allies. Incredibly, the new Moscow leadership rejected all former treaties signed between Russia and the West. Kremlin officials refuted former agreements and summarily refused to speak to any of the Allied diplomatic corps. Trotsky also renounced all war debts and declared the Western nations enemies of the state. Rumors began to circulate that the Bolsheviks had initiated contact with the Central Powers (particularly Germany). Could peace negotiations be far behind?

News of the October Revolution and Kerensky's fall from power hardly surprised Masaryk, Štefánik or former Družina leadership.[22] The Allies and Russia's neighbors felt immediately threatened by this about–face, but worse news soon followed. In November of 1917, amid an atmosphere of distrust between the Russian troops and their officers, ex-Družina Commander General Duchonín was murdered by his own men. Colonel Švec, now brigade commander, received orders to transfer from a Czecho-Slovak Army unit at the front to Russian headquarters in the rear. Later, Švec learned that he would be protecting the Russian staff from their own recruits. Švec and other Družina officers placed in similar positions found this new assignment highly repugnant. Švec wrote, "It would be grievous to me if I were obliged to take arms against the Bolsheviks, whom indeed I dislike on account of their German-bribed leaders. Yet, they are Russians with whom I have lived the gay and hard hours of military life."[23]

Admiral Kolchak, on an invited visit to San Francisco, had left his Black Sea fleet in the charge of his officer staff. While in San Francisco, Kolchak learned of the Bolshevik takeover. Immediately, he headed for home via Japan, where the Japanese Command impressed on Kolchak that he would be executed by the Bolsheviks upon his return. Already word spread of executions of Russian officers. For the time being, Admiral Kolchak became the guest of the emperor of Japan.

With Masaryk's network acting as diplomats and spies, France negotiated with Trotsky throughout November and eventually secured the transfer of a few units of Czechs and Slovaks in Russian uniform to the Western Front.[24] Though these troops would be under the patronage of the French military, Eduard Beneš made sure Czech and Slovak soldiers on all the fronts remained part of Masaryk's newly organized Czechoslovak National Council. For the legionnaires who would journey northward in late autumn, the route leading by way of Archangelsk would be filled with peril. Many wondered if they would not be safer to remain behind. It soon became apparent to the men who had remained behind, however, that those chosen to move northward would be a lucky few.

During the months of April and May 1917, Allied ships had been deploying marines in the ports at Archangelsk and Murmansk to protect stockpiled war materiel from falling into the hands of German spies. Lenin advised both the Archangelsk and Murmansk Soviets to accept the status of these U.S. units. Inexplicably, Lenin decided in the early months of the revolution that Allied assistance in the far north would not be "interventionist."[25]

On December 3, 1917, Trotsky announced to the world that peace negotiations would begin shortly in Brest-Litovsk between the Central Powers and the Russian Bolshevik nation.[26] Amid the resulting confusion, the newly organized Czecho-Slovak Army Corps, made up of POWs and Družina members, began to take precautions. Kerensky's Provisional Government, which had always appreciated Czech and Slovak military prowess at the front, had been obliterated and replaced by Soviet militias throughout the interior — men whose interest in the legionnaires extended only to possible Czech and Slovak recruits as Bolshevik supporters. Legion officers quickly realized that safety now lay eastward in the wilds of Siberia.

In early 1918, Masaryk petitioned the French Command for assistance. The French answered his call later in the spring by maintaining that the Czecho-Slovak Army Corps in Russia had always been a part of a Bohemian unit already fighting for the Allies on the Western Front. This designation invalidated any political claims the Russian military might make to ex-Družina units. More importantly, however, France proclaimed Masaryk and his entourage living in exile as the true Czecho-Slovak government — a government in absentia — and the Czecho-Slovak Army Corps in Siberia its national army. This maneuver, a brilliant tactic on the part of the French, did not improve the Czech and Slovak situation in the East after all.

Masaryk warned all units now pulling back from the Eastern Front throughout Ukraine to maintain neutrality. The Legion could only become involved if threatened personally; otherwise, its members must pledge to a man never to be embroiled in Russian policies.[27]

As Czech and Slovak troops retreated toward Kiev, the Ukrainian Front collapsed. Kiev, capital of Ukraine, occupied by the Red army, soon allowed 12 to 13 German detachments into the capital city. Overnight, German units surrounded the Czechs and Slovaks. However, detachments of the Legion met little to no resistance from Ukrainian militias in the area.

Seventh Regiment, 1918, near Kiev with balloon proclaiming, "Kiev to Prague," spring 1918.

Retreat through Ukraine became the only option for the legionnaires. With German units advancing at will throughout the countryside, Legion and Russian units still loyal to Kerensky covered one another as they evacuated to the rear. In order to retreat along the Dnieper River, the Czecho-Slovak Eighth Regiment had to secure a suspension bridge. Fighting for the bridge soon proved to be costly for both the Germans and the fleeing legionnaires. On February 28, 1918, as the battle for the bridge reached its zenith, the Czecho-Slovak First Division, acting as rear guard, surrounded German units that had encircled their colleagues. While other Czechs and Slovaks crossed to safety, the First Division stayed behind to keep the bridge open for any stragglers.

Captain Červinka, in charge of the Czecho-Slovak Sixth Regiment, was farthest west, collecting men in the rear. Supplies and trains had been remarkably easy to recover since boxcars and engines sat deserted along the railway. For Červinka it became a matter of placing Legion troops in contact with other units already moving into boxcars to his east.

Ahead of the Czechs and Slovaks lay the Bakhmach Depot, into which merged Ukrainian railroad lines heading east. While German units were in

Sixth Regiment commandeers trains outside Kruty near Bachmach in Ukraine, 1918 (courtesy Military Historical Archives, Prague).

heavy pursuit of the Legion, Lenin and Trotsky warned them not to trespass across the Ukrainian border. From Grebjonka-Poltava, Nezhni-Bakhmach, and Ichna-Kurtz, the Czechs and Slovaks pushed toward the depot. Lying like a wheel hub to approaching lines, Bakhmach Depot had to be secured at all cost or the Legion would be doomed.[28]

Disobeying orders, a few Soviet units planned to repay a debt they believed Russia owed the legionnaires. Remembering the Družina's courage in battle, renegade Russian soldiers occupied the Krontop line as yet another group held the railway station open for legionnaires to pass through. A similar incident occurred at Pilsky near Bakhmach as German troops advanced quickly hoping to halt the evacuation of the Czechs and Slovaks.[29]

The First Division, exhausted and hungry, trudged toward the railroad slowly falling behind. The Second Division, although farther along toward Bakhmach, was already in danger of being overrun by several enemy battalions. Neither division held much hope of reaching Bakhmach station before it fell into either German or Austrian hands. A fierce engagement lay ahead as the two Legion divisions merged into one on the outskirts of Bakhmach.

Approaching the station, they were pleasantly surprised to discover that a small band of legionnaires protecting the depot from their barricade inside had been successful in holding off the enemy. This ragtag group was in the fight of its life, however. The First and Second Czecho-Slovak divisions encircled the enemy. Ironically, it became the Germans who were overrun, and the Czechs and Slovaks who made it to freedom.

With still more German reinforcements following behind, Legion commanders worked frantically to move the last of the troops into boxcars.[30] Soldiers hung from open doorways and windows or lay on train rooftops — any place with a foothold. The First and the Second divisions made it through the junction to board trains and head eastward following the others. As the junction of Bakhmach receded in the distance, a cheer rose from the speeding boxcars. There would be no further contact between Legion and German troops either inside Russia or Ukraine after Bakhmach station.

Traveling as fast as possible, the First Division reached Kiev on March 1, 1918. By March 2 the entire Legion was said to have crossed the Dnieper River, crowding into additional trains waiting on the opposite bank.[31] Over 1,000 trains now headed east to an uncertain fate, but for the time being the Czechs and Slovaks felt safe.

Almost immediately, Ukrainian units began to harass them — impeding their retreat. Rumors spread that Germany had promised Ukraine political independence from Russia. In a few weeks, however, the Ukrainians regretted their behavior. A month after Russia signed the Brest-Litovsk Treaty, discussion of Ukrainian independence formerly promised by Germany became tabled. Instead, trains headed west into Germany filled with Ukrainian grain for German troops fighting on the Western Front. In no time, the breadbasket of Ukraine had been stripped bare and famine began to spread throughout the region. Western newspapers reported the Ukrainian catastrophe occurring under Germany's control. A reporter for the *New York Times* wrote, "An unprecedented dearth prevails in this rich country and the population of Kiev and other cities are suffering bitterly because of lack of bread."[32]

Though the Bolsheviks had won the day in the cities of European Russia, their following was weak elsewhere, especially the farther east one traveled. In all the confusion, rural areas consolidated under local warlords and pockets of antirevolutionary fervor began to develop. Much of the ex-tsarist opposition, though large in numbers, had been completely demoralized by the tsar's abdication. Since his arrest rumors of his fate spread throughout the countryside but nothing could be verified.

Ex-tsarist officers began to reorganize throughout the interior in competition with one another for authority over makeshift army units.[33] General Kornilov, ex-tsarist Provisional commander, quickly gathered more than 2,500 men along the Don River—turning on local Soviet militia in the region. In Orenburg, Ataman Dutov led Cossack troops against a fledgling Red Army being organized by Trotsky. Ataman Semenov and Ataman Kalmikov, both autonomous leaders of renegade bands of Mongol and Tartar mercenaries, began to prey on peasant communities bordering China and attacked Manchuria whenever the opportunity arose.

Resistance groups had as many reasons for opposing Bolshevism as they had men eager to fight. Some, like those organizing in Ukraine, hoped for autonomy from Russia. Others fought to restore Tsar Nicholas II to what they believed was his God-given right as leader of the Russian people. But others, like Ataman Semenov and Ataman Kalmikov, led bandits into areas suffering from the ravages of tsarist neglect to collect wandering soldiers who earlier deserted the eastern trenches with nowhere to go.[34]

In the early part of 1918, the world press took little notice of the Legion. Instead, newspapers covered Lenin's fledgling government and the progress of what was left of the Triple Entente (Britain, France, and Russia) on the Western Front. Rumors that the Central Powers and Russia had an agreement for an armistice began to spread throughout Ukraine and western Russia. A Russian armistice would mean that Austria, Germany, Hungary and Turkey could prosecute a one-front war even as the Allied effort in the west began to dim.[35]

The headquarters of the German Command on the Eastern Front at Brest-Litovsk had been chosen as the site for treaty negotiations. When the announcement of an agreement finally came, treaty terms shocked the world.

Under Trotsky's advice, fellow Bolsheviks rubber-stamped the Brest-Litovsk Treaty with Soviet congressional approval on March 12, 1918.[36]

In the Brest-Litovsk document Lenin and Trotsky had signed over much of Russia's Baltic States, eastern Poland, and the entire Caucasus, as well as more than six million marks in goods and services, and 120 million rubles. In total, Trotsky gave away 34 percent of Russia's population, 32 percent of its farmland — including 85 percent of its beet crop, 54 percent of its industrial capacity, and 89 percent of its coal reserves. Through the Treaty of Brest-Litovsk, Germany gained what Russia's enemies had dreamed of conquering for centuries. To a world that knew Russia was on the verge of famine, this seemed not only irresponsible but criminal.[37]

The Brest-Litovsk Treaty brought an end to Russia's part in the war effort, but at a hefty price. For the Slavic troops marooned inside Russia, the Brest-Litovsk Treaty worsened their predicament. In order to gain the return of all former Hapsburg deserters who served under the tsar in Russian uniform, Austrian and German delegations insisted that foreign troops be expelled immediately to the West.

News of the Brest-Litovsk Treaty reached the Legion as some of its more advanced units began to enter Siberian territory. The treaty came as a terrible blow, threatening all hopes of finding a route home. The minority peoples of Central Europe were dumbfounded by Russia's betrayal of their Slavic brethren.

Russia's formal withdrawal from the war followed shortly after the signing of Brest-Litovsk, but it hardly surprised the French or the British, who had already begun to worry about war supplies sitting on the docks in Archangelsk, Murmansk, and Vladivostok.[38] The Central Powers would surely push to dominate the entire Trans-Siberian Railway and grab these important ports as a result. The Allied Command staff members began to ask one another whether a new German offensive on the Western Front could be far off. Some in Versailles openly discussed the possibility of intervening in "the Russian situation" to keep the Germans at bay.[39]

As troop trains spread out across western Russia, Lenin surprised the legionnaires by pledging to help. Even though the Brest-Litovsk Treaty mandated the immediate expulsion of all foreign troops westward, the Moscow leadership contacted Thomas Masaryk's representatives to offer boxcars and equipment. Lenin wanted to help ensure that the Legion continued to travel eastward away from the Austrians, Germans, and Hungarians as quickly as possible. Lenin believed that the sooner these foreign troops fled Russian territory and were on Siberian soil the better, especially since German agents had begun to flood across Ukraine and into western Russia in pursuit.

The Trans-Siberian Railway, cutting across vast regions of isolated wilderness, also took the Czech and Slovak troops deeper and deeper into pockets of political instability. Across this hinterland, war lords and marauding bandits preyed upon vulnerable peasant communities. To compound Legion troubles, armed and aimless demobilized Russian soldiers wandered the countryside harassing settlements and banding together to overthrow existing city governments.[40]

Following the signing of the Brest-Litovsk Treaty, German diplomats stationed in Moscow petitioned Lenin and Trotsky to stop evacuating Czechs and Slovaks through western Russia and into Siberia. Count Mirbach, the German Ambassador to Russia, argued that the size of the Legion placed both Russia and Siberia in harm's way. Mirbach asserted that the Czech and Slovak Legion had secretly been acting in concert with the French and British. Mirbach warned Lenin that the Legion moving along the railroad through Siberia could easily overwhelm small town militias, isolating them from one another and, more importantly, from Moscow.

In fact, just the opposite was true. From the very first contact with local Siberian militia, officials harassed and abused Legion personnel. The fact that the Czecho-Slovak Army Corps had been given safe passage from Lenin only seemed to make matters worse. Instructed by their officers to keep the goodwill of the locals, Czech and Slovak echelons reluctantly handed over weapons and supplies. Movement from one depot to the next soon bogged down as local warlords and militia leaders extorted materiel from each train.

Many of these local militiamen represented the only armed force in the area and they exercised their control over surrounding villagers through brute force and intimidation. Foreign troops traveling through rural provinces not only represented potential revenue but also threatened local power. In addition, money issued by Kerensky's Provisional Government had proven easy to counterfeit so the Siberian population continued using the earlier Romanov currency.[41] Until the Communist government in Moscow could solve these problems, economic and political stability would be impossible. In the absence of any viable alternative, the population began to barter. This placed the Legion in a highly precarious position since some of the most sought after items to trade were war materiel.

After the majority of Czecho-Slovak troop trains cleared Bakhmach Junction, the First Czech Division proceeded toward Penza in Siberia. The division had planned to meet up with the Second Czech Division nearby. Both groups, however, encountered stiff resistance along the way. Town officials remembered the Belgian artillery which, enroute through Siberia from the Eastern Front, attacked locals. Since area commissars saw all uniformed foreigners as a threat, they petitioned Moscow to force the Legion trains to head northward for evacuation through the port at Archangelsk.

In debates over the safest possible route for their kinsmen, the Czecho-Slovak National Council (OCSNR), or *Odbočky,* considered many alternatives. The northward route to Archangelsk or Murmansk would lead the troops through the harshest of Siberian conditions — an incredibly hazardous journey for poorly equipped men. Proceeding to Archangelsk had also become impossible since both German and Finnish armies located nearby blocked the way. Traveling eastward, the route ultimately chosen, would also prove trying, but entail fewer complications with the Bolshevik authorities in Moscow. One of the greater fears was the possibility of trains becoming isolated from one another in the frigid Vologda region where fatal temperatures could cause more casualties than enemy fire.

As counterrevolutionary resistance to local Soviets took shape, Lenin and Trotsky worried over the added pressures caused by foreigners traveling through the countryside.[42] A few hundred remaining legionnaires joined the Red army while still others pledged allegiance to the counterrevolution, the sworn enemy of the Soviets. The defection of these men after swearing an oath of neutrality to Thomas Masaryk threatened to place the entire Legion in the middle of a quickly escalating civil war. Some individuals reportedly joined the Red Army out of fear of fighting on the Western Front. Further incentive had been a Red Army offer for higher rank at more pay, revealing the value Trotsky placed upon the education and training of Czech and Slovak volunteers.

Distrust was growing on both sides, however, as Czech and Slovak troop trains fled eastward. Legionnaires worried that the Soviets wanted nothing more than to dump them into the Siberian wilderness where food and supplies were scarce, and then offer only one way out: join the Red Army ranks or perish. On the other hand, rumors spread throughout Moscow that the Legion had been working secretly as mercenaries in the pay of Western capitalists.[43]

General Dieterichs, commanding general of the Czecho-Slovak Army, stationed in Vladivostok with the fourth Legion contingent, not dated.

Legion officials believed these stories had been deliberately spread by German agents who hoped to impede the Legion's transfer to the Western Front. It worked. Rural Soviet militia reacted violently, harassing trains whenever and wherever possible.

General Dieterichs, who had earlier commanded the Družina, hurried across the steppe to Vladivostok on the Pacific coast of Siberia; accompanying him was Dr. Girsa, representative of the Czecho-Slovak National Council (*Odbočky*), and the Fifth Regiment. They traveled swiftly eastward, installing a network of Legion telegraph operators, railway personnel, supplies, engineers and technicians to resuscitate the

Czech and Slovak communication specialists worked in depots all along the Trans-Siberian Railway, here Ekaterinburg, not dated.

Trans-Siberian Railway. Previously insolent depot officials who had harassed troop trains accepted Czech and Slovak technicians with a newfound gratitude.

Finally arriving at the port of Vladivostok, Dieterichs and Girsa arranged for a campsite and barracks to be erected on the outskirts of town. Though Vladivostok had also fallen to the Soviet militia, city officials remained accommodating. Rural Soviets, however, began to vie with one another to extort payment from Legion units traveling through their towns. Powerful warlords often saw Moscow's directives as an affront to their own political control. Siberian politics had long suffered from jealousies between rural and metropolitan regions within the provinces.

Worst still was the influence that German populations living throughout Siberia had begun to assert. Since April of 1918, the German government had been evaluating the suggestion of a Lieutenant E. Scholz, who had been repatriated to Germany from a POW camp in Siberia. Scholz reported that a population of over 80,000 Germans near Krasnoyarsk wanted to establish a German-sponsored free republic. Though the German foreign ministry never acted upon Scholz's suggestion, rumors persisted throughout Krasnoyarsk that unrest in the area had been due to the efforts of a German ring of spies.[44] Another rumor persisted that Germans intended to occupy Irkutsk in order to take over the entire Trans-Siberian Railway line.[45] Even so, Thomas Masaryk cautioned the Allied Command: "Nowhere in Siberia, between March 15th and April 2nd, did I see armed German or Austrian prisoners."[46]

Lenin agreed with the Legion Command's refusal to head north. His disapproval stemmed from entirely different reasons. The Bolshevik leadership did not want an entire foreign army of tens of thousands of men passing close to Petrograd at the very moment the Bolshevik's political situation had fallen to its weakest point. Moving Legion trains eastward would mean forcing these foreign troops farther and farther away from the Bolshevik epicenter.[47] Lenin also argued that trains carrying Legion troops to Vladivostok could be used to transport Austrian, Hungarian, German, and Turkish POWs back west from labor camps in Siberia.

In the depot at Penza countless boxcars discovered along sidings were parceled out to be connected to Legion troop trains. Men spread out filling these additional boxcars while the reorganization of the entire line under Czech and Slovak officers began. Though the Legion continued experiencing overcrowding and unsanitary conditions, the initial 40 to 50 men per boxcar became reduced by less than half.

Officer appointments had to be made since Russian officers could no longer command foreign troops. Several ex-tsarist officers who had been in command positions overseeing the Družina on the Eastern Front requested

Living conditions on board a teplushka *(boxcar). First Regiment, not dated.*

that they be allowed to accompany the Legion as it evacuated Siberia for ships that would take them to the Western Front. Stalin ordered the Penza soviet to appoint reliable commissioners to accompany the Legion to Vladivostok for its own protection.[48] He also ordered that each echelon of Czechs and Slovaks be allowed minimum numbers of arms. Any excess would be confiscated.

To soothe the regional soviets and to push the Czechs and Slovaks along, Antonoff-Ovsjenko, Bolshevik Commander of southern Russia, issued Order #26 on March 16, 1918, to train commanders and village officials up and down the Trans-Siberian line. Antonoff-Ovsjenko wrote, "The revolutionary army will never forget the fraternal assistance rendered by the Czecho-Slav [Slovak] Army Corps in the battle of the working people of the Ukraine against the thieving bands of imperialists. The military equipment given up by the Czecho-Slavs the revolutionary army accepts as a fraternal gift."[49]

Antonoff-Ovsjenko's message affected both sides but not in the manner he expected. The Legion regarded Order #26 as a threat, implying that rural strongmen had official permission to extort weapons and harass troop trains. In fact, Antonoff-Ovsjenko's order proved a portent of things to come. Immediately after Order #26 arrived, rural militia escalated threats to arrest legionnaires if weapons were not turned over. To move quickly through Penza and other Soviet depots in the hinterland, the legionnaires could keep 160 rifles, one machine gun, and a small quantity of ammunition. Local commissars believed that the French provided stores of weapons for these troops to proceed across Siberia on their way to Western Europe where they would fight.[50] Emmett Hoskins of the American Expeditionary Forces remembered:

> The Czechs [and Slovaks] agreed to refrain from hostilities against the Russians and the Russians guaranteed them safe passage to Vladivostok. The Czechs stood by their agreement. On the other hand, the Russians gradually became more hostile to the Czechs and abused them, and obstructed their passage in every way possible.[51]

Even though a resolution to reject Bolshevism had passed earlier in 1917 within Russian POW camps, a socialist left wing of the legionnaires traveling on boxcars succeeded in attracting some Slavic soldiers to its cause.[52] In the first weeks of April 1918, the Czech communist newspaper *Svoboda* began announcing Red Army recruitment drives in Siberia. Militias offered to accept any Czech or Slovak soldier wishing to leave the Legion and join Bolshevik revolutionary ranks. In April, Communist units from Moscow began arriving in towns throughout Siberia to intercept legionnaires.[53] In Penza the depot was outfitted with a special propaganda boxcar for recruitment of legionnaires.

In the midst of the resulting confusion, both the *New York Times* and the *New York Herald* sent correspondents to cover the Legion's progress eastward along the Trans-Siberian Railway. Neither newspaper wanted to miss an important human-interest story that appeared to be spreading across the heart of the Russian Far East. Readers in the United States and Britain began to watch for installments of the Legion's evacuation over more than 5,800 miles of rugged territory in the midst of a growing political crisis. For their readership, reporters also examined the history of the Slavic minority peoples of Central Europe and their centuries-old quest for autonomy.[54]

With pride, Czech-Americans and Slovak-Americans pointed to studies demonstrating that these communities had given both time and money to the Allied war effort in larger percentages than any other ethnic group. the *New York Times* of March 5, 1918, reported:

> They have aided our Allies and are aiding us to win the fight by the way that the French people aided the American Revolution; they have given of their blood and treasure to the Serbians, Belgians, French, and English. They are siding with the American government today both morally and financially, and have given more volunteers to the American Army than any other people of old country stock.[55]

Thomas Masaryk had no doubt that the Allies would repay his recruits for volunteering to fight in the trenches of Belgium and France. He knew that an armistice would surely abet the Czechs and Slovaks, as well as other Central European minorities, in gaining independence from Hapsburg rule at war's end. When independence came, the government in the Czech lands and Slovakia would need a well-trained and competent army to protect its borderlands. Legionnaires traveling through Russia and into Siberia along the Trans-Siberian would be that army.

Legion officers aboard troop trains knew that Masaryk had worked out an agreement for Legion troops to be transported by Allied ships to the Western Front from the Pacific port of Vladivostok.[56] On March 26, 1918, Masaryk visited the local soviet in Vladivostok to negotiate safe housing and a smooth transfer of the Czechs and Slovaks from trains and onto Allied shipping.

Within the long ribbon of Legion trains winding through Siberia, the situation appeared to be going from bad to worse. Several soldiers heard that the Omsk soviet had ordered the local guard to stop all troop trains from proceeding any further eastward. The Omsk militia, the *Tsentrosibir*, feared armed foreigners cutting through its land.[57] The Tsentrosibir pleaded with Lenin via telegram to reverse his earlier agreement with Masaryk and instead stop the flow of Legion trains to the Pacific coast. Czech and Slovak telecommunication officers working along the railway for Dieterichs and Girsa, however, intercepted the Tsentrosibir communication. While the telegraph operators sent this telegram on to Lenin, Czech and Slovak communications officers also passed it up and down the line to alert Legion train commanders.

As the lead of the most forward echelon, Colonel Radola Gajda knew that if
trouble occurred on the way to the
Pacific coast it would be his men who
would first encounter it. Gajda had
been born on February 14, 1882,
and christened under the name
Radola Geidl. Geidl spent his
childhood along the Dalmatian
coast on the island of Kotor. His
father had been a noncommissioned
officer in the Hapsburg navy. After
retiring, Radola's father moved his
family from Kotor to Kyjov, Moravia,
where he joined the provincial bureaucracy.

From 1908 to 1910, Geidl
studied pharmacy in the Bohemian
town of Votice. However, after
taking part in a raid on a wine cel-
lar with friends in 1907, he found
himself expelled from the gymna-

Captain Radola Gajda, commander of the Sixth and Seventh regiments, third con-tingent of Legion trains and later the com-manding general of Siberian troops under Omsk government, not dated.

sium. When Geidl finally ran out of funds, he decided to join the military as
his father had before him. He spent much of his service as an artillery regiment
clerk until his discharge in 1914. That same year, Geidl married the daughter
of a druggist by the name of Piron and began to work in the family pharmacy.

But the year of his marriage was also the year war broke out across
Europe. Radola Geidl found himself conscripted for service into the Hapsburg
army. It has been rumored that Geidl stretched the truth and began telling
colleagues during this period that he was a trained physician. Whether this
is true or not, Geidl quickly assumed the rank of captain in the Third Serbian
Regiment. As the Serbian front dissolved, however, Geidl traveled through
Korfu and on into Russia with the First Serbian Division.

Later, during 1915, while fighting on the Serbian front, the Russians collected him. Somehow Geidl finagled his way out of a POW camp. Again it
is rumored that he continued to maintain that he was a physician. By 1917,
Geidl had changed his German sounding name to Gajda and become a hospital assistant for the Legion's Second Regiment. His name appears and dis-
appears throughout the early months of the war along the Eastern Front only
to appear in 1918 as an officer in the Czech and Slovak Army Corps.

At the age of 27, Radola Gajda found himself a colonel in the Czecho-Slovak Legion, ushering troop trains across the interior of Siberia. Cool and moody, Gajda quickly made a reputation for himself as a leader with seemingly endless energy. A large man, mustachioed and thin faced, with a mop of medium-brown hair haphazardly brushed to one side, Radola Gajda became known for his icy blue eyes and captivating speaking voice. He had once led a shock battalion at Jezerna that broke through the German defenses and drove on toward Tarnopol. With this first success, Gajda began a long series of military actions that proved skillful. Yet it was his career in Siberia that would bring him both notoriety and success.[58]

Radola Gajda rose to this momentous occasion by challenging both himself and the men he led. Reputedly reckless, he was nonetheless respected for leading by example. Always at the head of his troops, he cajoled his units onward, and was reported to be the first up at dawn and the last to bed at night.

In the spring of 1918, Gajda desperately wanted to deliver the entire regiment safely to Vladivostok for evacuation to the Western Front. He willingly pushed his men to the extreme. They would be in Vladivostok by the end of summer. As local harassment by the militia continued to slow Legion progress, Gajda's determination stiffened. He called for the Czechs and Slovaks to defend themselves and to unite against town bullies like the Omsk Tsentrosibir.

Gadja publicly lobbied for the Legion to rise up against local soviets. His outspoken demeanor drew the attention of both Masaryk and Lenin. Gajda's disdain for Siberian local militia was shared by most of his fellow Czech and Slovak officers. Though Gajda's notoriety began in the late spring of 1918, later antics would earn him a place in Czech and Slovak history, where it remains controversial to this day.

Town henchmen made and broke agreements with Legion trains at will, often using the Bolshevik cause as their excuse. These warlords were no more loyal to the Bolshevik movement than to their bandits in the hills. The true concern of local militia leadership remained power and wealth.[59]

On March 26, 1918, Joseph Stalin published an announcement to mollify growing hostilities between the Legion and village administrators. Stalin guaranteed that the legionnaires would be free to travel with a certain amount of arms and ammunition for protection, especially against counterrevolutionaries.[60] Stalin's efforts proved fruitless, however, as Vasili Vladimirovich Kuraviev, the Soviet chairman of Penza, disregarded Moscow's orders and restricted Legion train movement on his section of railroad line.

For its part, the Czech and Slovak Army Corps believed fifteen of its trains would proceed through Penza unmolested on a daily basis. Instead, only one or two trains passed through the town depot from day to day, a rate that spelled disaster for others following behind. As a war correspondent reported,

> The Czechs [and Slovaks] were passing through an unknown country where the atmosphere was charged with rumors of plots and schemes. The Soviets not only were filled with anxiety as to the Czechs' intentions in Siberia, but they apparently felt that for foreign troops to pass through the country armed, would lower their dignity and would be an infringement of their sovereign rights.[61]

Legion Commanders became doubly concerned when Strombach, head of the Penza soviet, requested authority from Moscow to begin a propaganda campaign for a Czechoslovak Communist Party. Strombach wrote, "Enormous possibilities in the field of propaganda appear to be here, our task is to permeate the troops with ideas of internationalism. They [Czechs and Slovaks] are not at all familiar with socialist ideas. For this reason we cannot leave Penza and go to other places.... Large sums of agitation are badly needed; do not forget this..."[62]

Bolshevik leaders wanted to enlist what they saw as the proletarian core of the Legion while permitting what remained of the Legion, capitalist dupes and imperialists, to leave.[63] Many in the Communist Party believed that thousands of Czechs and Slovaks would rush to join the fledgling Red army throughout Siberia if given a chance to do so.[64] At the same time, rumors again spread that Lenin planned to turn the westernmost echelons northward, a complication that demanded Legion attention.

Chapter Four

By mid–April a few Czech and Slovak troop trains had arrived in Vladivostok. Contrary to their expectations, the legionnaires were not met by Allied vessels. Meanwhile, the majority of their comrades remained scattered along the Trans-Siberian Railroad from Russia through the steppe and on toward the Pacific Coast.

For the entire journey, the legionnaires were greeted with intimidation, beatings, and the confiscation of their weapons and supplies. They could no longer stay put. They could no longer proceed. And they surely could not retreat into the arms of the waiting Austrian and German armies.

Tracking them from the west, German and Austrian units pushed deep into Russian territory, determined to hunt down and execute as many of the insolent Slavic deserters as they could capture. In the meantime, Vladivostok Harbor remained empty of allied evacuation vessels.

The situation also grew increasingly worrisome for the Allies eager to place legionnaires under their command. As Japanese ships pulled into Vladivostok on April 23, 1918, France and Britain leaned heavily on the Japanese and United States governments to intervene in Siberian politics.[1] Britain skillfully negotiated Trotsky's permission for Allied intervention in order to secure war materiel sitting dockside in Archangelsk. The effort would use all available Allied forces, with the Japanese contingent being the largest. The French and British urgently pressed to reestablish an Allied front in Russia. U.S. president Woodrow Wilson, however, opposed such blatant interference in Russian and Siberian affairs.

The political atmosphere teemed with hidden agendas and secret alliances. When Japanese officials announced that they intended to place 70,000 troops in Vladivostok to "help the Legion," suspicions grew within Washington, D.C., and the Kremlin.[2] British concern over stockpiled armaments lying unused on the wharves in Archangelsk, Murmansk, and Vladivostok ineffectively veiled political agendas in central Asia. To complicate the matter, Bolshevik agitation in Germany and across Central Europe spread alarmingly, forcing Britain to support anti–Bolshevik independence efforts throughout the Caucasus and the Russian Far East.[3]

Military and political officials conferred privately and publicly over the fate of the legionnaires, who themselves possessed no knowledge of conversations occurring at the High Command in Versailles. The French and British reconfirmed intentions to transfer legionnaires to the Western Front. France had been pressing for the rapid transfer of these men as announced by Clemenceau: "All units of the Czech [and Slovak] Corps should be transported by the swiftest means to the Western Front, where the presence of these excellent troops is very important; for this reason I have taken appropriate steps with the British Government to obtain transportation for a part of these troops by way of Archangel."[4]

The Abbeville Resolution, a Franco–British effort, called for the evacuation of the Legion, but added that the Allies would suggest the Czechs and Slovaks maintain their position with regard to Russia.[5] This subtle compromise in the evacuation agreement kept open the possibility to change plans if necessary. The French and British promised that Thomas Masaryk and his newly recognized government in exile would be part of future Allied decisions concerning the Legion's situation in Siberia.

French and British discussions continued in secret, disregarding the Supreme War Council's input, opposition by the Unites States, or Czech and Slovak troop evacuation promises. Britain announced a plan to position the Legion in Siberia as a second front, adding a provision in the Allied evacuation agreement for "a portion of the army to remain in Russia to hold Archangel."[6] This proposal echoed Russian fears and alarmed both Thomas Masaryk and the Czecho-Slovak National Council. Masaryk and President Wilson pushed for Allied unity while vehemently advocating the transfer of all Legion troops to the Western Front as originally agreed.

Masaryk advocated for the Legion and against the Allies when necessary. During the preceding month he met with the Soviet leadership in Moscow. Masaryk assured the Russian commander in chief that Legion units would never be involved with an overthrow of the Bolshevik government. In turn, Moscow guaranteed that Legion trains would have free access to the Trans-Siberian Railway and the harbor at Vladivostok. No sooner had Masaryk departed from Moscow, however, then new cases of harassment erupted along the entire railway system.

Elsewhere in Russia, Count Mirbach, German ambassador to Russia, relayed to Russian foreign minister Chicherin a plot uncovered by members of the German government. Mirbach reported the placement of Japanese ships off the Pacific coast of Siberia, were intended, not to rescue legionnaires, but to attack Russia through her back door. Mirbach also intimated that Czech and Slovak troop trains were to play the central role in this unfolding scenario. Count Mirbach succeeded in resurrecting the age-old Russian phobia concerning Japanese interests in Siberia's Pacific coastline while including the Legion as part of it. On April 20, under German pressure, Minister Chicherin relayed the following message up and down the Trans-Siberian line: "Fearing Japanese attack in Siberia, Germany expressly demands the evacuation of German prisoners from eastern Siberia into western Siberia or European Russia to start immediately and effected as quickly as possible. I request you take all measures in your power. Czecho-Slovak echelons must not be sent eastward."[7]

Local Soviet militias quickly repositioned their scant resources. Minister Chicherin's orders sent thousands of Austrian, German, and Hungarian ex-prisoners on their way back home.[8] The hatred that Central Powers units felt towards the Czechs and Slovaks had only increased tenfold with every Hapsburg life taken by a Družina soldier.

Austrian, German, and Hungarian boxcars soon headed westward on their way home from camps in Siberia, passing troop trains filled with frustrated legionnaires who headed eastward at a snail's pace toward the port of Vladivostok. At depots, these old enemies often sat side by side in their respective boxcars hurtling insults and threats at one another. Railway employees alerted local soviets of the likelihood for an incident to erupt between the two groups.

Bolshevik leaders ignored most of these warnings along with Legion pleas for timelier passage through depots eastward. Tensions ballooned with the unrelenting ruthlessness of village strongmen. Word of Legion preparations to defend its property and members' lives reached the OCSNR, the Czecho-Slovak National Council. Isolated from their representatives, Legion train commanders invited Dr. Girsa of the Czecho-Slovak National Council to travel west from Vladivostok along the Trans-Siberian Railway to witness the Legion's situation.

Penza was a city at a strategic point on the Trans-Siberian Railway along the Sura River. Here all branch lines converged at Penza Station before merging into one major track leading across Siberia to Vladivostok Harbor. On April 23, 1918, the First and Fourth Czecho-Slovak regiments pulled into Penza Depot. As they arrived, three armored cars approached. Several Soviet officers ordered the legionnaires to give up more quantities of armaments and supplies. Major General Kolomensky, commander of the First Czecho-Slovak Hussite Division, had no intention of acquiescing to these demands, especially after hearing of Lenin's many promises for the Legion's "free transportation to Vladivostok."[1] Kolomensky refused to cooperate with the local militia leaders, believing their demands to be extortion.

Girsa hurried westward from Vladivostok accompanied by Professor Procop Maxa, another member of the Odbočka (OCSNR). Both men hoped to defuse further incidents like the one occurring at Penza Station. Girsa and Maxa began to experience what the Legion had been reporting:

At the first station east of Penza he [Dr. Girsa] saw what he would have to face. The orders had little weight with the local Soviets; and for several hours a day, the doctor had to negotiate with authorities, explaining to them that his men were Czecho-Slovaks, who were Slavs and friends to Russia; they only wanted to go home.[2]

Unknown to Girsa and Maxa, the Moscow-appointed commissar in charge of Red Army recruitment for Penza had his own agenda. He had received information that the best fighters and therefore best candidates for recruitment into the Red Army were traveling with the First Czecho-Slovak Army Corps. This unit above all others had a reputation for having experienced, decisive fighters, attributes sorely lacking in the newly organizing Red Army. Trotsky anticipated that inflating his ranks with skilled Slavic fighters would encourage recruitment efforts throughout Siberia.[3]

Militia units in major Siberian towns began to receive funding from Trotsky in order to persuade foreign troops to abandon their trek homeward. A Czecho-Slovak revolutionary regiment at Kobolevsky Barracks had already been planned for housing large numbers of volunteers. Though empathetic toward the plight of Russia, the legionnaires did not desire glory in battle, only freedom and independence for themselves and their families back home. For the most part, they steadfastly refused to join Trotsky's Red Army units.

Legionnaires felt more akin to the Siberian Socialist revolutionaries whose moderate position regarding the peasantry and the war resembled their own. The Siberian Socialist Revolutionary Cooperative also assisted Legion troop trains while Soviet militias continued to harass them.

Adding to the Legion's ambivalence toward the militias was Trotksy's rush to establish a military presence in Siberia, which further delayed Czech and Slovak evacuation plans. Czech and Slovak soldiers also blamed the Moscow leadership for signing the Brest-Litovsk Treaty, which they viewed as a terrible blow to Slavic brotherhood.

Village commissars insisted that Legion trains had proceeded slowly because of the lack of locomotives. Dr. Girsa countered these blatantly false excuses. Legion trains had their own locomotives. Girsa also pointed out that on the tracks running parallel, boxcars of Austrian, German, and Hungarian POWs continued unhindered in their progress westward.

Persistent German propaganda against Thomas Masaryk and the Legion convinced Trotsky it was necessary to reinforce the Siberian hinterland with more Red Army contingents. This action directly threatened the Czechs and Slovaks. Desperate over the slow pace of their trains, echelon officers turned to Legion Command for answers. Only two troop trains had arrived in Vladivostok by the end of April. General Dieterichs waited, helpless and frustrated at the lack of allied support in the matter. Dr. Girsa reported worsening

Thomas Masaryk with National Czech and Slovak Co-Council, Kiev, January 30, 1918.

incidents of harassment to the troop trains but there was little anyone could do. As May began, it became heartbreakingly obvious to the OCSNR that Moscow had finally succumbed to German pressure. Legion telegraph workers intercepted important telegrams between Moscow and Soviet militias in the field.[1] Correspondence between Moscow, Omsk, and Irkutsk advised soviets to delay all Legion trains.

Trotsky openly distrusted the seemingly unending cache of weapons concealed within Czech and Slovak boxcars. Likewise, just as Trotsky questioned the need for an armed but "peaceful" evacuation, train commanders declared that they no longer trusted Lenin's promises since the Legion was certainly not being given "safe and unmolested passage to Vladivostok."[2]

Making matters worse, counterrevolutionaries — especially the newly organizing White Army, commenced their own Legion recruitment efforts. Ex-tsarist officers hoped to sway Czech and Slovak legionnaires to join in their fight against the Bolsheviks. Despite the burgeoning aggression of both Whites and Reds, Legion units honored the neutrality they had vowed to Thomas Masaryk and the Czecho-Slovak government in exile. Legion officers made sure to steer clear of either Red or White Army units.

At Penza Station, legionnaires demonstrated to Professor Maxa their loyalty and patience. In May, he witnessed station guards manhandling, searching, and beating humiliated Czechs and Slovaks. These troops asked him to intercede, but Odbočka orders were to observe, not react. Maxa, in turn,

Confiscation of Legion weapons by local Penza militia, summer, 1918.

reported to superiors that Colonel Radola Gajda's assessment had been accurate: resistance had become the only answer in order for the Legion to proceed eastward toward Vladivostok.

Returning to Vladivostok from Penza, Maxa learned of discussions between a German delegation and Bolshevik leaders in Petrograd. These discussions meant to gauge the possibility of imprisonment and subsequent transfer of all legionnaires back to Hapsburg Command. At Tambov, Czech and Slovak echelon officers secretly voted on their options. If threatened, Gajda's First Division intended to fight its way through depot after depot until it reached Vladivostok Harbor.

The OCSNR understood, if not the scope, at least the intent of these train officers. Professor Masaryk, angered by the Legion's mistreatment, became resolute to evacuate his men at any cost and as quickly as possible. Along with leading elements of the Czecho-Slovak Army Command, 10,000 to 14,000 soldiers had arrived in Vladivostok only to be encamped in barracks on the outskirts of the city.[3] Masaryk wondered why no Allied vessels accepted them onboard.

On May 14, 1918, at the Chelyabinsk depot, busy with two overcrowded enemy troop trains, the tinderbox of Legion fears exploded. Shunted onto a siding, Czech and Slovak troops angrily awaited movement forward. Austro-Hungarian troops heading westward stopped alongside on the tracks next to them. Men onboard the two trains taunted and ridiculed one another. This was not uncommon, but in Chelyabinsk, a large piece of metal flew through an open window, striking one of the Legion soldiers in the head and mortally wounding him. Allegedly, the man who threw it had boasted earlier that he wanted to kill at least one Czech or Slovak before departing.

Several Legion soldiers jumped from their boxcar and wrestled a soldier they believed to be the culprit down from the boxcar opposite. Spoiling for a fight, both sides emptied from their trains and rioting ensued. Afterward, the accused Hungarian soldier lay alongside the tracks beaten to death. Chelyabinsk town militia arrested several Czech and Slovak officers and forced the troops back into their boxcars. Unfortunately, the Legion officers who had been arrested were not responsible for the death of the Hungarian soldier.[4] Colonel Vojcechovsky, a Russian officer who led the middle Legion contingent of trains, entered the town of Chelyabinsk demanding a meeting with the town commissar. Vojcechovsky hoped that investigating the incident would lead to the arrest of those actually involved.[5] The commissar refused to cooperate with Vojcechovsky. Instead, local soviet militia ordered Vojcechovsky and his entourage jailed. Their names were added to a list of Czechs and Slovaks to be executed at dawn the next morning. News of Vojcechovsky's situation filtered back to the troops sitting idle in Chelyabinsk Depot.[6] Within hours, Legion troops attacked militia headquarters. By midmorning of the following day, Vojcechovsky's echelon had taken over the town and imprisoned the local Chelyabinsk commissar and his men.

News of this uprising spread to Moscow where members of a visiting Odbočka delegation which included Professor Maxa, Čermák, and Janík were placed under house arrest. The incident occurring at Chelyabinsk convinced Lenin and Trotsky that the Germans had been correct all along: the Legion, represented by Maxa, Čermák, and Janík, really was in the pay of Western capitalists who had always intended to use the Legion to foment counterrevolution in Siberia. To Lenin and Trotsky, the Chelyabinsk uprising must have been the beginning of an effort to overthrow soviets all along the railroad.

Lieutenant Sergie Vojcechovsky, commander of the Third Regiment, second contingent of Legion trains, not dated.

Captured tanks near Chelyabinsk, June, 1918.

Leon Trotsky informed his three Odbočka captives that "it would be impossible to send any more Czech or Slovak echelons eastward."[7] The day Czechs and Slovaks feared had finally arrived. Order #115 mandated that "Czecho-Slovak troops be disarmed; those who do not do so voluntarily will be shot."[8] Local soviet militias were ordered to enroll Legion soldiers in the Red Army or arrest them for work in labor camps.

Trotsky's communiqués, sent up and down the Trans-Siberian line, fell instead under the care of General Dieterichs' appointed telegraph operators. Order #115 arrived in Legion headquarters in Vladivostok along with news of the arrest of the Odbočka officials. Under threat, Lenin forced Maxa and Čermák to appeal to all Legion trains to surrender.[9]

On the contrary, Legion officials interpreted these events as proof of Moscow's submission to German and Austro-Hungarian manipulation. Moscow had become an unwelcome enemy.[10] In the eyes of the Czech and Slovak troops traveling toward Vladivostok, Order #115 became Moscow's declaration of war on the Legion. From this point on it would have to forcibly occupy every inch of the Trans-Siberian Railway — neutralizing every town and station along the way. Poised to pass through harsh climates and brutal terrain, legionnaires readied themselves for constant battle. Each troop train quickly gathered to elect a council to represent it in the Odbočka in Vladivostok. In turn, Odbočka Command verified that each unit would be free to react according to its own unique situation along the railroad.[11] Echelons were to govern the segment of track occupied by their trains and the surrounding region; any other response would be deemed as inefficient.

Radola Gajda's trains passed Omsk, leading the chain of echelons. Gajda planned to occupy Novonikolayevsk up ahead in order to ensure a quick procession for all Legion trains following behind. Gajda had been contacted on two separate occasions by the Secret Organization of Russian Officers, an anti–Bolshevik group from Novonikolayevsk under the auspices of General Grishin-Almazov. Grishin-Almazov begged Gajda and the other commanders to wait until the anti–Bolshevik military groups could better organize in order to help the Legion cause. Siberian opposition leaders wanted to ensure the fate of the political administrations and civil control of their towns once the legionnaires had passed through. Grishin-Almazov's officers created the Siberian Volunteer Army, more than 150,000 Siberian members strong, to facilitate a controlled handover of towns and stations once the Legion evacuated to Vladivostok.[12]

Each Legion echelon became its own base of attack. If necessary the entire Trans-Siberian Railway would become a rolling theater of battle. The Czech-Slovak National Council believed it had unequivocal proof that the Bolsheviks never intended to allow the Czecho-Slovak Army Corps to leave Siberia.[13] Legion commanders also realized that trained Red Army troops would soon arrive to reinforce local militias. Time was of the essence. Legionnaires had to hurry to consolidate their positions.

The Polish Legion, which had passed through on the Trans-Siberian Railway before the Czechs and Slovaks, had also gathered together on its way to the Pacific coast. Polish Legion members, however, had disagreed about everything from who should lead them to what route to take. Unable to unite, they became easy prey for marauding bandits. After coming under attack, the Poles scattered into the woods where many were captured and held hostage by Soviet recruitment officers.[14] Forced to join Bolshevik units fighting throughout the Siberian countryside, legionnaires often came upon groups of these Polish soldiers hiding in the nearby forests. The fate of the Polish troops stood as a warning to the Legion to remain united in purpose or be lost alone.

With this specter in mind, Legion Command immediately launched attacks on depots up and down the line.[15] As news of the capture of town after town spread, hope began to grow. Controlling the entire steppe was impossible but managing large sections of railway through it was not. This plan, however, demanded an immense leap of faith. Indeed, any army attempting such a feat would have to have been insane.

The insanity began on May 25. For weeks troop trains to the west of Penza had been stalled and reports of escalating violence and harassment at the station made waiting legionnaires anxious.[16] Colonel Čeček's troops, numbering more than 10,000 and comprising the rear guard, attacked the town and depot. After three days of desperate hand-to-hand combat, Penza fell into Legion hands. Čeček quickly consolidated available arms and prepared to meet stiff resistance from European Russia to the west.[17] Čeček worked to keep this portion of the Trans-Siberian line open until all stragglers, whether Czech, Slovak, Rumanian, Bulgarian, or Pole, passed through and on to the east where they might find safety. To the west of Čeček, nothing but the Red Army and hopelessness awaited.

Lieutenant Stanislav Čeček, commander of the Fourth Regiment, rear contingent of Legion trains, not dated.

Spread across the Trans-Siberian line, smaller Legion units hurried to combine with larger echelons traveling ahead. To the east of Čeček another 8,000 to 10,000 men, newly freed from Chelyabinsk and low on arms, followed Colonel Vojcechovsky. They attacked stations and held them open for Čeček to follow. William Duncan, a minister and associate with the Young Men's Christian Association (YMCA), began to travel with these stragglers. Duncan wrote letters home to his family relaying stories about the heady atmosphere in which he found himself living. He described the incident at Chelyabinsk the day after:

> Just now a train of prisoners and refugees is standing opposite coming from further east with many Turks aboard. The Checks [Czechs] are searching to find hidden ammunition while people look on and wonder ... [the prisoners] were in Bohemia and they told of the bad conditions there, especially how twenty thousand of the Check [Czech] women were forced to work in the mines. You can imagine that such news does not make German sympathizers of these men.[18]

Reports circulated that legionnaires already believed the Bolsheviks acted under control of the kaiser.[19] The Legion heard of the immediate promotions of Austrian, German, and Hungarian POWs volunteering to enter newly organized Red Army units in Siberia. In one case, a Legion echelon had been forced to negotiate with the Petropavlovsk soviet. When Legion officials met with a Bolshevik delegation, they were shocked to find themselves talking to German ex-prisoners from a section of the local "international." In another example, legionnaires who attacked the garrison at Irkutsk said they heard the commander yell, "*Schleissen*," German for "close."[20] Presumably, a continued German influence throughout Siberia convinced the Legion of the inevitability of confrontation with this enemy. Though legionnaires formerly believed contact with the Austrians, Germans, and Hungarians had ended when they fled Ukraine, they now realized that old enemies had been nearby all along.

Deep within the Siberian hinterland, Colonel Gajda's units surged ahead. With little more than bayonets and stones, Gajda and his men quickly gained a reputation for the strategic use of trains in battle.[21] Only one field gun with six shells existed in his entire column but by moving it up and down the railway line, Gajda tricked the enemy into believing that the Sixth and Seventh regiments had many such weapons.

Under what were believed to be overwhelming numbers of well-armed legionnaires, local militias withdrew ahead of Gajda's echelon.[22] While the enemy on one train focused on what it assumed to be one column of Gajda's men, other legionnaires would circle back to disassemble the track behind the Soviet train before attacking. Militia units always assumed that they had been

Radola Gajda, seated, bottom center right, Boris Usakov seated, bottom center left, near Irkutsk, 1918.

surrounded by two separate Legion groups and would immediately back up their *broněviky* (armored train) only to discover the track had been destroyed behind. Panic ensued with disoriented militia men running into the woods for cover. Gajda's men would then board the deserted train, replace the track, and head up the line without firing a shot.

Despite Gajda's success, enemy sniper fire continued to reduce his ranks.[23] It became imperative to the survival of the Sixth and Seventh regiments that they secure munitions as soon as possible. Ahead, Gajda's troops faced 500 miles of track controlled by enemy troops who hid in the surrounding forests and shot at will.[24]

Colonel Gajda had been blessed with talented men under his command. Boris F. Usakov, for one, remained committed to the Legion's evacuation. Usakov, a Russian from Krasnoyarsk, became dedicated to the Legion as he traveled with the Sixth and Seventh on his way home.[25]

When Gajda rode into a town at the head of his trains, a tornado of excitement swirled around him. Peasants running to see the young colonel had no idea what a "Czech" or "Slovak" was but they recognized the name of "Gajda." His interest in the problems of local farmers led to a groundswell of popularity amongst the peasantry. On the other hand, Gajda's growing popularity also threatened local officials, who reported their concerns to Moscow.

Fourth Regiment aboard camouflaged troop train, Ufa, summer, 1918.

By the end of May, the entire Trans-Siberian Railway had become the site of a series of military engagements. As each town and station fell to Legion troops, the countryside surrounding it became secured for those Legion units following behind. From west to east, echelons hurried through depots in a never-ending flow of locomotives, boxcars, and men. As the westernmost stations became secured and Colonel Čeček's rear echelons passed through, control of towns once again reverted back to the Siberian populous at large.[26]

The day after Penza fell into Czech and Slovak hands, the Marianovka militia, from the outskirts of Omsk, ambushed a Legion train.[27] The outcomes of engagements at Chelyabinsk and Penza, along with Trotsky's Order #115, spurred the Marianovka Soviets into action.[28] Unfortunately, their resolve proved far greater than their prowess. In a relatively short time, the Marianovka militia members were captured, disarmed, and chased into the surrounding forest. Telegraph lines buzzed with official reports to Vladivostok's OCSNR headquarters. Within two weeks, Chelyabinsk, Penza, Marianovka and Novonikolayevsk had all surrendered to the Legion. As a result, the entire Volga region lay in Czech and Slovak hands.[29]

The Moscow leadership's influence began to be questioned. By the beginning of June 1918, news of legionnaire successes across the Russian Far East began to cause an uproar throughout European Russia. Simultaneously, organized counterrevolutionary fronts spread throughout southern and eastern Russia to confront local soviets.

German ambassador Count Mirbach advised Lenin and Trotsky to herd together all of the legionnaires and delegate their fates to their former Hapsburg commanders. Mirbach intended to contain the legionnaires in Siberia and prevent their transfer to the Western Front. Trotsky geared up units of the Red Army to move east against the Czechs and Slovaks. He knew that a protracted conflict with the Legion would probably ruin the Bolsheviks in Moscow. Not only might the Legion unite with the counterrevolution but the Russian people, sick of warfare, would never tolerate another protracted series of engagements while famine threatened in the cities. While Lenin and Trotsky planned their next move, the Legion overpowered Simbirsk, Lenin's birthplace.

The legionnaires seemed to advance against all odds. Town militias remained obstinate, so ambush and sabotage became the best strategy, especially when approaching an unfamiliar settlement. Miraculously, with fewer than one rifle for every six men, Legion troops prevailed with whatever tools they had on hand. By using each train as a base of operations, legionnaires marched on foot, combing the adjacent woods for snipers.[30] With every success, however, Czech and Slovak fatalities continued to mount throughout the summer, particularly near larger centers of population. Even so, legionnaires felt a sense of comradeship with the local peasantry — a sentiment that affected their fighting. Only a few weeks earlier, Družina members had fought together with the very same Russian recruits they now faced. Currently, their alternatives remained clear: fight or die.

Many Siberians hailed the Legion as a liberating force and blessed it for ridding towns and hamlets of cruel political bullies. Peasants passed on news of Czech and Slovak generosity. Legion Command provided food and medical care whenever possible. Later in the summer when Russian currency became scarce, Czech and Slovak troops paid for needed items with rubles to help the local economy. In return, villagers informed Czech and Slovak officers of enemy encampments ahead of their trains.[31] Former legionnaire Joseph Skelnička remembered this mutually beneficial relationship. "When I got to the station, I simply said, 'I need to bring so many pieces of cattle.' And they brought me that many.... Even the Communists gave us cattle, if we had written confirmation of our demand."[32]

Summer began with the division of the Czecho-Slovak Army Corps into four distinct groups. By midsummer, three remained west of Lake Baikal and the Baikal Mountain Range while the fourth settled in to wait for them in Vladivostok under the command of General Dieterichs. The westernmost trains under Colonel Čeček's leadership continued to act as rear guard for the entire column still proceeding toward Vladivostok. Acting as the middle echelon, Colonel Vojchecovsky's units pushed toward Chelyabinsk and Barabinsk where Colonel Gajda's Sixth and Seventh regiments struck out across the

Legion soldiers wounded at Chelyabinsk, summer 1918.

central Siberia steppe. Isolated and deep in enemy territory, Gajda moved toward the Baikal Mountains. Meanwhile, Czecho-Slovak Army headquarters regrouped to correct inefficiencies in the field under General Dieterichs' orders.

The entire Legion reorganized into two administrative divisions, each comprised of four regiments of three battalions. In addition, Czecho-Slovak Command established two separate artillery brigades of six batteries each to accompany two independent companies of engineers in the field. Two mobile field hospitals were established along with an aviation unit, field kitchens, mobile clerks, and a signal corps with courier units attached in order to streamline efforts on board the trains. Every echelon, housed in moving box-cars up and down the Trans-Siberian Railway, became an efficient fighting unit ready for contact with the enemy in the field.

Despite Dieterichs' best efforts, however, a large contingent of Soviet militias occupied the interior between Vladivostok and the Baikal Mountain Range. Telegraph communications had been severed, leaving Dieterichs' command stranded and living in barracks along the hillside overlooking Vladivostok Harbor. Frantic to hear the progress Gajda and the others were making, General Dieterichs worked to restore and secure communications. Legion Command in Vladivostok also continued to wait and watch for Allied transport vessels to dock at the port.

In Moscow, Germany's ambassador Count Mirbach continued to do everything in his power to halt Allied plans to transport legionnaires to the Western Front. German troops had made great strides into France and Belgium following ratification of the Brest-Litovsk Treaty in March 1917. An Allied infusion of well-trained Slavic troops to the west would threaten Germany's progress. Mirbach conceded, however, that though the Central Powers had reversed Allied advances along the Western Front, German influence in both Russia and Siberia, especially concerning the worrisome legionnaires, had begun to wane.[33]

Legion trains progressed along the Trans-Siberian Railway partly because large population centers were few and far between. In the urban centers, however, better-trained and better-organized Soviet militia congregated.[34] Samara, a town of more than 35,000, housed large warehouses stacked with Red Army weapons, munitions, and rations. Omsk, the seat of Bolshevik power in the western provinces, located between the Irtysh and Ishim rivers, would be especially difficult to attack. Summer runoff in June and July meant that the legionnaires would be forced to storm Omsk across swollen and treacherous river currents.[35] Adding to the demoralizing situation ahead, the roadways leading into both Samara and Omsk had become trenches of deep undulating mud. Horse hooves slipped and cart wheels stuck in ruts along these roads, delaying the Legion and making it easy prey for artillery fire.

After Samara and Omsk, Krasnoyarsk lay ahead. The city of Krasnoyarsk, Boris Usakov's hometown, held impressive numbers of well-trained Soviet militia men. Beyond Krasnoyarsk sat Kazan: an exceedingly well-guarded arsenal city. Yet, no community along the entire railway line held the importance that Ekaterinburg had since it spread out directly at the crossroads of the main Trans-Siberian lines from Petrograd to Chelyabinsk. Securing each city was the only chance these men had for survival. If the evacuation sputtered and died, the entire Legion faced annihilation.

Chapter Five

By the beginning of summer, Ekaterinburg and Irkutsk stood directly ahead of Gajda's troop trains — two giant enigmas — reputedly impervious to attack. The first, Irkutsk, perched on the west side of the Baikal Mountain Range astride a single railroad spur that ran straight through 39 tunnels and on to the Pacific coast at Vladivostok. Securing both cities was paramount for the Legion to proceed eastward. With one well-placed stick of dynamite the enemy could stop the Czechs and Slovaks quite literally in their tracks. Doing so would also ruin travel throughout Siberia for years to come and isolate west from east indefinitely. General Dieterichs' chief map expert, Colonel Vladimír Klecanda, remembered, "There still remained, however, this great obstacle: the strong, natural Baikal positions of impassable mountains and narrow defiles which lay along the south bank of the lake and which were defended by 5,000 men fully armed from the Irkutsk arsenal with powerful artillery and armed boats."[1]

The dilemma necessitated a surprise frontal attack on the fortified Baikal Depot, quite simply a suicide mission. Summer rains flooded the slippery shale mountain slopes, making earlier reconnaissance efforts to transport equipment impossible. Even if the Sixth and Seventh regiments could successfully overwhelm the Irkutsk garrison, command wondered if they could forestall the demolition of tunnel passes behind it.

Cut off by mountains and left with no telephone and telegraph communication, General Dieterichs and the local Soviet authorities in Vladivostok attempted to end fighting on the Trans-Siberian Railway. The following communiqué, sent by both Dieterichs and his Bolshevik counterpart in Vladivostok, was meant to defuse hostilities:

> Your departure from Vladivostok is assured and is delayed solely by technical reasons, by the absence till now of ships. There are already 12,000 of us here in excellent surroundings and impatiently awaiting your arrival. The local Soviet authority supports us in every manner. Any use of force on your part en route only delays travel and threatens the gravest complications. Therefore, we urgently insist that all clashes immediately cease, that complete order be maintained.[2]

But there were complications. Dieterichs knew Trotsky's Order #115 deeply affected his troops.[3]

Jan Syrový, privy to recent reconnaissance reports, rushed to link up with Colonel Gajda's trains heading toward the 39 tunnels. Scouring the hills surrounding their position, Syrový's men discovered that notorious ataman Grigori Semenov had been moving bandits south and into Chita. Semenov meant to use Chita as his headquarters in order to take advantage of the Legion's remarkable advances. Once the Legion cleared away Soviet resistance around Chita, Semenov intended to control the entire region. Presently, however, Semenov's position between Syrový's troop trains and the Baikal Mountain Range threatened Legion progress.

Echelon commanders could only guess the ataman's rationale, but little concerning Grigori Semenov had ever made sense. Making matters worse, Count Mirbach accused Legion Command of working to unite Legion efforts with renegade elements like Semenov. Jan Syrový's echelon sat out the silence of the telegraph wires west of the Baikal Mountains waiting to hear back from Odbočka headquarters.

The Legion despised Semenov, his tactics, and his followers. They believed him to be the worst kind of opportunist — a murdering brigand who lived by extorting and brutalizing his own people. The Czechs and Slovaks preferred any political faction, Bolshevik or Monarchist, Red or White, to someone like Ataman Semenov.

Ataman Grigori Semenov terrorizes Transbaikalia, not dated.

Grigori Mihailovich Semenov cared little for politics and even less for justice.[4] Born to a Buriate-Mongol mother and a Tartar-Cossack father, he grew up in a privileged Siberian class. Though having little formal education, military history, literature, and philosophy fascinated Semenov and lured him to the Cossack Military Academy in Orenberg. In 1911, he graduated with honors as an officer and a skilled horseman but also with a reputation for cruelty. During World War I, Semenov had been posted in Poland where he met another infamous Russian officer, Roman von Ungern Sternberg. As friends they often competed to outdo one another's penchant for violence. By February 1917, Semenov's cruelty toward his own men earned him a transfer away from the battlefield to a remote province near Irkutsk.

In relative obscurity, he began to gain control of a seemingly inconsequential region near the Baikal Mountains. With the tsar's abdication and the fall of the Mensheviks, Siberia became even further isolated, allowing Semenov to seize several factions and form a private army. His motley crew fashioned its own rules, indiscriminately victimizing anyone who got in its way. Semenov had himself elected to the position of ataman after first murdering the legitimate Cossack leader.

Soldiers returning from the Eastern Front who hoped to work toward autonomy in Siberia soon discovered that the new ataman cared only for himself. More reform-minded men in Semenov's camp quickly slipped away to join legitimate counterrevolutionary movements. By June 1918, Semenov's men patrolled the Trans-baiklia region in armored trains called the Merciless and the Destroyer. These behemoths preyed upon farmers in local villages, demanding bounty and murdering town leaders who refused to cooperate.[5]

Villagers quickly learned to recognize both the Merciless and Destroyer from a distance. To the Allies and the local militia, Semenov rationalized the killing of peasants by insisting on their allegiance to one faction or another. Of the wide array of Siberian autonomous movements throughout the provinces, Semenov's group remained the most notorious.

The Legion wanted nothing to do with factions vying for power throughout Siberia and intended to keep a safe distance from anything that could compromise its evacuation. Semenov had plans, however, and his plans included the Czechs and Slovaks. Colonel Gajda's trains headed eastward through the Baikal Mountains toward the 39 tunnels as Jan Syrový's echelons followed. Semenov decided to plant himself in Chita, directly in their path.

Grigori Semenov was not the only one mapping the progress of the legionnaires. In their imaginations, American and British citizens traveled with the Legion on a weekly basis by reading the Sunday supplements of both the *New York Times* and the *The London Review*. After the incident at Chelyabinsk, photographers and reporters from both papers joined the Czechs and Slovaks to live on and report from their trains. The status of the odyssey, the Legion's location, and the unique situation of each unit fascinated readers.

European and American press called for the quick evacuation of all the Slavic units moving eastward through Siberia. Immigrant communities in Canada, the United States, and throughout Western Europe petitioned for thorough evacuations of these men who represented homeland aspirations for independence. Public awareness and concern poured in from readers and focused on aiding the Legion's transfer to the Western Front. Several millions of dollars arrived for the Red Cross, the YMCA, and the Czech and Slovak Alliance, all organizations working to fund the evacuation of Legion troops or to back Thomas Masaryk's idea of an autonomous Czecho-Slovak state.[6]

After Gajda's impressive consolidation of the town of Mariinsk, his friend and confidante, Boris Usakov, left the unit to travel to the Bolshevik stronghold of Krasnoyarsk, his hometown. Boris Usakov was now a Russian officer of great renown. He had been traveling with the Legion since the beginning of the evacuation because he believed that Russia owed these men a debt. Usakov had become famous as a master of disguise — slipping into and out of Soviet strongholds dressed as everything from a peasant woman to an officer of the Red Guard. Earlier, he gained notoriety for fooling German troops in the same fashion. Few of his enemies knew what he actually looked like or that he was from Krasnoyarsk but many hoped to put an end to Boris Usakov's life on the run as a Legion spy.

Gajda's and Čeček's triumphant consolidation of town after town infuriated the Moscow leadership. So far, each officer had caught local militias off guard and, for the most part, found them lacking not only in supplies, but also training and resolve. Local units fought only when victory was guaranteed and abandoned territory and arms whenever seriously challenged.

Čeček's rear guard moved into Samara, proclaiming the town and the railroad open to traffic. In Samara, Čeček's units discovered large supplies of weapons which the fleeing Red Guard had abandoned. The Red Guard had, however, taken time to pilfer over 100 million rubles in gold from Samara's banks. For an army that prided itself on being against materialism, the Siberian soviets militias were adroit at stealing anything that wasn't pinned down. Čeček's men found Samara in a state of total chaos with 1,500 of its citizens lying dead in the city streets — casualties of pitched battles between the Red Guard and the Legion. Outside the city center, the flour mill, containing over 18,500 pounds of flour, burned out of control. After chasing the militia into the surrounding countryside, Colonel Čeček, in an unprecedented move, declared the city anti–Bolshevik and appointed the Constitutional Assembly delegates who had been in power before the Bolshevik takeover to act as Samara's provisional government.[7]

Explosion near Samara, summer 1918.

Legion units occupied towns and cities along the railway line, but seldom replaced administrators unless absolutely necessary. Čeček's actions directly violated his oath to Masaryk and to the Odbočka (OCSNR) by interfering in Siberia's internal affairs. The Czecho-Slovak National Council (OCSNR) knew that Colonel Čeček had the best intentions for the citizens of Samara, but because of his actions hostility towards all of the Czech and Slovak units traveling along the railway would increase. Predictably, Moscow's Central Committee viewed Čeček's proclamation as undeniable evidence that Count Mirbach and the Germans had been correct all along — the Legion really was acting under orders from Russia's former capitalist allies.

With Samara in Legion control, Colonel Gajda turned his sights toward the town of Nizhne-Udiinsk, a city that threatened to become Gajda's most difficult military target so far. Weapon supplies on board his troop trains had dwindled to severely low levels. Even though Nizhne-Udiinsk had a large military presence, Gajda's troops had to attack.

From the Legion trains, the landscape appeared incredibly beautiful as thick moss twisted over birch trees in groves above pools of black oily mud and amidst tufts of waving cat grass. From the boxcars legionnaires saw both men and women exotically dressed in animal hides who sported long black queues. The women rode roughshod on small shaggy ponies, skillfully herding groups of large-horned cattle.

In actuality, the thick spongy moss and swamp water encircling Nizhne-Udiinsk had become rancid in the summer heat. As the days grew longer, the humidity stifled the air, providing the perfect breeding ground for insects. From their boxcars, legionnaires noted the constant drone of buzzing mosquitoes.

One by one, Gajda's units poured out of their boxcars toward the advancing enemy. Reporters depicted a battle so hazardous that even Legion cooks and engineers joined in the fray. Later, as the battled raged, Gustav Bečvář watched in shock as wounded men with distorted and swollen faces passed by him on stretchers heading back to the hospital car. He remembered:

> Quite apart from injuries received in the normal course of battle, they were in a terrible state. Their faces were blotched and swollen in the most grotesque fashion, their eyes and noses being barely distinguishable....
> Mosquitoes! I have suffered from mosquitoes in many places and in varying degrees, but never before or since have I met a more virulent species than inhabited the surrounding of this small Siberian town. The Russian inhabitants, watching us pass, noticed our misery, and as we rushed on through the town towards the fighting line, many of them ran into their houses, returning with bottles filled with black liquid, which they told us to rub upon our faces and hands.[8]

Bečvář and the others were Gajda's most experienced fighters — skilled and tough, never surrendering ground once it had been taken. Gajda learned from locals, however, that the troops they would face that day were even more notorious in battle: Cossacks, literally meaning "horsemen." Having served near them along the Eastern Front, Colonel Radola Gajda knew that these fierce sword-wielding men might easily be the end of his unit.[9] Identified by their long flared coats, high black felt boots and gray fur hats, the Cossacks attacked on horseback with their usual flair and acrobatics. William Duncan, secretary with the YMCA, described a meeting he had with them that day near the swamps of Nizhne-Udiinsk:

> I heard the shout "the Cossacks are coming" and through the opening in the woods came these lovers of war. The horse and rider are one. [We were] tired, but there was something about them that made you feel the bugle blew [and] all that weariness would have fallen away. They are to a manner born — war is life to them. If a thing is worth having it is worth fighting for. Their leader was fully six feet seven inches tall with a beard that let you know he was a Russian of Russians. [They are] strong men who loved the out-of-doors life. As a sight to witness, I beheld them when we drew out ... standing around the fires singing the songs of war in which their spirits fed.[10]

The dank air and thick sludge of the Nizhne-Udiinsk swamp quickly swallowed up the Cossacks. As they slogged through the muck on horseback, their cloaks grew heavy with clinging mud. Once their pace slowed, mosquitoes bit their faces and swelled their eyes shut. The inhabitants of these swamps offered no help to the Cossacks, whom they detested for their reputed cruelty.[11] No one warned them of the Legion waiting, faces blackened with the secret mosquito repellent of Nizhne-Udiinsk. In the end, it appeared to many of

Fourth Regiment with mosquito netting near Nizhne-Udiinsk, not dated.

the legionnaires fighting that day on the outskirts of Nizhne-Udiinsk that luck had somehow changed their way. The tempo of fighting increased as spirits lifted. The Cossacks became sitting ducks.

Able to secure and consolidate stations ahead, Gajda's units repaired telegraph and telephone communications, rebuilt bridges, and moved on rapidly towards the mountains. Newspapers reported the Legion's victories as columns of troop trains began to unite into one unstoppable fighting force. Yet, serious obstacles remained ahead of Gajda and the others. Lake Baikal and the mountains that surrounded it could prove all but impassable.

A German engineer apprehended in the Lake Baikal region stunned his captors with the news that the local Soviets had plans to dynamite all 39 tunnel approaches. Destroying the tunnels would isolate the vast majority of legionnaires west of the mountains and could also eliminate travel across Siberia for years. Reconnaissance also revealed more than 40,000 Bolshevik troops hunkered down near Lake Baikal where the local militia had commandeered lake steamships fitted with artillery pieces to block any Czech and Slovak approach.

General Dieterichs, unable to help Gajda, awaited updates. Legion troops bivouacked in Vladivostok finally reported seeing Allied ships approaching the harbor. Their presence made the Soviet commissar and other city officials increasingly anxious even as Dieterichs worked to mollify them. Dieterichs, chief of staff of the Czecho-Slovak Legion, had been sitting for nearly two months in Vladivostok, his men in tents on the side of a mountain. His position had been very delicate as he watched relationships deteriorate day after

Legion engineers rebuilding a bridge, July, 1918.

Legionnaires guard the railroad tunnel accesses through the Baikal Mountain Range, 1918.

day without being able to prevent the destruction of good will. Worse still was his inability to assist beleaguered Czech and Slovak trains still on the railroad west of the Baikal Range.[12]

While Dieterichs waited for word from Gajda and the echelons following behind, Vladivostok Soviets ignored Japanese and American overtures to land vessels at the port. By June 25, 1918, 15,000 legionnaires had assembled in the harbor to board ships for the Western Front. The Legion Council quickly drafted an appeal to the Allies reiterating that they only wished to either go home or be evacuated to fight on the Western Front. Yet not one of the Legion units waiting in Vladivostok Harbor had been allowed to board the evacuation vessels. Worse yet, the Allied Command refused to provide a clear explanation why not.

After arriving in port, the Allies realized that the local Vladivostok militia had begun transferring large stocks of war supplies from the docks to the interior. These stockpiles left over from the tsarist war effort belonged to the Allies, not to local Bolsheviks. General Dieterichs, concerned that war materiel smuggled out of the city might be used against his own Legion troop trains in transit, tried to enlist the local commissar's help to end this subterfuge. City officials agreed to Legion demands that the militia confine itself to an area surrounding the Vladivostok fort and that all Allied materiel remain unmolested at dockside.[13] Unfortunately, the very week General Dieterichs signed this agreement, Czech and Slovak reconnaissance again reported arms and supplies heading west under the command of the local militia. On June 29, General Dieterichs and units from the Legion barracks marched to the fort of Vladivostok.

> The Bolsheviks and their soldiers, Hungarians and Austrians, refused to yield the fort, and inflicted considerable losses. During the battle, four Russian torpedo boats steamed out to assist in attacks on the Czechs, but a Japanese cruiser, the *Asachi,* swung across their path. The Japanese captain assured the Russians that he would sink them if they did not retreat. The Russian captains turned back.[14]

General Dieterichs' men succeeded in overthrowing the Bolsheviks in Vladivostok. This maneuver by the Legion's own military commander completely subverted its vow of neutrality and further complicated any Legion evacuation.

In an age of industrial competition, the port of Vladivostok and its stockpiled war materiel invited interest and interference from the far eastern provinces to the west. With Dieterichs in control of the strategic port, the Allies' true intentions concerning Legion troops came to light:

> The day after the Czechs' [and Slovaks'] seizure of Vladivostok, the French government gave formal recognition to Czechoslovakia as a nation...
> The question of Allied intervention in Russia had been completely resolved, and on July 1, a detachment of American Marines from the cruiser U.S.S. *Olympia* assisted the British military and naval forces in the occupation of Murmansk in the far north. Japan, Britain, France and the United States decided to move into Russia to keep the war materiel they had shipped from falling into German hands, and to prevent the Bolsheviks from helping the Germans.[15]

Although 12,000 troops under General Dieterichs celebrated the docking of the Allies in Vladivostok Harbor, Dieterichs privately nursed concerns. Czechs and Slovaks isolated west of the Baikal Range headed into confrontation with some of their most formidable adversaries. Militia encampments near the tunnels marking the Legion's only escape route barred the way. Whether these men would ever escape Siberia with their lives was uncertain. Dieterichs knew that over the next couple of weeks the fate of his men would be decided.

Once considered merely troublesome deserters on their way home, Legion troops had morphed into a major military presence across the entire Russian Far East. Lenin and Trotsky had to either obliterate the troop trains or increase the pace of Czech and Slovak repatriation and end extortion of these soldiers throughout the Trans-Siberian system.[16] Though heading in the opposite direction, Austrian, German, and Hungarian ex-POWs also found difficulty traveling homeward. The Central Powers put additional pressure on Lenin to do something about militia harassment of their own troop trains heading west out of Siberia.

The true cost of the Bolshevik Revolution and the Brest-Litovsk Treaty which pulled Russia out of the war effort had already severely strained the Allied effort on the Western Front. Though the United States had entered the war by April 1917, the Russian surrender reversed any advantages the Allies formerly enjoyed. Earlier in December 1917, reports reached Allied Command that large numbers of German troops in the western trenches had a few days of food rations left. When the United States suspended shipments of petroleum to Germany, its actions crippled German advances in the West.

The signing of the Brest-Litovsk Treaty changed all of that. The outlook of the war now turned in Germany's favor. The Brest-Litovsk Treaty opened Galician, Rumanian, and Caucasus petroleum supplies to the Central Powers. With Russia quiet to the east, Austria-Hungary, Germany, and Turkey took time to pause and rethink troop positions in all theaters of battle.

As the summer of 1918 heated up, lives and materiel continued to be squandered with neither army advancing along the western trenches. Several French divisions, caught in the most wasteful of the fighting, mutinied. Imperceptibly at first, the balance of power began to shift throughout Belgium and France. By mid–July, Austrian, German, and Hungarian supplies and men diverted from the Eastern Front arrived in the West by rail. Formerly successful Allied port blockades had now been rendered unnecessary as Russian materiel and foodstuffs traveled directly westward over land, bypassing the ports altogether. Allied reconnaissance reported that a German advance along the Western Front would soon follow — one that could succeed if the situation continued to worsen for Allied troops in the field.

Throughout early summer the Allied Supreme Command in Versailles heard German artillery pounding away at the outskirts of Paris. Its only welcomed relief had come from reports of Legion advances along the Trans-Siberian Railway. Desperate for more men and supplies, the Western powers looked to the Legion for experienced replacements.

By midsummer, Legion units had cleared over 2,000 miles of uninterrupted railway between Lake Baikal and Ekaterinburg. Czech and Slovak troops discovered caches of stored food and war materiel left behind by the tsarist officers in town warehouses and in forgotten boxcars alongside branch lines. The greatest problem facing the progress of the Legion became the *frontovik* bandits roaming the countryside — not a lack of supplies. Still there were more than enough random acts of violence occurring on either side to inflame an already desperate situation.[17] Ex-tsarist soldiers turned bandits destroyed tracks, tunnels, and depots to isolate and then pillage separated Czech and Slovak units and to prey upon the peasantry in towns that dotted the countryside.

Through representatives in Moscow, Germany demanded that the Volga region be retaken immediately, no matter the cost. With German troops entrenched along Russia's western borders and the Japanese present in the Russian Far East, Lenin's position in Moscow became untenable. Legion commanders continued to have the desire to demonstrate to Moscow that they had never been dupes of the Allies and that Czech and Slovak intentions had always been to evacuate to the Western Front as soon as possible. To prove this, towns taken and cleared of the Soviet militia by legionnaires were returned to local control once the last of the Legion trains departed.

Meanwhile, the nucleus of a Siberian Provisional Government began to coalesce throughout the countryside. The Siberian Autonomous Movement organized a regional duma, preparing for representative government throughout Siberia. The Czechs and Slovaks also held these ideals dear and empathized with the Siberian Autonomous Movement's crusade. Even as the atmosphere began to slide toward foreign interference and civil war, Legion Command hoped for a shift toward representative government and democratic rule in the Russian Far East.

The Siberian Autonomous Movement also appeared to have grassroots support among the peasantry. In Omsk more than 2,000 troops gathered to volunteer, while 1,000 reported to units in Tomsk, nearly 600 in Novonikolayevsk, 1,000 in Irkutsk, and 600 in Krasnoyarsk — a total of just under 7,000 men compared to 5,000 Bolshevik recruits from the same area.[18] Aware of this growing threat, Moscow enhanced Red Army troops with over 6,000 Austro-Hungarian ex-prisoners of war.[19]

With the rising tide of militarism from all sides, Russian and Siberian refugees began to flee toward Vladivostok from the west. The Allies had hoped to minimize chaos along the coast, but political unrest in the interior threatened their efforts. In the harbor area, war materiel and other supplies were stacked to capacity.[20] The port at Vladivostok had always been considered Russia's back door. Under the tsar, the harbor and city had been fortified with cannons mounted on concrete blocks on the hilltops partially encircling the port.[21] American, British, Canadian, Czech, French, Japanese, and Slovak troops organized international patrols of the entire city. With a Japanese commitment for more troops to be stationed deep into the Russian Far East, the French and British hoped that resistance in the Caucasus region would divert German troops to southern Russia.

At the turn of the century, American technical know-how had helped the Russian tsar push east toward the Orient. Japan continued to worry that Russia, whether under Bolshevik control or not, preferred a partnership with the United States.[22] Japan saw any effort to increase technical and economic support to Siberia on the part of the United States as interference in its national affairs. Japanese leaders believed that Siberia could prove an important route for expansion. Disguising its intentions, Tokyo promised to intervene in Siberia on behalf of the Czech and Slovak Legion.

The increase in Japanese troops aroused both Russian and American suspicion. With chaos in Moscow, Woodrow Wilson cautioned Britain and France that a sizable Japanese intervention might provoke Moscow to turn to Germany for help in Siberia.[23] President Wilson advanced the theory that the Brest-Litovsk Treaty had never been legitimate since the Russian representatives who signed the agreement had never been elected by the Russian people. They would not be recognized as representatives of Russia by her former allies.[24] If Lenin and Trotsky wanted to annul this treaty, Wilson proposed that the Allies would support them.

When Thomas Masaryk visited Washington in June 1918, President Wilson asked for his assessment of the situation in Siberia. Masaryk approved of economic assistance to Russia, believing that supplies of food, technical help, and engineering know-how might prevent a further slide into chaos. The American president was warned, however, that the Allies should not become entangled politically or militarily in either Russia or Siberia. Masaryk believed that any country becoming embroiled in Siberian civil issues would surely regret it. Support for the evacuation of all Legion units from Siberia remained Masaryk's chief concern. Secretary of State Lansing echoed this goal only days later on June 23, 1918, by urging President Wilson to act: "As these troops [Czechs and Slovaks] are most loyal to our cause and have been most unjustly treated by various Soviets, ought we not to consider whether something cannot be done to support them?"[25] The Legion units in the interior of Siberia had been left unaware of the political and diplomatic intrigue surrounding them. Over the spring and summer of 1918, they had instead been preoccupied with just staying alive.

Colonel Gajda knew that a respite for his men would be detrimental to their progress, so he pushed deeper into the mountains. The Sixth and Seventh regiments grew sick of Gajda's voice demanding, "Shoot and advance, shoot and advance." Still, Gajda could be seen running back and forth prodding and cajoling his men — placing himself at risk under fire, hardly eating or sleeping.[26] This constant advance left local militias in a state of confusion and placed them on the defensive. Colonel Čeček also moved swiftly through the Siberian countryside to keep up with Colonel Vojechovsky's trains. By July 12, Syzran had fallen, and the town of Bulgma was secure. Čeček's men, like Gajda's, ignored their consuming fatigue and continued eastward.

On July 22, the First and Fourth Legion regiments moved into Simbirsk. The collapse of the Simbirsk militia proved a terrible blow to Lenin and Trotsky. Commissar Jurenev, Bolshevik supreme commander of the region, fired off Message #345 to his Soldier Councils with the news:

Simbirsk has been taken by the Czecho-Slovaks and the White Russian troops. The Social Revolution is in peril. So that we have hitherto gained it is necessary to organize forthwith all the forces at your disposal and to send them out against the Czechs and the White Army. From the Germans we need fear nothing. You will be responsible in history for the success of the Revolution.[27]

Jurenev's impression that Czechs and Slovaks fought alongside the White Russian forces was an inaccurate assumption repeated over and over again throughout the coming months. Grisly descriptions of violence abounded in the Western press as White and Red army units began to prey upon one another, catching the Siberian villagers in between.

Many reports filtered through Sweden, Denmark, or Holland on the way to Western Europe and the United States. It was not until midsummer that the extent of the havoc overtaking Russia surfaced in the media. On Saturday, July 6, 1918, Yakov Blumkin and Nikolai Andreev, both employed by the Soviet Cheka and also members of the Left Socialist Revolutionary Party, burst into the office of the German consul. Dispatches described the two men entering Count Mirbach's private office where they had a short conversation with the German ambassador before shooting him. As they exited, Blumkin and Andreev lobbed explosives into the room. Both Blumkin and Andreev wanted the Soviets to rejoin the Allied war effort against Germany. Within days of his death, the German press began to connect Count von Mirbach's death with the overthrow of the Bolshevik military in Vladivostok and the Legion's successful campaign to evacuate from the Pacific coast. News of Count Von Mirbach's assassination reached the Western press by midmonth.[28] German rhetoric convinced the Allied nations that the Legion not only needed help, but that Russia was now a powder keg — no longer under the control of either the Soviets or German diplomacy.

At the Fifth Congress of All-Russian Soviets held earlier in July, recriminations surfaced on the part of the Social Revolutionary opposition. Maria Spiridonova of the Left Social Revolutionary Party announced that a majority of the provinces were still not and probably never would be pro-Bolshevik as Lenin and Trotsky asserted. The Congress had broken up into philosophical camps and finally bogged down under threats and intimidation on both sides. Along with many others, Miss Spiridonova was accused of helping to assassinate German ambassador Count von Mirbach.

Leon Trotsky now set the stage for further intimidation while warning Entente nations to stay out of Bolshevik business. Any involvement in either Russia or Siberia, Trotsky proclaimed, would be seen as a threat to both. As the Fifth Congress wound down, 11 former tsarist officials who had voluntarily returned from the West to assist the Moscow leadership in stabilizing the

Russian economy were arrested and executed. The Fifth Congress was only a portent of what would follow.[29]

On August 18, 1918, the *New York Times* carried an inconsequential-looking story, little more than one paragraph long, hidden on page 3.[30] It reported the execution of over 1,700 of Russia's best-trained officers. They had made the mistake of applying for emigration papers in an attempt to secure passage into the Polish territories. Several hundred Europeans had also been detained, many identified as British and French businessmen.

Though the Soviets had been careful to display a facade of brotherly love and common purpose, published accounts described a wildly different story. Lenin and Trotsky came under pressure from the citizenry to improve the desperate living conditions facing Russia's western cities. Assassinations in midsummer, especially those of Count Mirbach and General Eichhorn, reflected an atmosphere of distrust and growing hostility in the urban centers.

In his August 28 column Arthur Ransome, correspondent for the *London Daily News,* reported that postcard photographs were circulating throughout western Russia of Boris Donskoi's execution by hanging. Donskoi had been arrested for the assassination of German field marshal Von Eichhorn in Kiev. Eichhorn had anticipated his impending murder but the leadership in Moscow took no precautions to protect him. People questioned if Lenin and Trotsky maintained any control of the situation at all. As a result, Trotsky announced that all foreign consulate officials would be placed under surveillance.

As Russia spiraled into chaos, the White Russian Army, made up of former tsarist officers, tightened it's ranks. It organized to fight against the Red Guard while working to enlist Allied interest in the success of a counterrevolutionary movement.

Allied shipping in Vladivostok, supposedly there to evacuate the Legion, turned out to be warships.[31] Japan landed more troops in Vladivostok and publicly announced its intentions to financially back Ataman Semenov in Chita. In addition, Japanese units spread out into the borderlands along Manchuria and garrisoned near Irkutsk. The Allied Command began to worry that Japan's intention could be to cooperate with Chinese interests in Outer Mongolia and northern Manchuria in order to establish a satellite state in areas of Chinese occupation.[32]

Fear of becoming entangled in the growing counterrevolution festered among Legion troops. While the White Guard offered to help the peasantry, it did little more than victimize local citizens. Later, American General William Graves would write: "If the Allies were trying to get the Czechs [and Slovaks] to the Western Front, it seems peculiar that no arrangements had been made for ships to take them from Vladivostok."[33]

Chapter Six

From his destroyer in the Black Sea, Admiral Kolchak looked on as civil discord ravaged his beloved homeland.[1] Kolchak had been occupied in the Bosporus when Tsar Nicholas II abdicated his throne — effectively dissolving his faith in the invincibility of the Russian officer corps.[2] Even so, the young admiral continued to believe that the Russian military would succeed in its war effort against the Central Powers.

When Russia began to disintegrate under Kerensky's failed war effort, Kolchak's attempts to preserve morale and discipline in his own sailors at Sevastopol floundered.[3] Mutiny seemed imminent. Though he trusted Russia's allies, they were too far away to help restore order. For the first time Kolchak began to doubt the future of Mother Russia. Kolchak decided to travel to St. Petersburg to meet with Provisional Government representatives in order to salvage the situation facing his troops in Sevastopol. He traveled on the Trans-Siberian Railway through crowded village depots where Russian families congregated while fleeing eastward. Deserters from the front, frontoviks, milled about doorways begging for food. The young admiral witnessed the true desperation of his homeland. Kolchak wrote his wife, "In Petrograd I had reached the conviction that there was nothing ahead of us except defeat and shame. I thought that you too would turn your back on me, and this made it still harder to face the fact the war was lost, that everything was in ruins. I felt a bitter, almost an insupportable pain."[4]

As soon as Kolchak arrived in St. Petersburg, Admiral Glennon of the American Mission invited him to visit the United States. The young Russian admiral's successful Bosporus strategy had convinced the Americans that Kolchak's advice would help Allied naval plans in the region. They also hoped to gain Kolchak as a consultant to the United States Navy while the Allies figured out what to do about Kerensky's failed war effort.[5] Kolchak eagerly agreed to advise the Americans if only to salvage the Provisional Government's failing reputation. He was in San Francisco when news of the Bolshevik Revolution broke. Horrified, Kolchak immediately petitioned the British Army to join the fight. British Command posted the former admiral and Russian hero to Bombay in a Mesopotamian unit at the rank of private. Those who knew Kolchak reported that he never seemed disheartened by his treatment under the British.

On its way to Mesopotamia, Kolchak's ship docked in Japan long enough for the heart-wrenching news of the Brest-Litovsk Treaty to reach him. He was devastated that Russia reneged on its wartime alliance under German conditions. From Japan, Kolchak also learned from the British High Command of anti–Bolshevik units organizing to fight the Red Army in Siberia. He once again petitioned British High Command — this time to join the counterrevolution. Almost overnight Kolchak was named the commander of British forces in Manchuria. Aware that this new position placed him at the head of units that could slip across the Chinese border into Siberia, Kolchak graciously accepted the promotion.

Through the following months he watched as the White Russian effort coalesced and the Legion defeated one Soviet town militia after another. Russia's former admiral saw the vulnerabilities of the Red Army and recognized that Lenin would not allow his military to remain weak for long. The British Command began to realize its good fortune to have a leader of Kolchak's caliber in its ranks.

Carl Ackerman and Herman Bernstein, preeminent Western reporters, traveled in boxcars living among the Czechs and Slovaks through the summer of 1918. They noted that the Legion was, in fact, one of the most interesting armies they had ever encountered. It apparently consisted of professionals from every imaginable field — artisans, laborers, and academically trained specialists. From their rolling homes, the *teplushkas*, these skilled troops rebuilt

Legionnaires in gas masks, not dated.

Top: *Legion officer on a motorcycle, 1917.* Bottom: *Legion aviators of the First Division with airplane, Ufa, 1918.*

bridges and boxcars, produced medicines, salvaged old airplanes and weaponry, even published newspapers, music, poetry and maps. Physicians and butchers, chemists and carpenters, lawyers and tailors, engineers and postal workers, teachers and stone masons; all contributed to the progress of the evacuation. As the Allies later noted,

> Obviously, this was not an ordinary army aimlessly wandering across continents.... Each battalion had a number of professional photographers whose main duty was to take pictures of sentimental and historical interest to the group.... All officers spoke English, French, German or Russian as well as Czech and Slovak.[6]

In his waning years Joseph Skelnička, once in the Seventh Tatras Regiment, a unit comprised of 120 trains, vividly recalled his daily life aboard the teplushkas. The Legion's impeccable organization fascinated Skelnička. The soldiers' quarters were equipped with armor and interiors customized for whatever purpose Legion Command ordered.[7] Most troop trains contained an American-made coach at the center with a bakery and kitchen attached at either end. Officers lived together in a boxcar located near the center of each train, often connected to the pantry, tailor's facility, and shoemaker's shop. Every effort was made to make the Legion boxcars as comfortable as possible, since they offered the only retreat from the cruel realities threatening outside.[8] Regardless, comfort and safety were mere illusions. As many as 40 men slept on board beds stacked side by side, eight men to a bunk. Even in the middle of summer, Siberian nights could be very cool.[9] Where the sides of the boxcars met the ceiling, the legionnaires cut small squares for glass to be fitted in order to let in the sunlight. A second wall was fashioned to partner with the original siding and the space between both filled in with ash and wood shavings to add insulation.

Specialized trains answered a variety of needs. One teplushka housed cobblers, tailors, and leather workers who made and repaired uniforms and boots using leather and khaki material scavenged along the railroad or from field casualties. Despite such efforts, many soldiers traveled without proper equipment. Overcoats and boots were in the greatest demand. YMCA associate William Duncan reported to his superiors that legionnaires continually

Legion bakery car, not dated.

coveted his boots. Many Czech and Slovak soldiers were still wearing boots made originally in their homeland; others acquired infamously ill-fitting Russian boots. Along the Eastern Front socks had disappeared in the early months of the war, with rags replacing them thereafter.[10]

Technical positions, especially those occupations maintaining tracks, communication lines, and locomotives, were imperative for Legion survival. Siberian machinists and engineers were rare — rarer still in the volunteer Red Army. Local soviets often abandoned damaged locomotives instead of searching for parts or technicians to repair them. Czech and Slovak engineers salvaged discarded engines to add to the Legion's growing supply of rolling stock.

Legion mechanics also salvaged and reassembled a discarded printing press, and thus revived the *Československý deník*, a Czech-language newspaper first published in Kiev. The *Československý deník* reported lengthy accounts of international and national news for the legionnaires, locals, Allies and enemies alike, quickly becoming the primary news source for all of the Russian Far East. Pausing long enough to publish in temporary locations, the front page always identified what town the press passed through by press time.

Photographs of the Czechs and Slovaks began to circulate when Carl Ackerman and Herman Bernstein boarded Legion trains. Captions underneath these images explained them in English, French, Russian, and Czech. The

Veterinarians of the First Regiment, not dated.

Československý deník's editorial staff—comprised of Major Holeček, previously a Bohemian lawyer, and Colonel Rudolf Medek, schoolmaster and poet, relied upon personal accounts from the troops in the field. After an altercation, legionnaires immediately submitted their own stories. As the typeface wore down, Japanese and American units donated new equipment to keep the paper in print and the public informed.

This innovative spirit seeped into every element of Legion life on the trains. Captain Novotný, a former Bohemian postal official, instituted a postal system for Siberia.[11] Captain Novotný and his staff designed stamps reflecting conditions in Siberia. The first displayed a legionnaire in Siberian uniform, the second a Czech lion, symbol of the Czech lands, and the third a typical Russian Orthodox church, a familiar sight from teplushkas.[12] No matter how difficult conditions became along the route, Captain Novotný's postal system delivered the mail. Even when the enemy disrupted telegraph and telephone communiqués and later destroyed railway lines, Czech and Slovak postal workers connected isolated units in the field with Legion Command.

More awe-inspiring still was the Legion's banking system. Before the evacuation began, Družina troops earned their pay in rubles — currency that quickly depreciated. In Vladivostok, ex-bankers from the Czech and Slovak lands serving in the Legion advised General Dieterichs to establish a Legion banking system. The plan awarded every legionnaire a bank share valued at 200 French francs. As the ruble began to fail, the Legionnaires' Bank exchanged rubles for cargo and services. Bank officials notified legionnaires

Legion acting troupe near Novonikolaevsk, 1919.

Legion orchestra in Siberian field, with conductor Rudolf Karel, not dated.

of the worth of their stock and other relative information like locations of frequent counterfeit operations. At one point, Legion currency became so highly valued that even the Red Guard considered using it to replace the Russian ruble. For obvious reasons Lenin and Trotsky vetoed this proposition. YMCA secretary Charles H. Atherton traveled onboard a Legion train with a small reed organ that he had smuggled along. His bunkmates never ceased to impress with an unending repertoire of songs. Atherton learned innumerable folk tunes and marches that he published years later as a collection honoring his Legion friends called *Favorite Songs of the Czecho-Slovak Army in Russi, (Oblíbené písně našich hochů v československé armádě v Rusku).*

When time allowed, the men poured out of their teplushkas to spend time in the open air. Legionnaires performed intricate gymnastic routines from their Sokol days accompanied by their very own professional orchestra. Many Legion musicians came from the imperial court of Vienna, where the Hapsburg orchestra had been famous for over 300 years. Peasants watched in amazement as one field became the scene of a soccer match, while nearby a cavalry unit practiced maneuvers accompanied by Brahms, Bartok, Mozart, or Dvorak. All the while, engineers and mechanics repaired discarded equipment and supplies. On a lazy afternoon William Duncan sat composing a letter to his family back in the United States. He glanced out of his compartment upon a field of wildflowers and described the scene outside: "In the next car one of the soldiers is playing an accordion while out in the field some of the men are kicking a ball. Off on another track there are about 400 Serb refugees, for over three years now these poor people have been wandering around homeless, and now they are also on their way to Vladivostok, thinking that they will go from there to America."[13]

Legion decorating boxcars in Ukraine, 1918.

Duncan also described a contest arranged by Legion Command. Artist-soldiers had been ordered to decorate the exteriors of the teplushkas. Every train would be judged by a committee of officers picked by the men. Soon depictions of the high Tatra Mountains, snowcapped and mysterious, passed boxcars covered with the skyline of Prague with the Vltava River cutting through its cobblestone streets. Later, printed postcards of these decorated teplushkas became collector's items — published for legionnaires who prized them for sentimental reasons. These efforts served to divert troops attention from an atmosphere of violence growing outside their boxcars.

Cavalry soldiers who remained in one place longer than other units to care for their horses began to marry local women. Legion officers seldom supported these unions, but as time passed even they courted local women. Colonel Radola Gajda married during a respite in Ekaterinburg.[14] In response, the First Military Congress held on August 4, 1918, forbade any additional nuptials on the grounds that the teplushkas lacked space for couples and families. On board the boxcars, separation of the sexes became instituted. Efforts to forestall liaisons proved futile, however, and births continued with or without officer approval. When the marriage count exceeded 1,600, Legion Command demanded that at the very least nuptials be performed by an Orthodox priest or before a Legion consul.[15] Under rare circumstances, compartments became allocated to house couples.

Partisans fled in the wake of the arriving Legion soldiers, only to return again when the Czechs and Slovaks departed. Legionnaires found themselves protecting local villagers and peasants, many of whom ran to meet their units as Legion trains pulled into town. Joseph Skelnička recalled the kindness of locals. Aboard his teplushka, Skelnička and his comrades ran out of supplies. On one occasion, the situation became so dire that Skelnička's unit lived off of wheat chaff and kidney beans for days. A local Bolshevik mayor sold cattle to him and his unit, in effect saving their lives.

Empathy with locals and mutual generosity fostered various friendships. Soldiers often supported refugee families even after they moved on to another location. The Legion shared supplies from abandoned boxcars with the peasants and townsfolk. On one occasion, local townspeople received over 5,000 pieces of clothing retrieved in transit.[16] Skelnička's unit, the Seventh Tatras, encountered various political groups on its journey. Some were enthusiastically Communist, others not — for the most part, all wanted to trade with the Legion. Had Skelnička and his colleagues realized in the summer of 1918 that many more days on the railroad lay ahead, they might have held onto more of their supplies.

William Duncan remembered a boy he befriended:

> In this village, I was talking to a little fellow about 11 years old, clever and apparently normal in all respects, who couldn't tell me the name of the days, the number of days in the week. Who, in reply to any question that would require a little learning to answer, would answer that he was "*ne gramsity,*" meaning that he was not educated and therefore was not supposed to know. He smoked since he was six years of age and could roll a cigarette like a veteran.... There was no school in that village and the percentage of illiteracy must have been about ninety-nine.[17]

These friendships were violently frowned upon by the local militia and as civil war spread, atrocities against the peasantry grew more common and virulent. Joseph Skelnička reported being an eyewitness to this terror: "Once in a Volga marsh in early May ... when the trees were just beginning to cover their nakedness with tender, downy leaves, we passed quite close in to the swamp. Spreading throughout the surrounding forest, we were horrified to see at least 50 bodies hanging from the limbs." [18] Skelnička later found out the crime of the villagers in the marsh had been befriending a passing Legion train.

For many legionnaires, life unraveled as a lonely and exhausting string of hours. During periods of relief, units worked to resupply lines and perform tasks neglected during battle. Food and medical attention became hurried affairs shared with locals who had never heard of a "Czech" or a "Slovak," but who also reveled in the attention and hospitality shown to them by these peculiar-sounding foreigners.

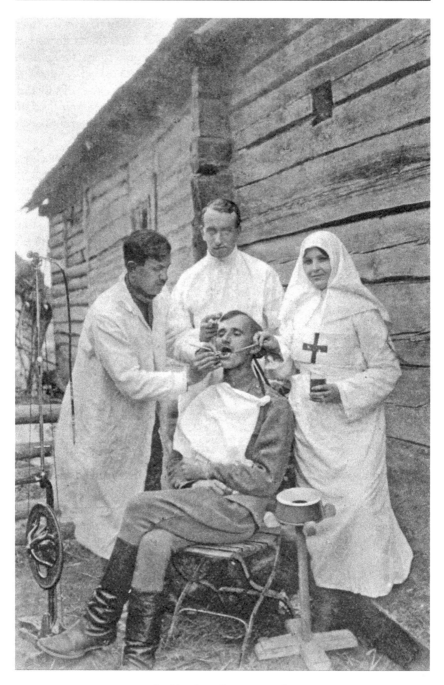

Teplushka dental care, not dated.

Down to the tiniest elements, the Legion trains became centers of efficiency both in battle and in the collection of supplies.[19] As travel time increased throughout the summer of 1918 so too did the casualty rate: the death of John Persic from infected water is a case in point. Adapting the Russian tradition of drinking boiled tea kept similar casualties to a minimum.[20] In an attempt to keep epidemics under control, every depot had a facility to boil water.

Reports from Moscow issued through Amsterdam painted alarming scenarios to the world outside western Russia. A German reporter from the Frankfurt *Zeitung* newspaper wrote, "The cost of food is highest, no bread is obtainable. Grain supplies to Northern and Central Russia have completely ceased."[21] In addition, families had reportedly been turned out of their homes in order to billet newly trained Red Army recruits.

In stark contrast, Harry Hoskins, an American second lieutenant, remembered being most impressed by the Transbaikalia where he saw "literally hundreds of miles of wheat. It's some of them most beautiful land I've ever seen. If they would use it properly, they [Russia] could raise enough beef to feed the world."[22] The conditions of Russia's poor stirred a basic socialist concern in not only the legionnaires, who struggled to maintain their neutrality oath, but also in hundreds of volunteers arriving from the United States.

American YMCA secretaries had been involved with charity work in Russia since the beginning of the war. While the tsarist effort on the Eastern Front was in full swing, more than 200 YMCA volunteers nursed the sick and delivered needed supplies for the orphaned, widowed, and injured. After the Bolshevik Revolution, both Red and White Russians sanctioned YMCA associates to work in Siberia dispensing donated food and clothing. With civil war looming, YMCA representatives arrived in the Siberian countryside to assist evacuation efforts of both repatriating POWs and the legionnaires. YMCA and Red Cross representatives guarded their neutral stance. Under Dieterichs' watch, the YMCA also secured supplies in Vladivostok warehouses, transferring material to areas of need in the interior.[23]

For some, remaining neutral became a struggle. Throughout the summer of 1918, political discourse grew ugly within the Legion. Large numbers of men upheld their socialist leanings, but others held monarchist beliefs and a number turned decidedly toward Bolshevism. For this last group, the Communist ideology brought them into direct conflict with fellow legionnaires, occasionally with tragic results.

Joseph Skelnička remembered an incident that occurred when a fellow legionnaire was caught working for the local Mariinsk soviet. The soldier had attempted to facilitate negotiations between the local Bolshevik commissar and his own troop commander, Captain Eduard Kadlec. Kadlec grew angry during the negotiations, and finally ended them by advising the Bolsheviks

YMCA with the Legion First Regiment near Irkutsk, 1919.

to clear out. Before the local militia left, however, Captain Kadlec warned the Czech soldier never to let his former unit catch him alone. If captured, he faced execution for charges of spying and sabotaging Legion progress. According to Skelnička, the ex-legionnaire boasted to Kadlec, "'You will never destroy us. We will destroy you!' Such a Communist, he was. It didn't take more than a week ... he was shot in the leg.... So we got him, and he was making a hero of himself. When Captain Kadlec told us, 'Put him on the bank over there and get twelve men here.' So we got men and put him on the bank, but before he was shot he said, 'Captain Kadlec, I want you to deliver my last greeting to my mother.'"[24]

With the Russian naval surrender of the city of Vladivostok, Dieterichs' legionnaires had been transformed from evacuating soldiers to an army of occupation.[25] In frustration and with the hope that Derber officials would prove more honest than their Soviet predecessors, Dieterichs placed the province in their hands.

In an environment rife with double-dealing, Thomas Masaryk, Eduard Beneš, and Milan Štefánik acknowledged their own political naiveté. General Štefánik led officials living abroad, including Colonel Vladimír Hruban, Captain Zdenko Gierlinger, and Jaromír Špaček, on recruitment missions throughout Canada and the United States. They hoped to ensure that Czech and Slovak immigrant communities maintained a high degree of interest and funding for the evacuation of the Legion to the Western Front.[26] To assist in their efforts, a Czecho-Slovak Information Bureau opened in New York City. On a regular basis, it disseminated Legion information to the Western press supplied mainly by the *New York Times'* Carl Ackerman and the *New York Herald's* Herman Bernstein. The Czech and Slovak odyssey through Siberia had quickly blossomed into one of the most significant human-interest stories of the summer.[27]

The Slovak League and the Bohemian National Alliance also worked in tandem in Chicago and Pittsburgh under the efforts of Professor Albert Mametey and Marina Pualiny, who organized a national effort to assist the Bohemian Red Cross. General Štefánik simultaneously collected funds for the Legion and recruited men from Czech and Slovak immigrant communities throughout Canada and the United States. On one occasion over 2,300 volunteered for the French foreign service — of this group most reported directly to Cognac, France, for training as infantrymen. Clement R. Nesnadny volunteered along with 300 other Czechs and Slovaks from the city of Cleveland, Ohio. He later stated: "I was young, believed in freedom and wanted to go and fight as soon as I could."[28] Over a third of these men died in the trenches on the Western Front. Though fighting for a homeland many had only heard about from their parents, volunteers focused on the dream of an independent Czech and Slovak nation.

By midsummer, soldiers from these Czech-American and Slovak-American communities had become seasoned soldiers fighting throughout Western Europe. They also took a great deal of interest in following the Legion's evacuation path along the Trans-Siberian Railway in the newspapers. The month of July heralded an appreciable upswing in both the ferocity and style of fighting by the German army in the West and the Red Army in the East.[29]

Contrary to any basic assumptions of it being a linear track, the Trans-Siberian Railway was, in fact, a series of complex systems.[30] A single line from Vladivostok on the Pacific coast led west, then broke into several spurs — one headed north and then west along the Ussuri and the Amur rivers, another ran west across Manchuria. The railway often double tracked or split into single tracks for seemingly little or no reason. The main line was also double tracked but had many single branch lines that moved into the interior in a number of directions.

The railroad branch that ran from Vladivostok northward turned at Nikolsk-Ussurisk and then proceeded westward through Khabarosk. This spur was controlled by more than 50,000 Red Guard troops.[31] General Dieterichs tried to warn Colonel Gajda of numerous enemy units lying in wait for his trains throughout the region. Czecho-Slovak units met the Ussuri Red Guard, which greatly outnumbered their own separated units as they moved toward Vladivostok.[32] Evacuation through Vladivostok had been the only option for the Legion, not only because of promises made to both Lenin and the Allies, but because German submarines patrolled the Baltic at the ports of Archangelsk and Murmansk.[33] General Dieterichs finally decided to send a portion of his unit from Vladivostok west toward Chita to help clear the way. This began what would later be identified as the Ussuri front. Ataman Semenov had also stationed his bandits in the midst of several Red Army units nearby.

Despite a reported lack of weapons and supplies, Colonel Gajda's exhausted men prepared to attack the stronghold of Irkutsk. Passing through the outskirts of town, they discovered and redistributed over 150 rifles hidden under a bed.[34] At dawn Gajda's men encircled the city.[35] Irkutsk fell to Gajda with relative ease. Later, he learned that several Bolshevik units had slipped away to move up ahead on the railroad. Reconnaissance pinpointed the train and the Bolsheviks who were commandeering carloads of explosives and moving them toward the 39 tunnels. If the tunnels were destroyed, the British estimated that restoring the railroad through to the other side of the Baikal Mountains would take at least two years.[36]

A train filled with explosives had been moved terrifyingly close to Kultuk's entrance to the last tunnel. Kultuk was bordered by a large meadow on the edge of Lake Baikal with snowcapped peaks rising sharply behind it. Gajda knew there was no time to waste. His men would have to take Kultuk and the Baikal Station simultaneously — a nearly impossible maneuver but one that had to be attempted.[37]

Five hundred men from Gajda's Seventh Regiment marched through the mountains to encircle Kultuk from behind. If the Seventh made it, these men would act as Gajda's rear guard while he launched a frontal attack on the Kultuk depot. If the Seventh did not make it, Gajda's frontal attack would be cut to pieces. Under cover of darkness, Cossack guides led soldiers over foggy, wet and slippery goat trails through pine forest toward the rear of the town.

During three days and nights, resting minimally, the legionnaires followed their guides through the steep wilderness, their silence interrupted only occasionally by the rumble of thunder or the crash of waterfalls in the distance. Before dawn of the third day they came down upon Kultuk's quiet mist-shrouded buildings. The Bolsheviks had not stationed sentries on the mountainside so maneuvering into place proved relatively easy.

As the Seventh Regiment descended upon the center of town, Bolshevik troops scrambled from their beds.[38] The Czechs and Slovaks made as much noise as possible, screaming, discharging weapons, and banging on nearby buildings to startle the enemy. Keeping watch over the train during the battle, seven legionnaires hid under an overhanging cliff by the depot. It was up to them to the keep local Bolshevik militia from moving the explosives.

Suddenly, a deafening roar stunned the soldiers as the ground jolted — rocks, earth and mountain foliage slid down into the streets, crashing through cottages. Soldiers broke and rushed to escape the ensuing shower of twisted metal. Water from Lake Baikal sprayed in violent plumes as hot metal pierced its surface. The Bolsheviks grabbed carts, horses, even engines, anything to make their escape. Suddenly, just as quickly, all was still. Where the station once stood, a deep red scar remained. The depot was a mangled wreck of steaming wood and twisted track. In the fighting, a stray bullet had struck the explosives hidden on board one of the boxcars.[39] No legionnaires were killed, but several of the station employees and Bolshevik guards vanished forever in the blast.

William Duncan reported to his superiors: "My stay at this place was too short-lived — just two hours, and I am now crossing the lake again and its beauty is intoxicating. At Baikal on the R.R. only the debris of the former station building remains where the Bolshevik trains were standing when the Czechs hit their cars loaded with dynamite and the buildings are no more, only the wreckage of wheels and cars strewn about."[40]

While Colonel Gajda's men worked to clean up Kultuk, Colonel Čeček, far in the rear, readied for Simbirsk. Ahead of him, Colonel Vojcechovsky led the Sixth and Second regiments directly behind Gajda's units. Vojcechovsky's trains headed toward the city of Ekaterinburg where the Volga River ran south and then west of the city. On the edge of a huge mining region in the central Urals, Ekaterinburg had become a particularly well-guarded tsarist city.

Colonel Vojcechovsky, the chief of staff and one of the few professional Russian officers still leading Czech troops, knew that his men had to take Ekaterinburg. This attack became especially lethal for both sides as day after day the Sixth and Second attacked and retreated, attacked and retreated. Though the Bolshevik stronghold was severely weakened, the militia held its ground. Casualties grew each day. Finally on July 22, Vojcechovsky and his trains breached the outskirts of the city and entered Ekaterinburg. Street fighting ensued with losses rising ever higher.

Vojcechovsky finally secured the city center but soon sensed something was amiss. Once the Legion controlled the streets, the city became eerily lifeless. Ekaterinburg held a secret — a secret so hideous that the world would never forget what had taken place here moments before the Czechs and Slovaks entered its downtown. Colonel Vojcechovsky and his legionnaires would have to live with the realization that they had unintentionally been party to a crime taking place on the outskirts of Ekaterinburg.

Chapter Seven

After abdicating to Kerensky's Menshieviks, Tsar Nicholas II became a captive in a land he once ruled. Under house arrest, he happily plowed the fields near his dacha before the gaze of astounded guards. By the summer of 1918, when Kerensky had also failed, news of the royal family faded from view. No one seemed to know where the imperial family had been relocated or what it was doing. Lenin and Trotsky had ordered the entire Romanov family moved around the Siberian countryside as prisoners of the Bolshevik state.

For a time, reports circulated that the Romanovs had been comfortably boarded in several locations. One such report in the spring of 1918 by Ivan Narodny described a Tobolsk monastery. Narodny contacted guards who had been friendly with one of the grand duchesses. Sergeant T. I. Klrpichnikoff reportedly lunched often as a guest of the Romanov children. He came forward with a presumably authentic account of his time with the state prisoners. Little Alexis, the heir apparent, had begun to flirt with notions of Slavic independence and democratic rule — a secret Klrpichnikoff kept to himself for quite awhile before sharing it with Narodny.[1] Young Alexis lived with his sisters in several rooms of the Tobolsk monastery. Alexis was reportedly growing strong. Rural settings far removed from stringent security measures pleased the little tsarevitch as he experienced fewer and fewer of his hemophilic attacks.

From afar, Lenin and Trotsky carefully monitored the Romanovs' every move. By February 1918, the royal family had unsuccessfully attempted to escape by bribing a guard. Consequently, the Romanovs were searched. More than 20,000 rubles had to be confiscated and the family once again moved. Nicholas and Aleksandra traveled by sleigh through the frozen tundra, leaving Alexis and two of his sisters. The two grand duchesses had been left behind to oversee Alexis, who suffered yet another attack of uncontrolled bleeding. News of the Romanovs ended at Tobolsk. Even though the family eventually reunited in a small dacha on the outskirts of Ekaterinburg, the world had no idea if its members were dead or alive.[2]

By the end of June, rumors surfaced that Lenin and Trotsky planned to bring the entire imperial family to Moscow for a trial and subsequent court-martial. Supposedly, Lenin had invited dignitaries from the Central Powers (Austria, Germany, Hungary, and Turkey) and the Entente powers (Britain, Canada, France, Japan, and the United States) to witness the occasion.

Both the king of England and the kaiser of Germany, the tsar's first cousins, were confident that Nicholas would soon be released to the Allies once this intended show trial ended. The Romanov family and servants imprisoned with them could then proceed into exile. England, Norway or Sweden appeared the best prospects for a fresh start for the royals.[3]

Newspapers in Amsterdam reported that Grand Duke Michael Aleksandrovitch, brother of the tsar, had proclaimed himself the new tsar.[4] The grand duke intended to lead the counterrevolution that had been coalescing in the interior. Aleksandrovitch's proclamation was a further catalyst for White and Red armies to increase efforts to recruit legionnaires into their units.

As Colonel Vojcechovsky's men advanced towards Ekaterinburg throughout the month of July 1918, the local Soviets attempted to contact Moscow for instructions regarding the fate of the imprisoned Romanov family in their midst. Ekaterinburg's militia believed that Vojcechovsky's troops acted as mercenaries in the pay of the counterrevolution.

The imperial family sat in its dacha unaware that a decision concerning its future had begun to take shape. Vojcechovsky would never be allowed to storm Ekaterinburg to free the ex-tsar in order to return the Romanovs to power. Frantically, messages blasted up the line from the Ekaterinburg soviet to Moscow. The coup de grace came when rumors spread that Vojcechovsky

Ekaterinburg Dacha where Tsar Nicholas II, his family and entourage were assassinated, July 1918.

might be carrying the Russian treasury with him. Ironically, Colonel Vojce-chovsky saw Ekaterinburg as just another impediment in a seemingly endless journey to the Pacific coast. Neither he nor his legionnaires had any idea that the tsar and his family had been hidden away in Ekaterinburg up the line.

On July 17, shortly after midnight, the Romanovs and their entourage awoke to confusion. They dressed and hurried downstairs for yet another move, this time possibly into exile in England. One can only wonder if they became excited as they dressed and gathered together with the prospect of freedom ahead. Their belongings had already been taken away for transport. Groggily they moved through the dacha's rooms together, but this time the guards herded them into the basement.[5]

Later, descriptions of the five children, Aleksandra and Nicholas, a family physician, and three servants stepping into a dimly lit basement abounded. Barely having time to adjust to the dark, the Romanov entourage felt the presence of several people. A line of soldiers facing the family immediately opened fire.[6] Rumor had it that all except the youngest daughter, Anastasia, and the heir apparent, Alexis, died instantly. Alexis and Anastasia had to be bludgeoned to death with rifle butts.

The survival of any evidence of a Romanov presence in Ekaterinburg had not been left to chance — not even the family dogs. The militia burned the Romanov belongings along with their bodies and threw everything down a mine shaft outside of town.[7] No one could foresee the reaction of the Russian people upon hearing of these murders.

> Among a superstitious peasantry, Imperial bones might acquire a counter–rev-olutionary mystique, and Yurovski's orders had included the destruction of the corpses. These were piled into a lorry and taken to an unused mine shaft 13 miles away which had been cordoned off by Red guards. Here they were stripped, dismembered with axes, drenched with petrol and sulfuric acid, and burnt on two enormous fires. The ashes, together with a miscellany of objects, including Anastasia's Pekinese, were then thrown down the waterlogged mine shaft.
>
> On the same night that the Tsar was murdered, the Tsarina's sister, the Grand Duchess Elizabeth, was also [killed], together with her husband, the Grand Duke Serge, and several members of the Imperial family. She was thrown liv-ing down a mine shaft at a place called Alapacievsk. Both women were grand-daughters of Queen Victoria, a troubling problem for the Moscow leadership, who were continuing to work out a diplomatic relationship with Britain.[8]

Within hours of the assassination of the royal family, Vojcechovsky and his unsuspecting legionnaires stormed Ekaterinburg. The city fell to Vojce-chovsky on July 25, 1918. Piecing together rumors, the Czechs and Slovaks realized something heinous had occurred just preceding their arrival. Later, the mine shaft and some of its grisly contents were discovered. Fragments of ash and bone found at the site were sent in a small wooden box to forensic experts traveling with an American army unit near Vladivostok. Vojcechovsky ordered information his unit gathered concerning the tsar's final days in Ekaterinburg to be included with the box.

For months the world press had been asking where the tsar and tsarina were, but information had not been forthcoming. As early as the first week in June, the *New York Times* began to question whether the Romanovs were still living. On June 26, 1918, Western papers printed questions they wanted Lenin to answer. Other members of the Romanov family joined this growing chorus. Lack of information concerning the fate of Nicholas, his wife, and children encouraged the spinning of wild tales: Alexis, the heir apparent, had succumbed to a bout of hemophilia; the family had secretly fled to freedom in the north; the family was under guard in Moscow awaiting trial.

Toward the end of July, a new story reverberated in the Copenhagen press: the Romanovs had been exterminated at an undisclosed location in Siberia. On July 28, 1918, Carl Ackerman of the *New York Times*, who had been traveling with the Legion, reported the execution of the imperial family in lurid detail. Soon so many inaccurate accounts circulated among the international press that Lenin and Trotsky decided to announce the trial and summary execution of the ex-tsar. The Moscow leadership laid the blame squarely at the doorstep of the Legion, which had, according to Lenin and Trotsky, marched into Ekaterinburg with only one goal in mind: to restore the Romanov family to power.[9] This accusation was followed by weeks of silence from Moscow. In the vacuum that resulted, only vague innuendo remained to fester in the world press. Why did Nicholas II have to be executed in secret and where were the other members of his family?

Legion Command wholeheartedly refuted Bolshevik accusations. It pointed out that not only had it never been pro-Romanov but it had always demonstrated its stance against aristocratic rule. Czechs and Slovaks would never restore the Romanov family to power against the wishes of the Russian people. Legion leadership repeated its ardent desire to evacuate troops from Siberia as soon as possible. Czech and Slovak troops did, however, admit that they found the manner in which the tsar died appalling and believed his body deserved a proper burial.

And what of the tsarina and her children? Aleksandra had been rumored to be resting quietly in locations scattered about Russia or Siberia. The Russian paper *Vjia*, a Soviet news source, described the tsar's death in simple terms, but mentioned nothing of his family members. Orders to execute the royal family did come from higher-ups but exactly who gave direct orders remained a mystery.

Details continued to be scrutinized in the Western press until a description of corpse mutilations appeared. The death of Aleksandra, the tsarina, placed Russia in a highly sensitive situation with both Germany and England, two enemies still at war but tied through family connections. Aleksandra's execution threatened to taint the reputation of Lenin and Trotsky with both governments. Aleksandra had been a direct descendent of the German royal family and one of Queen Victoria's favorite granddaughters. The murder of these royals personally affected the three most influential families of Europe — each closely connected through marriage. Even divisions caused by war could not equal the horror of this Bolshevik atrocity.

White Russian troops entered Ekaterinburg directly behind Vojcechovsky's troop trains and demanded that the citizens of the city divulge who had been personally responsible for the tsar's murder and the murder of his family. When no new information developed, the White Russian authorities arrested and executed innocents. More than 3,000 men, women and children from Ekaterinburg were later crammed into empty boxcars on the railway line outside of town. Throughout the following months the "train of death," as it became known, shunted back and forth from town to town along the Trans-Siberian Railway, its doors nailed shut with a hole cut into the siding at one end for ventilation. Legionnaires appealed to White Army officials to let these people go, but *the train of death* continued on its ceaseless journey.[10] It paused from time to time along a siding or in a depot where bodies were discarded before guards nailed those alive inside once again. American soldiers reported catching a glimpse of this train over the following months.

The unfolding political drama in Ekaterinburg afforded Colonel Čeček no peace as he pressed farther up the Trans-Siberian Railway with the Red Guard close behind. Earlier in the year, unbeknownst to the Czecho-Slovak Army Corps, Red army commanders had stored the entire Russian treasury first in Simbirsk and then in Kazan.[11] Kazan had been the center for an entire Soviet military district and it now stood directly before Colonel Čeček's trains.

After the Bolshevik revolt, many Allied missions had become isolated throughout the region. Two French officers traveling with Čeček, Major Guinet and Captain Brodes, convinced Čeček that an Allied intervention was on the verge of being established in Siberia through contacts in these missions. Čeček incorrectly believed that Allied reinforcements landing in Vladivostok would be heading into the Siberian countryside to help the Legion evacuate.[12] Proclaiming themselves Allied agents, Guinet and Brodes took it upon themselves to convince Čeček to launch a "new anti–German front on the Volga."[13] Hearing this, Thomas Masaryk and the Allied Supreme Command became alarmed. Guinet and Brodes never had privileged information from Allied headquarters as they asserted. The two Frenchmen were immediately threatened with courts martial. Colonel Čeček pushed ahead to attack Kazan.

The capture of Kazan by Čeček's men was doubtful since they had few arms and were relying on faulty topical maps of the area.[14] Even so, the local Soviet militia fled into the nearby forest in a panic a week before Čeček's trains approached. What Čeček hadn't realized was that a Serb unit under the leadership of an ex-tsarist officer, Blagotic, had already opened up the city for Čeček's trains on August 7. This incident was the first of many befuddled situations in which the Allied Command, White Russian officials, and the Legion misinterpreted one another's signals.

More than 200,000 citizens in Kazan opened their doors to the Czechs and Slovaks throughout August. Later it was learned that the population of Kazan had been hiding more than 4,000 ex-tsarist officers for months. Some of Nicholas Romanov's top commanders lived in Kazan right under the noses of the local Soviet after the Tsar's abdication. Eventually these Russian officers revealed yet another secret: the Romanov treasury, worth over 560 million rubles in gold bullion, had been moved on barges through Siberia in the early summer months of the Bolshevik takeover. Kazan had become the treasury's final resting place.[15]

White Army units surrounding the city demanded that Colonel Čeček, who had rearmed his trains with weapons located in Kazan, take responsibility for the Russian treasury before proceeding eastward. Čeček refused. He had already been misled into betraying his oath of neutrality to Masaryk and the OCSNR twice; transporting the Russian treasury on his trains for the counterrevolution would be a political misstep Čeček could ill afford. The White Army was not negotiating; either the treasury would be transferred to Vladivostok for safekeeping or Čeček's Legion trains would proceed no farther. Finding no alternatives, Čeček's echelon guarded the Russian treasury throughout its journey in Siberia, a mixed blessing for Colonel Čeček and the Legion.[16]

By the end of August, the Legion had accidentally secured the Russian treasury, stumbled into a disaster at Kultuk Depot in the Baikal Range, and become entangled in the Romanov assassination.[17] Lenin and Trotsky manipulated the effects of these incidents, tying them together in the world press. They accused Čeček of carrying the Russian treasury to secure the throne for Nicholas Romanov. Of course, Legion Command reiterated that evacuation remained its only goal. If Lenin would keep his original promise to the Legion, it would leave in a matter of weeks.

Hearing of Čeček's new troubles, the Czecho-Slovak Army Corp contacted Thomas Masaryk and his associates Eduard Beneš and Milan Štefánik. Čeček's situation transporting the Russian treasury threatened to place Czech and Slovak troops in the middle of a burgeoning civil war. It also meant that Čeček's echelon had become a particular target for marauding bandits like Ataman Semenov or Kalmikov.

During the summer months, the landscape surrounding Lake Baikal flourished with rich-colored pine forests and abundant animal life. Some species were unknown anywhere else in the world.[18] Near the town of Verchne-Udiinsk, the Selenga River that flowed vast and deep all the way from Mongolia moved up past the town and on toward the shores of Lake Baikal. For centuries trade moved along the Selenga from Urda into Siberia. Both the Selenga River and the areas surrounding Lake Baikal remained relatively unmapped. Colonel Gajda's reconnaissance teams gathered their own information and produced maps that defined the area for the forces now assembling there. Yet Gajda soon learned from the indigenous people nearby that an ancient overland trade route had long ago been constructed parallel to the river bed. Where the Selenga reached the Baikal Range, the mountains cut so close to the lake's edge that any attack by local soviet militia would occur along the railroad bed near the lake itself.

Colonel Gajda had secured the town of Kultuk with considerable damage to both the depot and railway line. The tangled mess threatened to stall Gajda's progress. Again he called for engineers in his echelon to report on the damage. After reviewing the situation, experts agreed that both would be in full working order in just a matter of weeks. Damage to the tunnels had actually been minimal. Colonel Gajda and his men had days, however, not weeks, in which to secure the other tunnels ahead. The lovely Kultuk Baikal peaks had offered his troops a short time to regroup, but Verchne-Udiinsk beckoned up ahead.

Gajda's strategy included three small lake steamers absconded from the shoreline: the *Siberian*, *Theodosie*, and the *Buriate*. Because the steamers could not hold his entire entourage, Gajda split his forces. He left the engineers to repair Kultuk's depot and railroad track, boarded Boris Usakov and one contingent on three steamers, and took his remaining troops to march through a mountain pass. Gajda intended to surprise the enemy in Verchne-Udiinsk from the rear.

Usakov proceeded at the head of his contingent. Once again he donned a disguise. Gajda owed a tremendous debt to this Russian officer and knew that the Legion's Seventh Regiment could not have made it thus far without Usakov's expert help. The Legion was not the only army in the area aware of Boris Usakov's reputation. The Red Army had grown tired of hearing about his successes. Usakov now had a price on his head and militia watching for him, disguised or not.[19]

This time, Usakov donned the uniform of a Red Guard officer and set off across the lake with the three Russian steamers. These dangerously overcrowded vessels faced a well-patrolled shoreline with less than adequate arms; they immediately came under fire by five militia vessels. Using artillery on the decks of the steamer boats, Usakov's contingent sank one militia vessel before realizing the enemy also fired from shore.[20]

Usakov sailed directly into neighboring Rosalskaya Harbor demanding to speak to the commanding commissar of Verchne-Udiinsk. Obviously both a Russian and an officer, Usakov was taken immediately to the camp commissar where he explained that his Red Guard militia units fighting across the lake had run into a regiment of legionnaires. Nearly overwhelmed, his men had become pinned down and suffered from a critical lack of arms. They needed immediate help.

As Usakov preformed his ruse, Colonel Gajda led his men into the town of Mysovaya where he defeated the local militia, chasing a Red army unit into the surrounding mountains. The Seventh Regiment quickly advanced toward the port of Rosalskaya where Usakov in disguise negotiated for war materiel and food. Reconnaissance reported that Usakov's men, also wearing Red Army uniforms, had begun loading the three steamers with stores of ammunition from the Verchne-Udiinsk militia warehouse.

Usakov's plan succeeded. The local commandant, concerned for Usakov's unit fighting the Legion on the other side of the lake, had been more than generous with his supplies and had even helped load them on the three steamers. As Usakov's unit boarded its vessels, however, the Soviet officer stepped forward and grabbed Usakov by the arm, informing him that he would be detained as insurance. Though Usakov feigned disgust at the insult, he remained in Rosalskaya waving from shore as his men departed.

Gajda crashed into Verchne-Udiinsk in unison with explosions placed by a separate forward unit of his men along the oil tanks lining the lake front. Legionnaires ran through the town screaming and making noise to spread panic. Though the local militia outnumbered the legionnaires by nearly two to one, the bulk of its weapons and ammunition had been loaded aboard steamers heading toward the opposite shoreline to be used on the other side of the lake by Usakov's men.

As the Seventh Regiment quickly moved from one building to another and the Red army fled, a huge blast ripped through the mountainside. The last of the 39 tunnels, over 350 feet long, had been destroyed. When Gajda's units attacked the town, the commandant of Verchne-Udiinsk heard the uproar at militia headquarters. He must have realized that he had been made a fool. Whether the Red officer also understood that the cunning imposter facing him was the infamous Boris Usakov is unclear. The commandant pulled out his revolver and shot Boris Usakov in the head at point-blank range.

When Gajda eventually discovered Usakov's body, photographs were taken, communiqués sent, and a full Legion funeral with honors planned. Usakov had been Gajda's friend and confidant. His death was not only a severe loss for the Sixth and Seventh regiments but a terrible personal loss to Gajda. Gajda's men would finally get the long rest they needed but at a heavy price.

The Czech and Slovak Army Corps now sat marooned in the middle of a growing civil war. In seconds the final tunnel offering its only exit to freedom to the east had collapsed, burying the hopes of legionnaires with it. Thus far the Czechs and Slovaks had endured German propaganda, the local militias' harassment, and weeks of violent confrontation along over 5,500 miles of railroad — only to become trapped on the wrong side of the Baikal Mountain Range. Even improvements in liberated villages seemed superficial as the Red Army moved in to stamp them out. Gajda and his men resigned themselves to final defeat.

On closer inspection, however, Gajda's engineers once again reported that only the tunnel walls had been damaged; the ceiling and floor remained intact. The entrance could be cleared of debris in a few backbreaking weeks if everyone worked night and day.[21] Miraculously, the tunnel was cleared and troop trains squeezed through in less than a month. The 39th tunnel would continue to be cleared for echelons following behind, but the tunnels were now secure and in Legion hands.[22] At the end of August Gajda's Sixth and Seventh regiments passed through the last in the network of obstacles and on toward the final stretch of railroad approaching Vladivostok. As they left Verchne-Udiinsk, the Sixth and Seventh regiments bid adieu to old friends left behind in the local cemetery, not the least of whom was Boris Usakov, whose bravery and cunning had often saved the day.

Under General Dieterichs' orders Jan Syrový and his trains left Vladivostok to move quickly westward on the other side of the Baikal Range. Syrový and Gajda finally connected on the western side of the 39th tunnel. With this meeting, the officers celebrated the entire length of Trans-Siberian Railway belonging to the Legion.

Five hundred miles from Chita, at Olaviana station, near the Manchurian border, they also met up with General Dieterichs' troops.[23] Up and down the Trans-Siberian Railway, the Legion stopped to celebrate the official occupation of the entire line. By the end of August 1918, Gajda, Vojcechovky, and Čeček connected together in a ribbon of over 1,000 trains moving undaunted to the Pacific coast, where evacuation awaited.[24] "The 50,000 Legion soldiers had established an organization in every important city along the great Trans-Siberian Railway. They maintained order; assumed direction of the railroads without interfering with any local government except those avowedly Bolshevik."[25]

By September 1918, British commanding general Alfred Knox convinced his superiors to recall Admiral Kolchak from Manchuria to Siberia.[26] Knox, head of the British Military Mission in Siberia, had been an attaché in St. Petersburg from 1910 to 1914. He witnessed the end of the Romanov regime with great regret, returning to London where he made the acquaintance of

Dr. Eduard Beneš. It was Beneš who told General Knox of Russian admiral Aleksandr Kolchak's availability. Inspired by Beneš, Knox traveled to Tokyo to meet the acclaimed Kolchak. Knox and Kolchak agreed on many issues, especially those concerning the growing civil war between the Reds and Whites in Russia and Siberia.[27] Knox pressed the British High Command to use Kolchak more proactively in Siberia.[28]

Japanese officials also recognized Kolchak's potential and were privately unnerved by all the British attention lavished upon him.[29] The Russian explorer and war hero worried the Japanese as much as he charmed them. A Russian scholar of international repute and a genius at military strategy, Kolchak had the ability to unite Siberia. Japanese leaders wanted no such thing. Kolchak had his orders and the Japanese were helpless to interfere — or were they?

After a two-month delay in Tokyo, Kolchak sailed directly to Vladivostok. There he stayed with Dr. Václav Girsa, Czech National Council representative. Kolchak spent several nights discussing problems facing the Legion and Siberia with the Czech representative. Girsa explained the worsening conditions in the interior of Siberia. He spoke of the infamous Ataman Grigori Semenov of Chita and of the hardships Semenov's band inflicted on the local population, which was also the constant victim of the Red Army, the White Army, and other bands of frontoviks.[30] Dr. Girsa shared troubling news concerning the Omsk government. Czech and Slovak officers reported that the Directory of Five that governed Omsk had become hopelessly bogged down in factional disputes and petty squabbles. Though suffering from a mysterious ailment, Kolchak expressed an abiding interest in the Omsk situation and a strong desire to help in any way possible.[31] Dr. Girsa arranged for Kolchak to board a train heading to Omsk as soon as possible on the Trans-Siberian Railway.

Eduard Beneš, working in both London and Paris, and Thomas Masaryk, continuously globe-trotting, eagerly awaited permission for legionnaires to board evacuation vessels sitting in Vladivostok Harbor for transport to the Western Front. Earlier, the British government had announced that it would regard the Czechoslovak National Council as the voice of Czech and Slovak aims for statehood. On June 3, 1918, British foreign secretary Arthur James Balfour had written a letter to Eduard Benes on behalf of the British empire. In it he wrote,

> I have the honor to assure you that his Majesty's Government, who have every possible sympathy with the Czecho-Slovak movement, will be glad to give the same recognition to this movement as has been granted by the Governments of France and Italy. His Majesty's Government will thus be prepared to recognize the Czecho-Slovak movement in Allied countries, and they will also be

prepared to recognize the Czecho-Slovak Army as an organized unit operating in the Allied cause, and to attach thereto a British liaison officer as soon as need for this may arise.[32]

The letter delighted Czech and Slovak officials, but successive British and French announcements did little to hide deeper political implications. Balfour's communiqué echoed the call for Czech and Slovak self–rule by recognizing Thomas Masaryk and his colleagues' efforts as an allied government in absentia. With an armed force in Siberia, French and English recognition effectively placed the Legion directly under the Supreme Allied Command — layering another authority between the Legion in Siberia and Masaryk's organization in Western Europe and North America.

After General Dieterichs' earlier takeover of Vladivostok, the United States government publicly recognized the Czechs and Slovaks working through Masaryk, Beneš, and Štefánik as an allied nation in absentia. Colonel George Emerson, United States first assistant to the Russian Railway Service Corps, received a telegram from Washington, D.C. The message warned that Gajda's success in uniting the entire Trans-Siberian Railway would most likely result in Czech and Slovak troops being placed under French and British control. Emerson informed his superiors in Washington, D.C., that he believed because of the Legion's position, France now controlled Siberia.

News of the Legion's unification across all of Siberia came as a startling blow to the Bolsheviks in Moscow. Even so, Lenin and Trotsky faced more pressing issues. Convinced that Japan planned to invade Siberia, Lenin looked to the United States for help.[33] Although President Woodrow Wilson agreed with Lenin's assessment, Japan remained a U.S. ally throughout the war. Taking any action against the leadership in Tokyo would have been dangerous and counterproductive for the United States. President Wilson regarded the Japanese call for military intervention with its tens of thousands of troops as not only absurd but highly threatening. President Wilson turned to the Allied Command to assist in restraining Japanese ambitions. Instead, London appeared to mimic Tokyo as Lord Robert Cecil, Assistant Secretary of State for Foreign Affairs, wooed the Legion with flattery in the press, announcing that "the presence of a Czecho-Slovak Army in Russia at this time is, I believe, one of the miracles of history."[34]

As early as 1917, French and British diplomats covertly discussed the plausibility of dividing not only Siberia but Russia into spheres of influence. If spheres of influence existed, Britain would control all Russian approaches to India and the oil fields, and an interest in the Cossack, Armenian, Kurdish, and Georgian lands. France would control Russia's coal and iron fields, the entire railway system, and interests in Ukraine, Crimea, and Bessarabia.

In response to President Wilson's apprehension over Japanese aggression,

France and Britain proposed that Japan simply carve up Siberia and share it with the United States. Britain preferred that the United States retain control over the Trans-Siberian Railway in order to maintain it in running condition. It appeared that Great Britain's politicians believed it logical for the Japanese to control all territories bordering China, an area Japan had coveted for decades. Upon hearing these suggestions, President Wilson realized that all the while Tsar Nicholas II and his army had been fighting to uphold the Eastern Front, Russia's own allies had been plotting to divide his country among themselves.[35]

Once the tsar had been forced out, France and Britain made plans to step into the vacuum left behind. After the Provisional Government faltered, this became ever more probable, but neither country had counted on the Bolsheviks taking and remaining in control. When interventionist forces finally docked in Vladivostok, detractors pointed out that France's and England's spheres of influence had begun to be realized. Woodrow Wilson was horrified.

Irtysk and Tanalyk, two British corporations, as well as other mining interests in coal, copper, and iron ore, combined to make Siberian intervention a valid and lucrative economic prospect for England. As soon as the Legion overran the Trans-Siberian Railway, England saw an immediate rise in mineral exports.[36] The Czechs and Slovaks had unintentionally maximized distribution systems all along the railroad, immediately increasing British profits. This new windfall did not go unnoticed by Britain's White Hall or its counterparts in Tokyo and Paris.

The Legion's relationship with France had already fallen to a new low by the end of May 1918 when OCSNR officials uncovered French diplomatic papers in Siberia. These documents revealed that throughout 1917, France, the Legion's sponsor and friend, attempted to negotiate a peace agreement with Austria-Hungary. It sickened Legion commanders to learn that France had opened up channels with the Austrians and Hungarians to deny the birthright that the legionnaires had been fighting for so valiantly. France not only promised away Bohemia, Moravia, and Slovakia but the Legion would also have been returned to Austria-Hungary to face charges of desertion and certain execution.

The situation in Russia and Siberia, not the war in Western Europe, now became Thomas Masaryk's greatest obstacle in gaining independence for the Slavic minorities suffering under Austria and Hungary. From exile in Western Europe, the Czech National Council frantically contacted the Entente leadership to once again demand the Legion's immediate departure for the Western Front. The Allied Command answered Masaryk and his colleagues with only vague assurances.

No country gave the Legion double messages more than the United States. To answer the Legion's call for help and to counterbalance troops sent by Japan, an American Expeditionary Force (AEF) began to organize units of both the 27th and 31st American infantry divisions originally stationed in the Philippines. As General William Graves readied his troops in San Francisco for their transfer to Siberia, he received orders from Washington, D.C., curtailing their freedom of action.[37] Graves worried that this made little sense especially since he had reports that there were still many Czech and Slovak troop trains in precarious situations west of the Baikal Mountain Range. Legion officials soon found themselves equally confused by Graves' peculiar command. Did he intend to help them or not?

President Wilson's desire to intervene and yet remain unobtrusive confused and complicated the American Expeditionary Force mandate. Graves informed his men that both the Moscow leadership and the president of the United States had ordered that they remain neutral or suffer the consequences.[38] After receiving a memorandum and a ten-minute briefing, Secretary of War Newton Baker warned Graves, "Watch your step; you will be walking on eggs loaded with dynamite."[39] Graves' transport, the *Thomas*, left San Francisco Harbor on August 14, 1918, carrying over 5,000 men of the Eighth Division from Fort Mason, California, apparently under orders to do nothing. Graves and his men headed to the wilds of Siberia poorly apprised of what they would encounter there.[40] His troops were to remain neutral while helping the Czechs and Slovaks evacuate.

By mid–September, the entire Trans-Siberian Railway buzzed with expectation. As Ernest Lloyd Harris described to superiors in Washington, "it is nothing more or less than [as if the] Siberian railroad line, which would extend from Liverpool to San Francisco, has been handed to the Allies."[41] Again the Legion gave the Supreme Allied Command in France hope that Czech and Slovak troops might provide the solution to a collapsing Western Front. No one could blame the Allies for taking advantage of this highly skilled army.[42]

For the Legion troops still traveling in the field, however, the Allies had little to do with their feelings of excitement. Legionnaires gathered around campfires to discuss the miracle they had just accomplished, the takeover of the entire length of Trans-Siberian Railway. They would soon be fighting on the Western Front, finally facing their true enemies: Austria, Germany, and Hungary.

Gustav Bečvář, the college student who had nearly faced hanging in the Ukraine, sat amongst celebrating comrades. Bečvář and the others had been in many bitter fights during this Siberian summer and lost many friends, but the tenacious Radola Gajda had led them through the steppe while forging a way through the tunnels and the Baikal Mountain passes. Bečvář, like his fellow legionnaires, stopped to rest and remember the past three months. He looked forward to leaving this inhospitable land. Unfortunately, he, like all the others who celebrated with him, was about to discover what a few Legion officers already knew.

How little we knew the future. Had we but known it, the most dramatic moment of the campaign was now hard upon us.

It was on September 22 that the blow fell. Charlie Kovář was the officer in charge of Verchne-Udiinsk station, and I went over to tell him the story of our recent expedition to the south. I thought that my friend looked unusually solemn that morning.

"Well, Charlie, we've been halfway 'round the world,'" I said as we sat down in his room. "The other half will be easy now that the way to Vladivostok is clear."

Charlie stared at me for a full minute without saying a word. Then he spoke slowly: "Vladivostok be damned!" Then more quickly: "Why Gus, don't you know? We're not going to France at all. New orders have come through, and they are that we must return west to the Ural Mountains to reinforce the line troops are holding there against the Bolsheviks."

We sat staring at each other for a long time. But neither of us spoke.[43]

Chapter Eight

far off I see
A little band of heroes, like a wreck
Abandoned and forgotten in the waves.
So steadfastly they stand amid the smoke
of burning cities and the grime of war.
Dim-eyed they stagger onward, they are bent
and they have lost their dream of victory.[1]

On August 3, 1919, the cruiser *Suffolk* docked at Vladivostok Harbor to the welcoming notes of a Czech and Slovak military band. It did not take on legionnaires; instead, the Middlesex Regiment, a British contingent docking in Siberia, unloaded its belongings and left the ship.

Two days later, General Dieterichs reported to Vladivostok headquarters to find representatives of the Allied Command deep in discussion. The French had decided to back a British proposal to alleviate pressure on the Western Front by resurrecting a second front in the Russian Far East. Great Britain would now facilitate overall communications in Siberia, with France controlling both northwestern and southwestern operations in Russia. In addition, Britain's General Knox was appointed to oversee the mission of British and American troops on their way to Siberia with full cooperation of General William Graves, the head of the American Expeditionary Force in Siberia.[2] The united Anglo-French policy toward Russia would favor a fundamentally anti–Soviet position. France and Britain were merely counting the days until the Bolsheviks fell to open revolt since they intended to step into the void before Germany could.

As early as July 1918, French general Maurice Janin began exchanging dispatches with the British. In the case that the Allies supported the White Russian effort, French General Janin would be made commander of Allied troops in Siberia — a command which extended over the Legion. General Dieterichs and the men of the Czech National Congress became familiar with this scenario when in June detailed military dossiers argued for the establishment of a second front in Siberia under leadership of the Supreme Command.

On June 17, 1918, as the Legion fought its way across Siberia, the British section of the Supreme War Council in Versailles had begun to distribute an analysis of Red Army division capabilities. This report confirmed Allied fears: Germany had already begun exploiting Ukraine and western Russia. If Lenin's government did topple, the Central Powers could access war materiel scattered throughout Siberia to use against the Allies on the Western Front. France and England maintained that Russia was in effect aiding Germany and Austria by freeing up over 70 divisions of soldiers from the Central Powers when suing for peace.

Austrian, German, and Hungarian troops that had formerly fought against the tsar and then Kerensky were now being transferred from western Russia to the Western Front. The dossier advised that the British section oversee locomotives and rolling stock in order for sufficient personnel to begin a second front near European Russia.

The Trans-Siberian Railway could carry 45 divisions out of which 30 would move on to the Ural front. With Siberian populations in this region already facing famine and deteriorating political conditions, the Allies hoped to take advantage of any ensuing chaos. A second Allied front hinged on one element: the Legion. The Czechs and Slovaks steadily arriving in Vladivostok on the Trans-Siberian Railway would neither return home nor fight on the

Western Front; instead they would retrace their heroic journey through the Baikal tunnels to retake every village that had just been returned to locals. Every inch of Siberian countryside that legionnaires fought and died for would now have to be retaken. Completely disregarding earlier promises made to Thomas Masaryk and the men he represented, the Supreme Allied Command offered up the exhausted Slavic troops as a vanguard for their new second front.[3]

Under pressure from both the French and British, President Woodrow Wilson finally agreed to a limited Allied intervention in Siberia.[4] On August 21, 1918, 1,421

General Maurice Janin, commanding general of Allied forces in Siberia, 1919.

men of the 27th and 31st U.S. regiments disembarked from the cruiser *Brooklyn* under the command of Admiral Knight. They joined the British cruiser *Suffolk*, the smaller French vessel *Keraisnt*, and warships from Italy that sat waiting for orders in Vladivostok Harbor.[5] These Allied troops occupied Russian barracks in the north end of the harbor district some distance from officers headquartered in central Vladivostok. By September, General Graves had arrived in Vladivostok with the rest of his contingent. This added more than 7,000 fresh troops to the Allied Expeditionary Force.[6] American, British, Canadian, French, and Japanese units awaited their assignments.

Thomas Masaryk warned the Supreme Allied Command in Versailles that intervening in Siberia would be foolish. Since mid–August, he had been compiling disconcerting data collected by contacts in the field.[7] The previously weak and disorganized local Soviet militia had been replaced in many areas by Trotsky's well-trained Red Guard. Furthermore, enemy units had been augmented with numbers of Austrian and German ex-prisoners of war. Estimates reported that four companies of Red Guard reinforcements currently awaited the Legion in Kazan. Worse still, the Red Guard was rested and well supplied — just the reverse was true of the Czechs and Slovaks being sent back to face them. As Professor Masaryk pleaded with U.S. Secretary of State Robert Lansing to stop this madness, winter conditions were looming.

In a message sent to Masaryk in Washington, D.C., Girsa, Špaček, and Houska of the Czecho-Slovak National Council asked, "How much longer?"[8] Masaryk needed no clarification; the troops were frustrated and becoming angry with the Allies. Only the recognition of "the rights of the Czechoslovak nation to independence" on the part of the British government on August 13, 1918, followed by that of the United States through Secretary Lansing on September 2, 1918, had placated Czech and Slovak leaders.[9] An Allied victory at the end of the war now guaranteed them their goal of nationhood.[10] Given no other choice, the OCSNR, the Czech National Council, was finally coerced into agreeing with the establishment of a second front.[11]

Soon after Balfour's communiqué reached Eduard Beneš, England called publicly for the Legion to remain in Siberia indefinitely. Lloyd George admitted, "It is not too much to say that the presence of the Legion was the deciding factor in our Siberian expedition."[12] On the eve of what would have been the Legion's evacuation from Siberia through Vladivostok, General Dieterichs formally received the order of the day: "The Czecho-Slovak Army Corps is to form the advance guard of the Allied Armies for the purpose of re–establishing an anti–German line in Russia."[13]

Learning that 200 Legion trains had already been turned around and sent back into the interior without his knowledge, General Dieterichs became infuriated.[14] Legionnaires would also be rushed back to the Urals and the Volga as foundational units for all future anti–German activity that followed.

Presumably to rally the troops, France furnished General Dieterichs' contingent with new uniforms before cramming the men into waiting boxcars. With incredible speed, troops raced back across the Siberian landscape where only days earlier colleagues had died fighting to travel eastward. Already Czechs and Slovaks were returning to guard the Omsk-Baikal line, scene of the most exhaustive fighting in the provinces.[15] Radola Gajda's Seventh Regiment had only just returned from fighting in the south when it was sent back. Towns and depots whose names had already become a footnote now became blurred as legionnaires sped past them heading west. Centers like Harbin, Chita, Khabarovsk, Blagoveshchensk, Omsk, Krasnoyarsk, Irkutsk, and Verchne-Udiinsk had to be neutralized all over again. Especially difficult would be control over important transfer points like Nikolayevsk at the mouth of the Amur River.[16] The Legion saw its current situation as an Allied betrayal of massive proportions.

Cossacks, peasants and ex-prisoners (mostly Poles, Lithuanians and Serbians) gathered around the departing boxcars to pledge unity with the Legion. As the ranks swelled with volunteers, optimism began to resurge. Maintaining order on the railroad once again became crucial as jurisdiction over the countryside and town administrations required the organizing of Italian, Lithuanian, Polish, and Rumanian troops also traveling with the Legion.[17] In time, many legionnaires rationalized their plight, acknowledging that they were needed more in Siberia than in the trenches of Belgium or France. By September 1918, there were more than 300,000 men returning to the Ural and Volga fronts, a front that stretched along more than 3,000 miles of railway track.

Sullen and disgruntled, Legion Command also departed Vladivostok, preferring to live and fight with its troops rather than share quarters with Allied officers. Under Pavlů's advice members of the National Council mollified many of the more vocal Czech and Slovak officers with promotions. Many of these promotions went to Czechs over Slovaks, which caused rancor among the Slovak troops.

The Czechoslovak National Council moved to centralize army command.[18] Although both Čeček and Gajda were considered for the highest office of commander in chief, neither had been found "suitable." French general Janin found Gajda "too much the wild lion"[19] and it seemed that Čeček had showed "too much egalitarian spirit towards his men."[20]

Lieutenant Syrový, commander of the second Regiment, a less emotional and far more obedient officer, was awarded the post instead. General Syrový, a former bank clerk from Warsaw, assumed supreme command of the Czecho-Slovak Army Corps, appointing General Dieterichs as the chief of staff. Dieterichs opted to work from a train housing both the telegraph and reconnaissance units of the Legion. His 27-year-old quartermaster, Lieutenant Colonel Vladimír Klecanda, worked closely with him, continuing to map unfamiliar regions of the Siberian steppe.[21]

A newly organized Siberian front, the creation of anti–Bolshevik movements and Allied Command, was readied to face the Red Army. This second front would be broken into three separate sections with the first forming under Radola Gajda's leadership. Newly promoted to the rank of general, the youngest in the Czech and Slovak Army Corps, Gajda gathered his troops outside of Ekaterinburg to face more than 25,000 Red Guard nearby. General Ljupov led the second unit, renamed the Birsk Group, which would be stationed between General Gajda and General Ĉeĉek. While the Red Army consciously prepared to suffer great losses, the Czechs and Slovaks knew they could never sustain large numbers of casualties.

> To the west of Lake Baikal, the Legion waited for help with winter closing in. These units were over six days by train from the nearest supply line. Most of the soldiers were weary, having fought nonstop over the past three years, first along the Eastern Front and then joining the Russians in Serbia or the Ukraine.[22]

From Moscow, Trotsky groomed the Red Guard for the heavy fighting ahead.[23] Furthermore, the Bolshevik leadership had decided to act against the United States — whose insistence of "neutrality" while landing troops in Siberia had grown tiresome. On August 2, 1918, the Soviet Republic had notified the American vice council Imbrie, who was stationed in Petrograd, that a state of war existed between Russia and the United States. Imbrie had hurriedly contacted superiors in Washington, D.C., detailing his concern over the safety of American citizens working throughout Russia and Siberia. Imbrie's notification of war was misfiled and lost, however, and United States Secretary of State Robert Lansing never received this pertinent information. For 20 days Lenin and Trotsky waited for a reply from President Woodrow Wilson.[24] When notification finally surfaced it was no longer of use to either side.

> The general attack of the Bolsheviks against Kazan started on September 5. Trotsky promised a reward in cash to that regiment which would be the first to succeed in smashing its way into the town. Moreover, he permitted all his men to pillage the town for three long days.[25]

While Lenin trusted Trotsky's military leadership, many in the Soviet elite felt this was no way to fight a war, and as Soviet troops marched steadfastly into battle, ideological disputes strained the unification of their leaders. Before long, resentment and division spread throughout the cities and farmlands under Bolshevik control. Lenin, forced to choose between the peasants of the countryside and the workers in the cities, began to order the confiscation of grain from farms. Efforts to strengthen the position of the central committee by establishing a wedge between factions in the party included characterizing rural villagers as "selfish" and "parasitic." The laboring classes of the city soon turned against their counterparts on the farm. "Civil War in the Villages" and "Down with Rich Peasants" replaced earlier Bolshevik slogans.[26] The vast majority of agricultural areas still maintained neutrality, but many farmers began to turn to the counterrevolution for help.

This growing anti–Bolshevik feeling finally split into three main factions: the extreme reactionaries, constitutional monarchists, and social revolutionaries. Whether in a city or in a village, life became increasingly more difficult for all Russians and Siberians throughout the autumn of 1918. Political division manifested itself violently in every forum. Months earlier, on January 16, 1918, a young man had entered Lenin's offices and fired his pistol, missing the Russian leader by only inches.[27] Lenin's luck had taken a turn for the worse, however, on August 30, 1918, while he visited a factory in Murman. Dora Kaplan, an avid revolutionary, ran up to the Russian premier, shooting him twice at point-blank range before turning to bolt out into the street.[28] Dora was apprehended and brought in for interrogation before she could take her own life with the poisonous cigarettes hidden on her person. Lenin lay critically wounded in the hospital while Dora Kaplan refused to reveal her accomplices.

Not long after news of Kaplan's murder attempt, the successful assassination of Moses Urinsky, chairman of the Petrograd Commission for the Suppression of Counter-Revolution, occurred. Both acts led to a series of official reprisals that deepened factional divisions within the Bolshevik movement. Russian newspaper headlines screamed for mass terror against the bourgeoisie. Thousands of suspects were suddenly arrested and transported out of Moscow and Petrograd to undisclosed destinations in the countryside as terror gripped all of European Russia. The Bolshevik Party searched homes and placed buildings under siege as Socialist Party members were arrested. *Pravda* reported "that in accordance with an order of Commission Extra-ordinary for Combating Counter-revolution, all subjects of Entente States between the ages of 16 and 45 were being interned and would not be released until they had explained their reported anti Soviet actions."[29]

A proclamation issued by M. Peters, chief of the Extraordinary Commission in the Russian capital went on to describe how any individual caught with a weapon would be immediately executed. In addition, any person agitating against the soviet would be arrested and sent to a camp after his or her private possessions had been seized. The *Krasnay's Gazeta* demanded vengeance against all Socialists: "Blood must flow, that they be exterminated."[30] One of the first to be exterminated was the editor of a rival newspaper, the *Bourse Courier*.

Leon Trotsky warned the anti–Bolshevik leader General Alekseev that the Bolsheviks were ready to retaliate against all non–Bolsheviks. For every Bolshevik soldier killed, an ex-tsarist officer or official in custody would die.[31] Grand Duke M. Verkhovski, war minister in the failed Kerensky government and Prince Schakowsky, minister of public aid, joined a long list scheduled for a speedy execution. The Western press began to report that Russian prisons overflowed with ex-tsarist authorities. Over 10,000 anti–Bolsheviks became incarcerated while the gallows and firing squads kept busy day and night.

Alekseev understood the extreme nature of Trotsky's promise, and made a threat of his own appealing to Trotsky's Jewish lineage. The old general announced that he would quarter (cut into fourths) every Jew in Russia if Trotsky's threat were to be carried out. Alekseev's bluff worked. Thousands of soldiers were soon released in both Moscow and Petrograd, but only those of low rank. Later, however, hundreds of these men went missing, never to be seen again. Hostages continued to be taken, homes looted, and foreign consulates closed.

When Soviet officials ransacked Petrograd's British Consulate and British naval attaché Captain Cromie was murdered while attempting to protect British property, the world press took note.[32] For days, his mutilated body hung from the British Embassy window, greeting foreign dignitaries arriving for work. Cromie had worked in Petrograd to establish cooperation between his government and Lenin's. He sympathized with the Bolshevik Revolution's goals and had eagerly pushed Trotsky to allow the Czech and Slovak Legion to evacuate from Vladivostok. It seemed nobody could escape Russia's violence.

Lenin would recuperate from his wounds, but not Russia. It had become too late for either the citizenry or its politicians to stop the cycle of bloodletting that overwhelmed Mother Russia. Pitiless vengeance replaced patriotism while slogans touted brotherhood in the mass media. By mid–September, 107 Americans fled Russia along with other foreign dignitaries across the Ballosproff Bridge leading from Russia to Finland. In Harparanda, Finland, those fleeing reported that for every Bolshevik soldier killed in rioting, 1,000 middle-class Russians had been executed.[33]

In the midst of this chaos, U.S. Army reconnaissance confirmed that the Czech and Slovak Legion needed help in the interior, where it had become dangerously outnumbered and badly overextended.[34] General Gajda's troops took positions against the town of Verchne-Udiinsk, where they had fought so valiantly only weeks before. This time heavy Czech and Slovak casualties resulted. Gajda fired off message after message to General Graves, head of the American Expeditionary Force, begging for reinforcements. Gajda was not the only Legion officer in need of assistance from the allies, yet pleas for help to the AEF seemed a waste of time. The American forces were being micro-managed from thousands of miles away as President Wilson mandated that all AEF soldiers remain east of Lake Baikal. General Graves reluctantly shrugged off Gajda's messages.[35]

Aristocrats and landed gentry also waited in exile for the Allies to intervene in the civil war. They hoped for a leader who would combine anti–Soviet forces into a unified front and win back their lost estates. As the Allies organized the second front manned by Czech and Slovak legionnaires, Russia's exiles quickly realized that the Entente powers intended to work safely from behind the scenes. Someone else's son would have to do the dirty work.

Only Ataman Semenov announced that he and his men were willing to help carry the Legion's burden. For a short time Russian exiles believed Semenov and sent money from abroad to fund his anti–Bolshevik front. Later, Semenov's representative, Ilia Shemelin, also garnered aid from rich landlords in exile in the Amur Province.[36]

The Japanese had long seen a valuable ally in Ataman Semenov. They had no intention of allowing a secure state to rise again in either Russia or Siberia.[37] Fearless, cunning, and conveniently positioned between the Mongolian borderland and Chita, Semenov and his men lived on a healthy stipend from Japanese commander general Kikuzo Otani.

By claiming that the United States had far exceeded the Allied troop quota, Japanese officials raised their own troop levels by more than 10,000 men. Allied Supreme Command disliked and distrusted General Otani's overblown arrogance and belligerence.[38] Much like Semenov's men, Otani's soldiers were gaining notoriety for brutality in the field.[39] Allied attempts to curtail the Japanese fell short as Ataman Semenov's army descended upon supply lines, Soviet or not, murdering anyone who tried to stop them. The resulting chaos gave Japanese officials in Vladivostok further excuses for incursions deeper into the Siberian countryside. As the Legion received approval to keep the Trans-Siberian Railway open to traffic, it learned that Ataman Semenov had already grabbed control of major portions of the Transbaikalia line.

Ataman Kalmykov, a colleague and friend of Semenov's, also curried favor with Japanese general Otani. Ivan Palovich Kalmykov, son of a Ussuri Cossack lieutenant, lived in Grodekovo, a town on the Manchurian border.[40] Kalmykov had been highly decorated after suffering a war injury on the Eastern Front and when Tsar Nicholas II abdicated, Kalmykov returned to Siberia. At home, he made the friendship of Dimitri L. Horvath, who later employed Kalmykov to organize an army to fight against local Soviet militias. From May through July 1918, as the Legion rose victoriously and moved across the Russian Far East, Kalmykov's troops suffered a series of disastrous defeats in the Maritime Province.[41] During August, Kalmykov moved his band to the

Amur Province, where he established himself as a candidate for the position of Ussuri Ataman.[42]

There would be more than 19 rival governments in the Volga and Maritime provinces throughout 1918 and 1919, each claiming the popular support of the majority. All wanted to defeat the Soviets, but none was willing to share power. As early as the fall of 1918, conflict had already begun to exist between two large centers of counterrevolutionary power: Samara and Omsk.[43] The Samara Committee of Members of the Constituent Assembly vied for recognition throughout Siberia with the Siberian Provisional Government in Omsk, each reluctant to place its armed forces under the leadership of the other.

Desperate for military aid yet attracted to the ideals of Omsk's opposition party, the Czechs and Slovaks felt caught between Omsk and Samara. The Social Revolutionaries of Omsk seemed more interested in the needs of the peasants and less interested in military conquest. Yet monarchist forces tied to Omsk continuously victimized local peasants. The Socialist position, although closer to the Legion's, appeared too naïve, especially concerning the rapidly deteriorating conditions on the Siberian front. As one Legion officer described it:

> There were many sincere officers who sympathized with the Revolution and there were many Social Revolutionists who were beginning to realize that it was impossible to administer a government in wartime on purely theoretical patterns.
> The Samara-Ufa group was far more intractable. Their appeal for a unified Russia could not fail to exert a considerable influence on Russian thinking, but their insistence upon the creation of an all-Russian government which was to use Siberia merely as a base until the recovery of Moscow turned their own attention and that of all groups to general problems which were outside the scope of their resources and their practical capabilities.[44]

Masaryk, Beneš, and Štefánik agreed that it was not in the Legion's interest to restore the old monarchical system in Russia or to legitimize the policies of either the counterrevolutionaries or the Socialists.[45] Under the current conditions, Czech and Slovak officers were forced to become diplomats. Legion officers earned a reputation as proficient commanders in the field, better than counterparts in the Red Army and incredibly more empathetic to the poor than the counterrevolutionaries.[46]

The anti–Bolsheviks and the Soviets had accused each other of despicable acts. Unfortunately, as autumn slipped into winter, both sides had been proven correct. Civil wars are seldom civil, but this one had quickly turned excessively brutal. Peasants caught in the middle of the Red and White armies often had to choose sides or take a chance of being accused of sympathizing with the enemy.[47]

Of all the Allies pushing for a widening of the Ural and Volga fronts, few openly discussed political constituencies gathering throughout the countryside. This did little to hinder international press coverage, however. On a weekly basis reporters like Carl Ackerman and Herman Bernstein brought descriptions of the strife overwhelming Siberia to a disbelieving public back home. In some cases, Americans read about their own fathers, brothers, sons, or husbands heading into the region.

Throughout the United States fundraising continued in conjunction with the YMCA, the Jewish Welfare Board, the Knights of Columbus, the Salvation Army, the American Library Association, and the War Camp Community Services. These efforts raised more than $190 million.

Allied Command specifically demanded that the Czech and Slovak troops return to areas where they had fought to secure the Trans-Siberian Railway earlier in the summer. Allied Command deemed these missions not only too difficult for their own troops, but too dangerous as well. Only charities, specifically the Red Cross and the YMCA, sent volunteer workers into the interior west of the Baikal tunnels.[48] Eleven units representing 28 nations worked from Vladivostok to provide assistance in just such a way.

YMCA headquarters in Archangelsk and Murmansk coordinated more than 6,000 miles of Siberian railroad with expenditures of $200 million for Russian relief.[49] The YMCA was considered a unique organization since it demanded neutrality from its workers in order to offer assistance to any and all soldiers and noncombatants regardless of nationality, political affiliation, or religion. This remained true even after the United States entered the war in 1917.[50]

Compatriots of the Legion throughout Canada and the United States became familiar with sentimentalized versions of the legionnaire's plight as they returned westward to the Ural and Volga region. News from the Ural and Volga fronts became ever more complicated as numbers of refugees fleeing to the Pacific coast for safety expanded. In European Russia, systematic executions added to the ever-growing flood of exiles heading to the Russian Far East. The port city of Vladivostok, already severely low on raw materials, stretched its capacity to handle the new influx of humanity.

As chaotic conditions began to overwhelm the Russian Far East, the British High Command cast about for an authority figure who understood the variety of political concerns developing throughout the region, a leader who could unite the peasantry with the local political front and both with the Allied effort. The man the British sought was already in their own ranks, eager for a chance to prove his mettle.

On September 21, 1918, Admiral Kolchak boarded a train to travel west on the Trans-Siberian Railway. He shared a compartment with a young Legion officer returning to his unit on the front. After being in Vladivostok for more than a month, hoping to arrange for reinforcements and supplies for his men in the field, Radola Gajda, frustrated that his requests had been ignored, hurried back to his command. The train trip to Omsk took more than 17 days, with long delays throughout. As the two men traveled together, they shared their impressions of the Allies and the intervention. The civil war and the counterrevolution would wait for no one. Both Kolchak and Gajda agreed that the Allies appeared naive — lacking expertise and knowledge concerning the growing chaos in the Russian Far East.[51] Kolchak became interested in his young travel partner as he probed the Slovak general's stories of battle.

Gajda, like many of his compatriots, was familiar with Kolchak's reputation as a brilliant explorer and with his success in the Russian navy. Gajda felt validated by Kolchak's respect and friendship; it pleased him to share ideas concerning the Siberians and their plight with such an impressive leader. In Omsk, the two parted as close friends, aware that the civil war surrounding them would most probably bring them back together again.

The first week in September had brought relatively good news for Legion units in the area. Samara, halfway between Moscow and the Siberian border, had been reoccupied, a feat hailed by Allied Command despite the heavy losses in Čeček's unit.

Gajda, still one of the youngest officers in the field, returned to his men only to discover that in his absence, Bolshevik troops had advanced swiftly on both the Ural and the Volga fronts. Kazan, the city of Čeček's triumph only a month before, had fallen once again to the militia on September 10. Within a few days of Kazan's fate, Samara also fell to the Red Army.

> It can be said that his [Cecek's] situation was none too secure.... As for the Allies, it is true that one French and two British battalions, as well as a British coast battery, reached the Czech's Western Front [in Siberia]. But elsewhere, the Allied aid did not amount to much. Japanese troops penetrated as far as Irkutsk, while American and British contingents guarded Vladivostok. Yet it was neither at Irkutsk nor Vladivostok that the Czechs were threatened.[52]

Legionnaires found the White Russian units fighting alongside them more trouble than their worth — lacking leadership and resolve. On the day when the soldiers of the First Czecho-Slovak Regiment were a few miles from Kazan, stubbornly fighting against the Bolsheviks (under Gajda's leadership), a good many Russian officers took their leave at the local races.[53]

Both the Ural and Volga fronts had already begun to show signs of approaching winter. As the days grew shorter, rumors spread that Trotsky had greatly enlarged the Red Guard, consolidating efforts and supply lines for a long winter siege.[54] News of growing Czech and Slovak fatalities combined with rumors about the Red Army to erode Legion morale. Discipline plummeted to an unimaginable low among the Czechs and Slovaks. A few soldiers packed up their belongings, telling superiors that they would rather walk home or die trying than take part in the abomination that had become the second front.

General Graves began to realize that he had disembarked from his ship in Vladivostok Harbor and walked straight into countervailing forces. American troops had been ordered to accompany and support Allies whose behavior General Graves often found reprehensible. Reports that British general Alfred Knox spoke openly of Siberian peasants in a derogatory manner disgusted Graves. Knox was overheard to say, "The Russian peasant is a pig, and the way to talk to him is not to his head but to his back via a whip."[55] In addition, the French appeared to back any scheme, no matter how crazy. The French also believed that Moscow used Austrian and Hungarian POWs instead of repatriating them homeward.[56] Tens of thousands of ex-Austro-Hungarian prisoners were rumored to be joining the Bolsheviks in order to fight against the Legion.[57]

Chapter Nine

Throughout 1918, Soviet rule had been struggling in the provincial centers of Siberia. Strict policy authorized food and equipment needed by Red Army units to be confiscated from anyone. Many in towns across the hinterland saw the return of the Legion as protection from marauding units of Soviet militia. They welcomed the return of the Czechs and Slovaks to the Ural and Volga fronts.[1]

Before the war, the liberation of the Austrian and Hungarian minorities depended upon Russia, with Moscow as the center of the Pan-Slavic ideal. With the signing of the Brest-Litovsk Treaty, Lenin and Trotsky gave up any alignment against Pan-Slavism's historical enemy, Germany. In the ensuing havoc, the Slavic minorities in the Hapsburg Empire struggled under the harsh rule of their scorned emperor, Charles I, who succeeded Franz Joseph in 1916.

Colonel Švec's highly decorated troops were among the units returning to the Ural and Volga fronts. Josef Jiří Švec had been an original Družina member, well liked and spiritually inspiring. Nonetheless, his men felt betrayed and downtrodden by the actions of allies they once trusted. In mid–October, when Švec asked his troops to prepare for yet another engagement, they refused. A man and an officer with ideals born of the Sokol, Švec could not imagine such a mutiny. He read their actions not as a problem of morale, but as his own personal failure. Švec returned to his teplushka, wrote his men a note of apology, and then shot himself through the temple.

Chelyabinsk, site of the first revolt of the Legion on the Trans-Siberian Railway, received yet another Czech in its cemetery. News of Švec's suicide spread throughout the Legion like wildfire while his men, dishonored and ashamed, volunteered for any and all missions. On October 28, 1918, Colonel Švec was laid to rest, with many fellow Legion officers and noncoms in attendance. Like Boris Usakov's, Colonel Švec's death settled upon the Legion as a heavy blow and a reflection of the Allies' negligence and abuse.[2]

The months of waiting were finally over for Švec, but the timing of his suicide would prove to be ironic.[3] As if to make Švec's death even more poignant, the very day he was buried, Czechoslovakia was proclaimed an independent nation state. The streets of Prague, Brno, and Bratislava filled with celebrating Czechs and Slovaks. After 300 years of struggle, the dream of freedom from Austria had finally been realized.

Quite unexpectedly the war on the Western Front had begun to sour for the forces of Austria and Germany. Infusions of American troops in France and Belgium had turned the fate of the war in favor of the Allies. This news from the Western Front reinvigorated the hopes of the Slavic minorities in Central Europe. With full Allied approval, the Czecho-Slovak National Council worked quietly with Czech and Slovak separatists throughout the homeland to negotiate with the current Bohemian puppet government.[4] On October 23, 1918, Viennese officials granted permission for Bohemian leaders to travel outside the provinces in order to meet with members of separatist and nationalist movements. Throughout Bohemia, there was a growing fear among the population that Masaryk would be lulled into accepting the current leadership in Prague.

Dr. Karel Kramář, a renowned Prague politician and colleague of Masaryk's, had also worked to secure a free and independent Bohemia. Dr. Kramář had always been a monarchist but popular feeling went counter to his approach. With the puppet government of the Czech lands absent, the people of Bohemia held a spontaneous yet nonviolent revolution. Czechs and Slovaks took to the streets to pressure the emperor to abdicate. As the war in the West turned decidedly against the Hapsburg dynasty, fighting its minorities at home seemed out of the question.

On October 28, 1918, Charles I stepped aside and the new state of Czechoslovakia was established. As a free nation, Czechoslovakia unified Bohemians, Moravians, Ruthenians, and Slovaks under one government with Prague and Bratislava as its capitals. Members of the democratic Czecho-Slovak National Council were named as representatives for the fledgling government. Professor Thomas Masaryk, 69 years old and in exile, was quickly proclaimed the first president of Czechoslovakia, the first democratic nation to rise from the ashes of the Hapsburg Empire.[5]

The Czech and Slovak state named Eduard Beneš as foreign minister. Beneš remained in Paris to represent Czechoslovakia in discussions with the Allied Command. Milan Štefánik was appointed to the position of war minister. Štefánik concerned himself first with the establishment of the nation's borders and the progress of the Legion's evacuation from Siberia. It had been generally assumed that Masaryk's choice to follow him into the presidency when he stepped down would be the Slovak war hero, Štefánik. He was popular and certain to win any election. Even though Czechoslovakia had no official army, Štefánik would work to change the fate of the Legion marooned in Siberia along the Ural and Volga fronts.

*Dressed in traditional Czech and Slovak village outfits (*kroje*), sokol members salute the new homeland, not dated (courtesy Military Historical Archives, Prague).*

Czech and Slovak immigrant communities rallied in the streets of the United States. Thousands in Chicago and New York paraded in their *kroje* (folk dress), passing out leaflets, maps and the Czechoslovak tricolored flag. A huge map placed on display in front of the New York Public Library illustrated the new nation of Czechoslovakia for the American public.[6] The map traveled between American cities, educating the population about this new country's location and ethnic composition.

Bohemia, Moravia, and Slovakia were now free and independent, but the legionnaires in Siberia would not be in Prague to partake in any celebrations. After 300 years of oppression, 70,000 soldiers remained fighting in mud and freezing temperatures in someone else's war while their own country pleaded for them to be returned home. Landlocked and low on provisions, the Legion held onto territory it no longer wanted and waited for reinforcements that never came. William Duncan, YMCA representative, watched as betrayal changed the fortunes of these men:

> At night I have reached this place with a train of good things for the soldiers at the front. My regiment, the Sixth, is along the Ekaterinburg front for which place I will probably start tonight. The Czech [and Slovak] soldiers do not

know that the American troops are not coming through to help at the front and daily they await their arrival. The men are tired after the long months of fighting and are being heavily pressed by superior forces which adds to the seriousness of the situation. I am glad to be back again but I know not how to tell these poor fellows that help is not coming. I wish that our folk could feel the need the way it impresses us here.[7]

American, Canadian, British, and French citizens wanted explanations why the Legion continued on as a presence in Siberia. After all, wasn't that the justification given for intervening on Russia's sovereign soil in the first place?[8] Reports from the interior painted a dire picture of Red and White Army abuses and political entanglements. Thomas Masaryk demanded the return of his men before winter, but his words failed to penetrate indignant ears.

Admiral Kolchak arrived in Omsk with no authority, no funding and little preparation. The situation in Omsk deeply disturbed him. The provincial government, the Directory of Five, lived on the edge of town in a series of shabby boxcars. Backed by both the right-wing Siberian government and the left-wing Samara faction, the Directory of Five had been entrusted with the unification of the population under one regional entity. Instead, the Directory of Five had become entangled in political intrigue and pointless infighting. Under the Directory of Five the region was no closer to stability than it had ever been.[9] The Directory had become the butt of jokes, ridiculed and ignored by the citizenry.[10]

Omsk itself was clogged with refugees. City avenues were caked with mud and teeming with uniformed men and homeless pets, rummaging for bits of food in piles of garbage. Kolchak saw both Cossack and Russian soldiers in groups brawling together, drunk and filthy.[11] Aleksandr Kolchak's arrival immediately attracted attention. Many Omsk officials saw the former admiral as a natural-born leader who could ensure a better future for both the people and the soldiers of the provinces. Kolchak had little time to waste and little experience in political circles, but at 45 years old, he had become a seasoned military officer who seemed a unique and skilled leader of men in crisis. General Knox reported that the ex-admiral in Omsk displayed "two characteristics uncommon in a Russian, a quick temper which inspires a useful awe among his subordinates, and a disinclination to talk merely for talking's sake."[12]

As Kolchak settled in to contact the Directory of Five, Bolshevik troops rallied in the field, advancing quickly against the counterrevolution in both the Volga and Ural theaters. Caught in the middle, Legion troops had been hit hard. Kolchak realized that the Allied Command had bungled many aspects of the intervention, but he believed they were trying to correct their mistakes.

Alexandr Kolchak's political leanings had become indisputably pro-British due to his close friendships abroad with businessmen like Mr. Fedosev, managing director of the British mining firms, the Irtysh and Tanalyk corporations, both highly visible English concerns in Siberia.[13] British influence over Kolchak did not escape the attention of the American administration or the French Command, and certainly not that of the Japanese.[14]

Immediately upon his arrival in Omsk, the Directory of Five asked Kolchak to accept the position of war minister. Kolchak accepted. Fearing the failure of their plan to control the Russian Far East, the Japanese reacted immediately. Admiral Kolchak admonished the Japanese for Semenov's presence in Chita where the ataman's ruthless behavior had become unacceptable. Japanese-sponsored chaos and destruction would have to be curtailed. Kolchak demanded a meeting with Ataman Semenov. Later, the British reported Kolchak's impressions:

> He [Semenov] needed nothing, he got everything he wanted from Japan, no requests to make, no plans to disclose. "I saw," said Kolchak, "that there was no use talking with him." He told Semenov, in effect, that he washed his hands of him, and the two men parted on the worst possible terms.[15]

Kolchak appealed for more counterrevolutionary recruiting at military headquarters in Omsk. Expecting 60,000, Kolchak was delighted when more than 200,000 men reported to fight for Omsk's new minister of war. The Allied Command believed that it had finally found a leader who could unite the political factions of Siberia and rebuild a cohesive front line in both the Ural and Volga theaters.

Among the tens of thousands of volunteers who arrived in Omsk were a few hundred former tsarist officers. Assigning many of these trained officers to advisory positions in Omsk would be Kolchak's first misstep. Before long this inner circle began to openly discuss the establishment of a "new Tsar." While these pronouncements made Kolchak and his British counterparts uncomfortable, some in the Allied Command rethought their enthusiasm for Aleksandr Kolchak, wondering what "changes" the new war minister had in store for Siberia.[16]

On November 9, 1918, all Allied representatives, Siberian army commanders, and the war minister Admiral Kolchak reported to Ekaterinburg for ceremonies honoring the Czecho-Slovak Legion. Kolchak remembered, "My first mission was to be present at that ceremony, where I for the first time made acquaintance of Czech officers and of Syrový. Foreign representatives were present there. There also I saw Gajda for the second time."[17]

Colonel John Ward of the Middlesex Regiment led the regimental band playing the British national anthem as Czechs and Slovaks marched before a reviewing stand of Allied officers. Standards were bestowed upon the Legion and colors presented.

Passed over for recognition and still waiting for reinforcements and supplies for his troops at the front, Radola Gajda harbored growing hostility.[18] His soldiers, exhausted and sick, were ill-clothed for the coming winter. They lacked even the most basic combat equipment. Units that had fought valiantly for Gajda on their trek eastward were now dying in large numbers because of the Allied's neglect. Gajda's complaints remained unanswered but his growing anger did not go unnoticed. After the Ekaterinburg ceremony, Gajda gave the leadership an ultimatum: resupply the Legion at the front, or he would turn his troops on Omsk. Gajda demanded that Siberian troops be forced to fight equally as hard as the legionnaires. After the ceremonies ended and without the approval of his superiors, Gajda stormed the seat of the Siberian government in Omsk as promised.

Though they understood Gajda's frustration, his aggression embarrassed members of the Czecho-Slovak National Council. His ultimatum had, however, been fully supported by other Legion officers. Within days, the Allied Command answered Gajda with supplies and reinforcements. Radola Gajda had won this round, but at the risk of losing good standing with his own National Council, the OCSNR.

Admiral Kolchak found Gajda's headstrong push toward Omsk inspired.[19] Gajda's decisiveness and integrity, his willingness to lose everything for the sake of his men, made the young general the kind of leader the war ministry needed to reorganize the Siberian front.[20] Kolchak returned to Omsk with thoughts of Gajda's potential.

On November 11, 1918, German and Austrian armies surrendered along the Western Front. The Triple Alliance had collapsed in one last brutal gasp in the trenches of Belgium and France. Thomas Masaryk's farewell address to the United States before assuming the presidency of the new state of Czechoslovakia was capped-off by news of an armistice. The war had ended.

In Paris new national borders were carved out of the old Hapsburg Empire throughout Central Europe. Thoughts turned to Versailles, where diplomats negotiated the return of soldiers and prisoners of war. Men stranded in distant locales the world over would surely be able to leave, to return to their prewar lives, their homelands, and their families.[21] Throughout Russia and Siberia this meant that former prisoners would no longer menace the countryside, stealing from peasants and hoarding stockpiled war supplies. Surpluses would be redistributed to help the growing number of refugees caught between the White and Red troops.

Throughout the new state of Czechoslovakia, border squabbles with the Poles, Hungarians, and Germans erupted immediately. Masaryk's fledgling government found itself in desperate need of an experienced army. The only men who could provide such expertise had been marooned in Siberia. Masaryk did what he could and immediately began organizing armed units to patrol the borderlands of the Czechs and the Slovaks.[22]

Marshall Foch, commander of Allied forces in Europe, proclaimed that Hungary had forfeited her titles to Slovakia. Areas under dispute by the Hungarians now became annexed to the new nation of Czechoslovakia.[23] Hungary had just lost a war, and although demoralized, its leadership remained adamant that these ancestral lands belonged to her, not the Slovaks. Street rioting systematically erupted in the streets of Bratislava, Košice, and Komárno. Foch could make proclamations, but the Czechs and Slovaks had to defend these towns and cities with the few trained men they had on hand.

Instead of sending Masaryk's Legion home, Allied Command reaffirmed the need for continued maintenance of an expeditionary force in Siberia. With the war collapsing in Western Europe, these interventionist arguments rang hollow. By mid-November, the Legion Army still balanced precariously amidst the politics of the Allied Command at Versailles, the Bolshevik government in Moscow, and White forces reorganizing in the field under the Directory of Five. Under the command of the Allies, the Legion found itself irrevocably bound to the Allied's efforts in Siberia. The Trans-Siberian ran directly through areas of the most violent fighting between Whites and Reds.[24] Orders were to direct the collection of equipment and enhance the stability of the railroad.

On the night of November 17, 1918, Ataman Krasilnikov, a minor Cossack leader, called upon the Directory of Five in Omsk. Krasilnikov arrested all five of the ministers and moved them to an undisclosed location before boldly reporting his actions to officers of the counterrevolution. Krasilnikov's coup d'état immediately became denounced by every Siberian faction in the region along with the Allied Command. While privately satisfied to see the end of the Directory's incompetence, the Allies called Ataman Krasilnikov's actions blatant kidnapping.

Kolchak demanded the immediate release of all five hostages. As Cossack troops milled about Omsk, tempers flared, threatening a violent revolt in the streets of the capital. Minister Kolchak prepared Siberian units to subdue any violence. His efforts seemed to settle the situation for the time being.

In a meeting between military and ministry officials, representative Boldrev announced that in the absence of the Directory of Five, he wished to nominate himself as head of the Omsk government. Kolchak seconded this idea. Minister Vologodski instead suggested that the new war minister Kolchak would make a better choice.[25] This suggestion was also eagerly seconded.

Aleksandr Kolchak reportedly watched the unfolding of these proceedings, dumfounded as one after another the men assembled voted for him to take the helm. Later, the ex-admiral remembered: "I saw that there was nothing more to say, and gave my consent."[26] In the morning Kolchak made a general announcement to the citizens of Omsk to state his objectives, which included the creation of an effective army that would be victorious over Bolshevism. Kolchak also promised law and order so that in future the populace would be able to choose the form of government it desired.

Allied Command tentatively supported Kolchak's government if not the manner of his ascent to power.[27] The Soviet leadership in Moscow immediately accused Kolchak of organizing a British-sponsored coup d'état. Lenin warned that Kolchak's regime would fail and that the end of the directorate signaled the beginning of a renewed Red Army effort in the field — a new stage of suffering for the people of Siberia.[28] General Janin echoed accusations against Kolchak that he had acted under confidential orders from the British to overthrow the Directory of Five. Among Allied officers, Legion Command, and the vast majority of White Army officials, General Janin's warnings meant little. They held Janin in contempt for earlier efforts to discredit White officers.[29]

Legion Command certainly could never officially support a regime that had come to power without a democratic election by the people. The Czech National Council also refused to back Kolchak as supreme ruler, a title laden with monarchist overtones. The command structure in Omsk consisted of ex-tsarist officers who reportedly sang the tsarist national anthem at meetings, alienating Allied officials and Legion Command. Even the citizens of Omsk seemed squeamish with what appeared to them to be flirting with the trappings of a defunct Romanov era.

Press accounts characterized the first days of Kolchak's rule as full of "irresponsible military circles [who] saw the opportunity to act on their own initiative, and in no time were completely out of hand."[30] Amidst this volatile atmosphere in Omsk, Kolchak announced his new choice to command and reorganize the Siberian troops in the field: General Radola Gajda. Passed over for commissions, the young Slovak general felt he had earned this post and the responsibilities it entailed.

The OCSNR proclaimed that Gajda had not only broken the Legion's oath of neutrality but turned his back on fellow legionnaires and everything the new state of Czechoslovakia represented.[31] Though the Czechs and Slovaks yearned for a strong and respectable government for Siberia, they were aghast that one of their own had become entangled in the politics of Omsk with all its countervailing forces.

In December 1918, Štefánik, Czechoslovak Minister of War, arrived in Siberia to visit with the troops, and gauge for himself how they fared under the command of General Janin and the Allies.[32] The minister found the front disorganized and the Legion troops demoralized. Štefánik communicated

Masaryk's prepared statement to the Legion, explaining why its presence in Siberia had helped Beneš in the ongoing discussions at Versailles. The Czechoslovak Minister of War also reported back to Masaryk that, for the most part, the troops remained uninspired.[33] While Štefánik's grace and charisma impressed the troops, he departed failing to restore the discipline that Legion Command demanded.

In answer to Legion objections, Kolchak requested Štefánik's approval of Gajda's appointment. Štefánik answered that he had no objections, but warned Kolchak of Gajda's penchant for rebellious ambition. Furthermore, Štefánik forbade Gajda from punishing mutineers. Gajda, however, accepted the new appointment on his own terms. He advised Kolchak that a future expedition to Perm' ordered by Siberian officials would prove difficult at best.

By the winter of 1918, Supreme Ruler Kolchak and his new commanding general, ex-legionnaire Gajda, had become close friends and confidantes. Rumors spread that Gajda might one day be groomed to take Kolchak's place, when and if the supreme ruler stepped down. Gajda seemed to be under this impression as well, believing that somehow he could become a power broker in the Russian Far East. Gajda's dreams proved illusory though, as he would forever be seen as an interloper by Kolchak's staff.

In the Siberian army ranks, Gajda quickly realized that he lacked cohesive support from any of the factions vying for control over the people of Siberia.[34] When Kolchak named his *Stavka* (general staff), it reflected a decidedly tsarist bent. Gajda supported the supreme ruler, backing his war effort, but as an ex-Legion officer he could never sway indignant Stavka officials to back his own efforts.

The Stavka staff of 900 officers worked with a support staff of 5,000.[35] The exponential growth of officers in Omsk concerned Gajda immensely. Allied Command also sensed a change in the Legion's attitude toward the anti–Bolshevik front after the Stavka took over. General Knox warned his staff, "They [the Legion] are sick of the fighting, sick of the Gilbert-and-Sullivan quality of the Allied military efforts, and especially sick of the Russians, whom they saw as listless and incapable of making up their minds."[36] The Czechs and Slovaks outspokenly voiced outrage. Their hero, Radola Gajda, had thrown his support behind a political usurper — a White Russia.

Kolchak set about to gain the support of the citizens of Omsk, the Siberian army, the Legion, and especially the Allied Command. Initially, efforts to stabilize and reorganize the Ussuri and Volga fronts reassured each of these groups.[37] Not everyone could be convinced, however. President Woodrow Wilson, urged by both British and French advisors, agreed to give Kolchak a chance but only if Kolchak established a democratic regime from Omsk. After the new supreme ruler equipped an army of nearly 250,000 men with more than 500,000 rifles, 346 million rounds and more than 6,800 machine guns originally stockpiled by the former tsar, he turned his offensive against the Red Army.

The Bolsheviks, also fully equipped and organized, had begun to solidify the Ural theater. General Gajda's first task, Kolchak ordered, was to stabilize areas recently lost to the Red Army. Gajda had plans of his own. He demanded that White Army officers fight alongside their units in the field. The peasantry found it difficult to trust these ex-tsarist officials and even soldiers in the Siberian Army needed to see more action on the part of this officer class. Disregarding General Gajda completely, White officers continued lounging at Stavka headquarters in Omsk.

General Janin also voiced concerns over the ballooning growth of the number of officers on Kolchak's staff. As head of the Allied intervention, General Maurice Janin expected an immediate meeting with the supreme ruler. Janin had met Kolchak once before in 1916 and, though envious of the young admiral, knew Kolchak's fame had been well deserved. As a young naval officer Kolchak had always shown a fresh outlook on the prosecution of the war effort. He understood the importance of having a united front against the enemy.

After returning from the meeting in Omsk, Janin reported to his superiors in Paris that he had found Aleksandr Kolchak changed. In fact, Kolchak seemed an entirely different person. Janin wrote,

> He had aged and I find him very much changed from the day in 1916 when I saw him brought by Admiral Rusin to the Imperial table at General Headquarters, on the Black Sea Fleet. There is a hollowness about his cheeks; his complexion and his eyes are feverish; his nose, which is very pronounced, seems to jut out more than ever.... He is emaciated, worn out, his eyes are haggard, and he appears to be in a state of extreme nervous tension. Suddenly he stops speaking, jerks his neck back, closes his eyes, becomes rigid. Can it be that the allegations of morphiomania are true?[38]

No matter how Kolchak appeared to General Janin, his initial report fell on deaf ears with superiors. Kolchak seemed in control of his troops, made intelligent and necessary decisions, and appeared to be of sound mind and body. Fighting at the front had, in fact, begun to turn in favor of Gajda's troops. Kolchak's centrist government was gaining support within the countryside. Under his leadership the government of Omsk gained respect and appeared to be evolving into a democracy as President Woodrow Wilson demanded. If this was possible, the Allies wondered, could Russia be far behind?[39]

In the press, Kolchak announced that he had discovered where the Directory of Five had been held. He demanded the Directory of Five be released and sent a British unit to escort them to the Manchurian border, where the ministers would be safe from further Cossack harassment. Kolchak fully expected this effort to win over naysayers including French General Janin and the Legion Command. Instead, Kolchak's actions met with queries as to why the Directory of Five had effectively been sent into exile across the Manchurian border.

This new onslaught of skepticism infuriated Kolchak. He began to question whether he could ever gain approval of the Allies or the Legion. The OCSNR, in fact, continued to voice concerns over Kolchak's choice of Gajda as commander in chief of a Siberian army with so many Stavka officers in Omsk who had been rumored to be referring to Aleksandr Kolchak as the "Second Tsar." Other Legion officers wondered aloud why anyone, including Kolchak, would want to run the government in Omsk even though it appeared a strategic center:

> Omsk, as the capital of the new regime, had much to recommend it. It was the center of navigation on the Ob'-Irtysh river system, a Trans-Siberian junction, and had extensive railroad and machine shops, enormous barracks, and several good military hospitals. But it had nothing around it to compare to the industrial heartland....

"The thought kept running through my head," one Czech officer recalled, "how lonely and how dreary was the stage which Kolchak had selected for his empire–building. In the midst of this treeless steppe six feet deep with snow in winter, windblown and brown in summer...."[40]

No matter the criticism, the supreme commander announced that he would prove that his people exercised choice: democratic elections would be held within a year. Kolchak admonished his detractors by saying that he desired democracy for the Siberians as much as the Allies demanded it. Kolchak proclaimed: "Within a year one of two things will happen: either the Constitution Assembly will have met in Moscow or I shall be dead."[41]

Chapter Ten

Throughout December 1918 and January 1919, Legion trains sped back into the interior. Nothing the Czechs and Slovaks had experienced so far could have prepared them for the Siberian cold they now experienced. Frozen, silent farmland stretched into the surrounding forests in an endless oppressive gray mist that hovered above the icebound scenery. Only a strip alongside the tracks was cleared away and free of deep drifts. Week-long blizzards trapped everyone indoors with temperatures plummeting between 20 to 50 degrees below freezing.

When the howling blizzard wind slammed into the Legion trains, snow piled high above boxcar roofs and ice fused metal train wheels to the tracks.

Legionnaires in Kirgis dress guarding locomotives in 40-degrees-below-zero weather, not dated.

Winter conditions on the Ural Front, winter 1918.

The infamous Siberian permafrost mutilated soldiers, torturing fingers, ears, nose, and feet. To survive the Legion turned to the experts, mimicking Buriate herdsmen and prospectors.[1] Lessons on erecting Siberian *naide* huts saved hundreds caught out in the open while on patrol. Similar to the Eskimo igloo, the naide's construction took only minutes and provided priceless insulation from the elements even though made out of snow.

As winter conditions worsened, the pace of violence increased. Panicked masses rushed toward the Pacific with their belongings on their backs. Families huddled together against buildings and boxcars, slept in doorways, congregated around garbage heaps, and begged for food and a place to stand on the next eastbound train. American Railroad Service Corps reported these conditions to superiors back in Vladivostok; an engineer described his eerie surroundings:

> I snapped [photographed] three little refugee children who refused to pose until we whispered the charm, "chocolate." Then they stood with broad smiles despite their pitiful rags and pinched faces. They had lived at Tatarskaya over four years; had fled from Russia near the beginning of the war. Their mother lived at Tatarskaya but their father was from old Russia. The oldest child was not old enough to remember anything about Russia, or even what part of Russia they came from. Most of the refugees in Siberia have no idea of geography. They simply crowd on to a train and let it take them wherever it goes.[2]

Ice bound locomotive at Perm (not dated).

Flu and typhus spread through the countryside in what would become the worst flu epidemic of the twentieth century. In Verchne-Udiinsk, site of Gajda's greatest achievement just months before, the 27th U.S. Army Regiment settled into position. Suddenly it became overrun by a killing influenza epidemic. The death toll rose so quickly that General Graves ordered the dead to be hidden in order to control panic in the town.[3]

Allied transport vessels continued to dock in Vladivostok Harbor as idle rumors filtered west that reinforcements would arrive to replace the Legion on both fronts. Until then and with no other options, the Legion pushed on against the Red Army, amassing more than 400 punitive expeditions. While soldiers and peasants suffered, Allied officials spoke to the media back home of victory. Winston Churchill declared to the House of Commons: "The foul baboonery of Bolshevism was on its deathbed."[4] It never entered the Allies' perception that the Soviet system could emerge victorious.

As the days grew shorter, the isolated lands of Siberia hosted ever more violent confrontation between the Reds and the Whites. Neither the White Army nor the Allies demonstrated concern over the Legion's misery. In return, Czech and Slovak units along the Ural and Volga fronts cared little for updates from Allied Command.[5] When several Legion officers admitted to General Graves that they no longer had faith in England, Japan or France, the American general reported to Washington, D.C., that this could be a turning point in the intervention and not in the direction the Allies had hoped.

The Legion reported that a detachment called the "internationalists" had recently joined the ranks of the Red Army. To legionnaires the term "internationalist" implied that Austrian, German, or Hungarian ex-prisoners of war were involved.[6] People in the countryside suspected that the Hungarians ran the entire Bolshevik front. With the signing of the Brest-Litovsk Treaty thousands of Prussian troops had been released from Siberian work camps to migrate homeward, foraging in towns and across the Siberian wild for available food and shelter. Small bands of ex-POWs wrecked property and stole from the railway, fomenting resentment by locals.[7] William Duncan of the YMCA once reported witnessing Russians brutalizing Austrian ex-POWs and stealing their woolen-soled shoes.[8]

The number of atrocities against noncombatants spiked on all sides of the front. Czech and Slovak soldiers, demoralized and hopeless, were no longer the heroes of the peasants. Legion officers increasingly found themselves trying to excuse the poor behavior of men caught robbing locals. In one case Cossack troops beat, lassoed and dragged three Russian prisoners before hacking them to death. The incident reached official channels as Legion officers had to admit that their investigation revealed the involvement of their own men.[9]

Under the pay of the Japanese, Ataman Semenov and Ataman Kalmykov hired newly released criminals to join their units. Semenov, who dressed as a prince and lived in a luxurious van aboard his broněviky, encouraged men to violently collect booty whenever possible, providing they swore allegiance to his cause. Both Semenov and Kalmykov meandered through the countryside, stealing and murdering, and inevitably scattering villagers in their wake. All knew Kalmykov's camouflage painted trains.[10] The atamans and their Japanese sponsors were the most loathsome of the troops victimizing locals. Britain learned from a brief association with both Semenov and Kalmykov of the Cossacks' tendency towards unnecessary and unpredictable ruthlessness. Britain cut off all contacts with both, yet Japan continued to sponsor discontent and lawlessness under the guise of intervention. General Graves found himself and the troops of the 27th and 31st Regiments, the "Polar Bears and Wolf Hounds," respectively, impotently witnessing Japanese excesses with orders from President Wilson to remain neutral.[11] Emmett Hoskins, an American sailor, wrote home of an incident he witnessed dockside in Vladivostok: "They [Russians] passed close by two Japanese battleships anchored in the [Vladivostok] bay and close by the USS *Brooklyn* making towards the wharf.... The Russians pantomimed to the *Brooklyn* crew by shaking their fists at the Japanese 'battlewagons' and making faces, and to the *Brooklyn* they bowed low and smiled."[12]

American patrols concentrated efforts in the South Ussuri and Vladivostok regions, stationing units at 100 mile intervals.[13] Throughout 1919, only the Red Cross and YMCA organized within the interior. Under the leadership of Dr. John R. Mott, YMCA General Secretary, 100 Americans volunteered to educate more than 200 additional workers — some of whom were Czech, Polish, Rumanian, Russian, Slovak, or Siberian. After learning of how destitute ex-prisoners of war from Austria, German, and Hungary had been found, the YMCA began providing aid to these men as well. Reports that more than 60,000 ex-prisoners had gathered in forests moved the British quartermaster to send blankets and clothing to Chelyabinsk by way of the YMCA. In addition, YMCA representatives purchased boots, caps, shirts, and gloves to ship to ex-prisoners. Though legionnaires continued to consider these soldiers enemies, they could not deny how dire these ex-POWs' situation had become.[14]

> All had only dirty light underwear made out of plain cloth and all were barefoot. The uniforms, shirts and boots were needed for the men at the front. Some of the wounds looked as if they had never been dressed, the blood still caked on them. Their hair was matted. The poor fellows had no combs, and they were all, oh so dirty.[15]

The YMCA also asked a pool of genial ex-prisoners to join its effort in the field as charity workers.[16] YMCA associates distributed cigarettes, films, and lectures in the appropriate languages.[17] Coffee houses supplied rolls, coffee, and cheap meals and often converted into churches every Sunday morning when troop trains arrived for services.[18]

Abandoned barracks and railroad depots allocated for use by the Red Cross and YMCA also were converted into hospital facilities fitted with electric lighting plants, huge Russian funnel stoves, and phonograph, motion picture, and library equipment.[19] YMCA "secretaries," as they referred to one another, made sure that individuals placed in their care received at least one cup of tea, hard tack, and a spoonful of sugar per day.

Letters and reports from enthusiastic young American men and women arrived at YMCA headquarters in New York from across Siberia. Many of the YMCA secretaries spent weeks with no other English speakers available in the field. Others traveled for months in boxcars with the Czechs and Slovaks. The Legion marveled at these American men and women who put their lives on the line daily in order to care for total strangers. The YMCA secretaries were the only other foreign presence the Legion saw in the interior and they were not even armed.

One report from the Krasnoyarsk region detailed how a local Soviet *Zemstvo* granted a YMCA worker access to more than 284 villages in his soviet. The area encompassed 80,000 people, most living in impoverished communities of less than 1,000 inhabitants each. If truly lucky, townsfolk might have the services of a priest to oversee town business but normally these hamlets had only one local leader and most had never seen the services of either a doctor or a dentist.

YMCA workers reported that they rarely met anyone who could read. The dirt roads leading into these villages fronted simple huts built in clusters to keep out the wind near communally cultivated fields. In Siberian homes the entire family slept huddled together around an enormous stove. In winter everyone slept in the same clothes they had worked in all day. Bathing was rare and precarious in the extreme cold.

The Legion suffered much the same conditions. A female nurse traveling in Legion boxcars for the YMCA wrote, "The cracks were stuffed with cotton and the room lined with paper. Often they [legionnaires] have no light in the evenings and having no place to go, are compelled to sit in the dark, and think — they have few pleasant things to think about."[20]

As famine spread yet again, the Bolsheviks and the counterrevolutionaries looted and burned granaries and water towers and destroyed railroad equipment. The potential collapse of the entire distribution system throughout Siberia threatened not only YMCA efforts but basic services. Transport that had formerly run smoothly along the highways and roadways now became hopelessly clogged as the Trans-Siberian Railway began to atrophy. Only the Czechs and Slovaks moved far enough inland to make any meaningful impact on the entire system of transport. Even in the best of times the Trans-Siberian Railway had been maintained at standards well below those of Western Europe or the United States.[21]

Studying the lack of supplies along the proposed second front, the United States Army estimated that even with 300 transport vessels traveling nonstop to and from Vladivostok Harbor and carrying only railway supplies, the Trans-Siberian Railway could not survive. Machinery and parts needed to supply even minimal levels of maintenance had already become rare. In addition, partisan factions throughout the countryside continued to attack and destroy bridges, tracks, and depots at will. To make matters worse, even the more populated centers like Vladivostok, Harbin, Chita, Krasnoyarsk, Omsk, Perm,' and Samara had stations and repair facilities more than 25 years old. Workers knowledgeable in repairing railroads and equipment had long since joined the stream of humanity fleeing toward Vladivostok. Depots built 100 miles apart housed pumping stations to service locomotives, but even they were failing.

The Worthington Pump and Machine Company of New York City had been the manufacturer of much of the Siberian railway equipment.[22] In 1919 a desperate attempt to save the Trans-Siberian system under the Inter-Allied Agreement proposed financing the supervision of the railroads under the care of a Technical Board of Engineers. American John Stevens was appointed to head the operation and he announced that every line would be placed under the protection of Allied troops. American, British, Canadian, Chinese, Czech,

French, Japanese, and Slovak troops would comprise a miniature League of Nations to protect the viability of the railway system and all of its branch lines. Engineers representing each country would report to Mr. Steven's team, attacking problems of long-distance transport, broad-gauge and heavy-grade incompatibility, and the effects of winter temperatures on staff and equipment. Unfortunately, however, civil war and epidemics began to interfere with the railway board's progress.[23]

The relationship among the Legion, the White Army, and the Allies accurately reflected the disintegration of the countryside. Despite Washington's telegram to the United States consul at Vladivostok on January 29, 1919, informing him that the Czecho-Slovaks had been given a $7 million loan for the purchase of war supplies, the Legion continued to suffer huge numbers of casualties in Kazan and Ufa due to inadequate arms. The promised Allied reinforcements never came. Legion hopes had long since been replaced by skepticism.

Legion officials complained of widespread mistreatment of Siberian troops by their own White officers. Ill-equipped soldiers had actually been left to die by commanders; if troops complained, many were beaten or executed on the spot. This resulted in a dangerous increase in desertions at the front and a greater need for legionnaires to make up the ever-decreasing numbers of White Army troops.

> The forces of their Russian ally, with huge reserves of manpower behind them, were constantly eroded by desertion; 3,000 men of the Samara Rifle Division deserted in the month before the city fell. A few gallant Russian officers — Usakov, Kappel and Vojcechovsky among them — were trusted, followed and admired; but the main lesson the Czechs [and Slovaks] had learned since the Chelyabinsk incident at the end of May was that in the civil war, you could rely on nobody, depend on nothing. They were serious people; they wanted no more part in a bloody farce.[24]

President Wilson had hoped that an American economic intervention could ensure the establishment of a Siberian democratic government. The American president encouraged non–Bolshevik elements to rise up and fight for their democratic freedoms. In a letter to President Wilson, Secretary Lansing admitted that he was optimistic with the Legion on the scene: "Our confidence in the Czech [and Slovak] forces has been justified.... The fact that now a Russian military force of equal strength has joined them combined with the gratifying reception given the Czechs [and Slovaks] by the civilian population of the localities occupied, is strong evidence to prove that the Russians are entirely satisfied to cooperate with the Czechs [and Slovaks] in Russia and that assistance to the Czechs [and Slovaks] amounts to assistance to the Russians."[25]

When interviewed by a newspaper correspondent, French General Janin was asked why the Allies had intervened to help the Legion only to leave them stranded in the interior. Janin answered with a quotation from the Old Testament: "There are some who have eyes and do not see, and ears and do not hear. Often and often I tell them."[26] The world press was not satisfied as its questions continued to be ignored.

Throughout January 1919, a congressional investigation committee held hearings in Washington, D.C., to define American interventionist policy in Siberia. Acting Secretary of State Polk was confronted with questions concerning recent Legion complaints at the front and the Legion's delayed evacuation. In February 1919, General Graves once again warned his superiors: "I consider the morale bad and the Czechs [and Slovaks] do not constitute a dependable force for use against the Bolsheviks."[27]

The British and French, however, believed in unlimited intervention using the Legion to lead the second front. But the war was over in Europe; there was no western or eastern front anymore. Russian policy broke down completely between America and her allies as Anglo-French policy making subsequently bypassed President Wilson. Either way, the Allies were not being candid concerning the Legion's fate.

Czech and Slovak soldiers began laying down their arms. Small groups headed for home. No one, it seemed, had a fixed route in mind, but most believed that staying to fight for the Allies was equivalent to a death sentence. Some headed south while others traveled west into European Russia where they had to evade both Red and White factions.[28]

Most Legion troops, however, remained united and in the fight as ordered. These men hoped against hope that the Allies would end their interventionist dreams or begin fighting themselves. In fact, Allied units were being sent into the interior but only in rear positions to prevent the sabotage of mining, manufacturing and warehouse interests.[29] As winter deepened, the Legion's number thinned out until units of 250 became responsible for vast areas of railway track. General Štefánik and General Syrový published an address in the *Ceskoslovenský deník* at the beginning of 1919 urging their troops "to fight for Russia, for Slavic brotherhood and freedom...." On January 20, 1919, Štefánik left Omsk for Europe. He had tried his best in the short time he had with the Legion. However, since he could not keep his promise to repatriate the Legion with him, he had only managed to increase general confusion."[30]

To keep both traffic and communications flowing, the Legion maintained its positions. In the end, the Stavka, Kolchak's ruthless yet lackadaisical officer staff in Omsk, ended Legion participation along the Ural and Volga fronts. General Janin and General Štefánik were rumored to be warning Legion officers not to move against Kolchak's officers.[31] Left with no further recourse, Czech and Slovak officers announced that the Legion would continue to guard the Trans-Siberian Railway to minimize partisan attacks and to allow supplies to reach soldiers at the front. But the Legion would no longer take part in the fighting.[32]

The Red Army's numbers had climbed to more than 500,000 men with still more in reserve. Facing an adversary of such size, Kolchak saw the Legion's withdrawal from fighting as a monstrous act of cowardice. The supreme ruler of Siberia announced to General Janin: "The sooner they clear out, the better."[33]

Only one ex-legionnaire remained exempt from Kolchak's declaration. Under General Gajda's personal command successful advances in the Ural front began turning favor against the Soviets. Even the newly organizing Siberian Army gained ground along the steppe.[34] Kolchak's experience combined with Gajda's capable advice to give hope for a united Siberia. POWs under the watchful eyes of the YMCA felt that Kolchak was one of few counterrevolutionary figures capable of uniting Siberia and defeating the Bolsheviks.[35] Exactly under what type of government this unification would occur remained unclear. Kolchak admirers still spoke of the revival of a new tsarist regime. British colonel John Ward, a frequent visitor of Gajda's in early 1919, was one such admirer; he maintained that if England had both a democratic government and a monarch, Russia and Siberia could as well.[36]

Gajda remained focused on the field and steadfastly trusted his leader, but Kolchak's highly influential Stavka staff was another story altogether. On one occasion Gajda discovered a plan for aircraft to drop leaflets over local villages declaring, "You have stolen the land, and payment will have to be made."[37] Believing in land reform and having developed a warm rapport with peasants living near the front, Gajda refused to distribute this material. It became obvious that any supporter of land reform would be labeled a "Communist."[38] A true legionnaire, Gajda refused to take part in this victimization.

Many Czechs and Slovaks shared in the hope that Kolchak and Gajda could unite Siberia and stop the devastation that encircled them. Some believed that Kolchak and Semenov had to be severe and ruthless to stave off any coming disaster. For a time, legionnaire Joseph Skelnička thought Kolchak and Semenov worked for the same cause:

> Kolchak was one of the commanders who worked with us, was helping us to clear away these individual troops. That's Kolchak, then Semenov, he was after the Baikal. He was helping us to go forward. And Dutov, he was in the South. So we had three helpers with their armies, they helped us. We were working with them together because all were against Communism and we were, too. That's why they gave us priority.[39]

Quite suddenly, however, the Legion and their officials no longer cared what these men of foreign affairs did in their own countries. If the Allies were not going to evacuate the Legion then it would evacuate itself. Minister Štefánik chartered former Red Cross ships and readied them for service under the tricolors of Czechoslovakia. The *Legie* became the first vessel paid for by the new state of Czechoslovakia in a navy belonging to a landlocked country.[40] A second vessel, the *Roma,* under the command of officer and physician Dr. Raše, left Vladivostok on January 15, 1919. Raše's staff included 35 medical students, all volunteers from the United States, Korea, Germany, and Estonia. The *Roma*'s capacity totaled about 1,500 passengers, but Dr. Raše permitted more than 2,500 troops on board in order to ensure the immediate evacuation of the sick and injured. Seriously injured soldiers slept in the most comfortable cabins. As the ship traveled through the waters of southern Asia and eastern Africa, four shell-shocked soldiers jumped overboard and drowned. Docking in Naples, Italy, on March 11, 1919, ambulances transported the ill and wounded from the *Roma* to trains waiting at the Naples depot for transport to Czechoslovakia.[41] Despite the loss of the four soldiers, General Raše expected the *Roma* to set the standard for all subsequent trips.

Thomas Masaryk's government purchased and leased vessels from Britain, Japan and the United States. Some of these vessels sailed into the ports of Trieste and Marseille. Although most of the sick and wounded followed the *Roma*'s established route, those under United States' authority stopped en route on the Pacific coasts of Canada and the United States. After evacuation of the sick and wounded, regular Legion troops could follow.

Czech and Slovak troops in the field began to face the same desperation they had seen Siberian troops experiencing throughout the fall and winter. Weather, violence, and Red and White crimes made movement from the front to Vladivostok increasingly more difficult. Kolchak complained openly of Legion belligerence toward his troops and Allied officials worried what the

Baikal Mountains in winter, 1919.

further disintegration of Czech and Slovak morale could mean for the transportation of supplies and people along the Trans-Siberian Railway.

Partisans took this opportunity to step up raids against the railroads and the Legion protecting them. Bridges, sections of track, telegraph and telephone equipment remained heavily damaged up and down the line. Several troop trains and refugee cars came under attack, leaving large numbers of casualties.

Aleksandr Kolchak had been unarguably one of the great patriots of Russia — one of the country's most decorated explorers and a truly remarkable military mind of his day.[42] A tall figure with dark intense eyes, Kolchak even looked the part of supreme ruler. Only his ruddy complexion gave a hint of his mother's Turkish blood. He had always been considered a handsome man but lately there had also been a look of strained preoccupation in his face. Kolchak had reportedly been working long into the night with little food and even less rest. The overwhelming responsibility he had accepted as leader of the Omsk government had left him exhausted and gaunt. His English friend, General Knox, noted: "I confess that all my sympathy is with Kolchak, who has more grit, pluck, and honest patriotism than anyone else in Siberia and whose difficult task is being made almost impossible by the selfishness of the Japanese, vanity of the French, and indifference of the other allies."[43]

Despite Kolchak's good intentions and former loyalty to the peasantry, word reached his allies and former friends that his Stavka officers had been repressing the populous. The supreme ruler was said to be separated from others and surrounded by personal guards who kept meetings to a minimum and strangers at a distance.[44] Stavka staff previewed reports meant for Kolchak, questioned visitors, and refused most an opportunity to speak with him in person. Stories portrayed the supreme ruler as a man on the edge of insanity who accused those who opposed any of his ideas of being mercenary cutthroats. Kolchak was said to turn the other way when his own officer staff flaunted its power and victimized the weak.[45]

General Gajda worried that the Siberian people might reject the counterrevolution if they continued being mistreated by Kolchak's officers. The Bolsheviks had many brilliant leaders and given time they could summon more men to join the Red Army from the ranks of the disenfranchised. In vain, Gajda insisted that White troops occupying the countryside be responsible for atrocities committed on their watch and that White officers live with and care for their own troops.

When his recommendations went ignored, Gajda made them public. He reproached Russian officers by name for cowardice and behavior unbecoming their rank. While none of this served to endear him to the Stavka in Omsk, Gajda remained one of Kolchak's most favored generals. When Gajda flirted with a plan to unite General Deniken's efforts in the south with his own in the north, Stavka officers grew concerned. They worried that if the Slovak upstart was successful, his influence over the supreme ruler might become greater than their own. Russian generals in Omsk demanded that Gajda be transferred farther north.[46]

Kolchak did what his commanding officers requested. Gajda marched north even while continuing his public reproaches. He accused White Army officers of living in comfortable accommodations, gambling, drinking and whoring to the rear while their men fought and died along the Siberian steppe. In Tomsk, citizens complained to Gajda that White Russian Army troops had begun to roam the streets begging for food and warm clothing.[47] In his investigations, Gajda discovered that the soldiers involved had not eaten for days while their White general Matkovski remained in the rear, safe and warm. Gajda reported this incident to Kolchak, who rebuked Matkovski. When the uproar subsided and greater problems preoccupied both Gajda and Kolchak, General Matkovski ordered a firing squad to execute the soldiers involved.

In an inspection tour, Kolchak arrived at the front to find his men in tattered uniforms without coats or socks and wearing boots with gaping holes. He soon discovered that Allied supplies had not been reaching counterrevolutionary units because they had been pilfered.[48] White officers, sometimes through incompetence or neglect, but usually as a result of black market activity, grew rich by selling off vast amounts of Allied supplied material meant for soldiers fighting at the front. Similar complaints by Gajda and others did nothing to end this practice even after Kolchak returned to Omsk.[49] The supreme ruler later explained:

> This picture did not become clear to me until later — that actually, there were some intentional activities for the non–delivery and detaining of military supplies; but this was chiefly not in the Western but in the Siberian Army.... We had a very difficult situation with the deliveries of the Army because during the initial period, we did not get anything. Deliveries of arms began approximately in March; until that time, all units lacked arms, boots and clothing. At that period, the situation was very bad, but I do not think that it was of a premeditated nature.[50]

The average soldier knew that his supplies were being squandered and he could find them to the rear in cities like Omsk or Tomsk where officers dressed in boots, coats and uniforms meant for the men at the front. These officers, safe in staff positions, adorned themselves with elaborate gold-braided epaulets and the latest military medals.

After warning Kolchak of his general staff's behavior, General Gajda asked to secure the territory surrounding Perm', Samara and Kazan before taking any further offensive steps against the Red Army. Again Kolchak chose to follow his Stavka general staff and ordered Gajda to march directly toward Moscow instead. Gajda's 200,000 troops soon became overextended along an 800-mile front. As Gajda watched helplessly, his units were ground down by a better-supplied Red Army. His soldiers lacked medical supplies, food and equipment, which continued to severely tie Gajda's hands.

In the end, Gajda was forced to leave his men at the front and travel back to Omsk to beg for supplies. He did his best to convince the supreme ruler that he had been misled by his Stavka staff but Kolchak seemed nonplussed, listless and emaciated. To the north of Gajda's position, desertions severely weakened the Murmansk front and similar events threatened to destroy the counterrevolution near Petrograd. Both areas trapped Gajda's men in a hopeless vise-grip.

The supreme ruler's disregard so affected Gajda that he went against orders and pulled what forces he had left back from the front before they were completely annihilated. Unlike other White Armies, Gajda's troops fell back without huge casualties. The precarious situation of area peasants had so affected Gajda that they accompanied his men to the rear. This retreat became one of the greatest retreats in military history for its size and success in saving tens of thousands of individuals.

> It has been said that the accomplishment of this without disaster will be acclaimed by strategists of the future as one of the finest military genius in history.... It was only by this northern wing of Kolchak's army that the peasants were decently treated. There, they were neither plundered nor thrashed, nor summarily deprived of the land. Great masses of them withdrew with Gajda's army. In other regions, the peasants remained when the army retired, for they said that the Bolsheviks could be no worse. They remained and shot Kolchak's officers in the back.[51]

While the Legion and the Allies heralded Gajda's retreat and the salvation of thousands of peasants as a minor miracle, Kolchak and his general staff thought no such thing. Even General Graves noted the improper treatment of Gajda by the officers he wanted to serve: "Gajda took vigorous action with reference to these dishonest transactions and had some officers court-martialed and dismissed.... One would think that the Russians, especially the higher ranking officers in Kolchak's forces, would have rallied to Gajda's support for his action in trying to eradicate dishonesty from the Army."[52] Instead, the supreme ruler demanded another meeting with Gajda. "A painful audience took place, during which Kolchak, in his agitation, broke several pencils and an inkpot. 'After all,' he cried, 'What else could I expect, for you have not attended the military high school?' 'And you,' replied Gajda, 'You have commanded a few ships. Does that qualify you to govern an empire?'"[53]

In the end, the supreme ruler once again demanded that Gajda deploy

General Radola Gajda's broněviky, *the Orlík (Falcon), Irkutsk, 1919.*

yet another offensive against the Red Army. This time Gajda lost all faith in the counterrevolution. The Slovak general questioned the soundness of Kolchak's emotional state and effectively ended their relationship in one final ugly scene. After recriminations, Gajda renounced command of counterrevolutionary troops and departed for his waiting broněviky. White troops had been decimated everywhere, even at Orenburg as the Bolsheviks soundly turned the tide of the fighting at the front.[54]

In the end, the Red Army gobbled up territory once held by the Siberian army. Peasants and villagers took to the roads and railway lines en masse as they headed toward the Pacific coast where they assumed they could find safety. Others joined partisan brigades that worked with the Soviet militia from the interior. Gajda felt that he had failed and wondered, after so much loss surrounding him, would nothing ever be gained?

Chapter Eleven

Easter 1919 coaxed the warmest temperatures of the winter, yet 15 below zero was not exactly how the tens of thousands of refugees heading toward Vladivostok on foot would have described warmth. Siberia appeared to be a country fatally imploding as partisan units, formerly targeting only the Legion troop trains, now descended upon the indiscriminate hamlets.[1] The Czecho-Slovak National Council (OCSNR) bemoaned abuses against the peasantry on the part of both the White and Red Armies. Even so, no one seemed to be listening. Czech and Slovak officers in the field demanded that the OCSNR disassociate itself from heinous crimes occurring all across the steppe.

More and more often the Legion became the target of miscellaneous violence. In April, two Legion soldiers guarding a section of isolated track were ambushed, dragged into the surrounding woods, stripped and shot. Left to die in below-freezing temperatures, one of the soldiers crawled for miles back to a road where villagers discovered him half dead.[2]

In order to save the railroad track and its rolling stock from further theft, Kolchak stationed his units on Trans-Siberian trains and announced a governmental order to end partisan collaboration. Minister of the Interior Pepelayev began to arrest hundreds with little consideration of whether they were guilty or not. Kolchak later admitted that over 90 percent of those jailed had probably been innocent, an admission that came too late for many forgotten, lost to exposure, or dying from epidemics within Omsk's prison walls.[3]

While innocent souls rotted away under Kolchak's care, others languished and died at the hands of Ataman Semenov and Ataman Kalmykov, both under the pay of the Japanese. Forced to choose between multiple evils, Siberians turned against the counterrevolution in ever increasing numbers.[4] Desertions could not, however, deter the Japanese in their campaign against the peasantry. On March 22, 1919, Japanese troops set fire to homes in the village of Ivanovka and then shot its citizens in the back as they fled the flames. When asked why by the peasantry and their own allies, Japanese officials had no comment.

Koreans fighting in the Japanese Army complained bitterly of Japanese-sponsored brutality and frequently deserted into partisan ranks. The Japanese treatment of the Siberians and other ethnic groups appeared devoid of any respect. An order issued by a Japanese captain to the elder of the village of Voznesensk indicated this attitude: "I order you, elder, to appear tomorrow the 24th of December, 1919, at 5:30 in the morning at my office at the Japanese staff headquarters in the village of Nikolaevski; and if you, elder, do not appear with your assistant at the appointed time, then I shall have to go with my detachment and destroy all of your village and shoot the people both old and young, along with your assistant."[5]

It could only follow that acts of retribution against Japanese units escalated in answer to this type of behavior. Near the village of Uspenskaia, a partisan unit ambushed a platoon of Japanese soldiers as it waded across the nearby stream where the current was strongest. Hidden in the reeds, the partisans opened fire, killing the entire column. Nonetheless, Japanese units continued fomenting anarchy. As a result, the Japanese mandate to intervene in Siberian matters remained a special concern for Allied Command. Japanese-sponsored terrorism of Tartar and Mongol bands made the situation ever more dangerous for other Allied troops in the field.

Resentment of the Japanese did not, however, lead to confrontations between Siberian citizens and other Allied units.[6] In fact, when General Graves sent a Marine unit under Lieutenant Channing to Uspenskaia after local frontovik raids, American attitudes greatly impressed village leaders.[7] Lieutenant Channing met unofficially with area partisans to negotiate the peaceful placement of Marine units along sections of the railway line outside of town. With American units acting as guards, this agreement soothed hostilities and both parties involved remained true to their word.[8]

In a hurried effort to evacuate the Legion, Minister Štefánik once again journeyed throughout Italy and France calling upon Allied dignitaries. His colleagues in Prague knew he suffered from fatigue and a recurring old wound. Štefánik was due for a long-needed rest after he returned to Czechoslovakia. For the present, however, he worked at a frantic pace to keep the Kolchak regime from interfering with the continued evacuation of Czech and Slovak soldiers from Siberia. Štefánik's efforts in Western Europe proved fruitful. Heading back toward Bratislava, he remarked that he was satisfied that the Legion's troops would all be home soon.

On May 4, 1919, as Štefánik's mother stood in a large crowd waiting at the Pressburg (Bratislava) airport, the Czechoslovak minister's plane crossed over the outskirts of the city. This had to be the moment Štefánik had waited for his entire life. His Slovak countrymen were finally free of both the Austrians and Hungarians who had ruled over their land. Milan Štefánik had not seen

General Milan Rastislav Štefánik's plane crashes, Slovakia, May 4, 1919.

his Slovakia in a very long time. The crowd waiting below became excited as it heard the plane engine overhead. On its approach to the landing strip it suddenly nose dived and fell from the sky. Later, no one could believe that the three men on board had all died.

The people of Czechoslovakia were stunned. Legionnaires and especially Slovaks everywhere fell into a deep and irreconcilable period of mourning. They had lost so many compatriots and yet this accident seemed too unfair. Štefánik was the nation's most highly decorated war hero, a founding father of his nation, and a man whose name would remain synonymous in decades to come with the fight for freedom. To Beneš and Masaryk waiting for their friend in Prague, Štefánik's death came as a deeply felt personal loss.

But there was little time to spend on anything personal in the summer of 1919. By June, border disputes stemming from newly drawn maps threatened the new nations of Central Europe. In Czechoslovakia several border raids brought into question the efficiency of Thomas Masaryk's state building. Hungarian Communists near Pressburg hoped to recapture portions of Slovakia that had formerly belonged to Hungary for almost 1,000 years. On June 9, 1919, in Košice near the northern border of Hungary and Slovakia, Hungarian forces attacked. After two days of armed confrontation, Hungarian forces pushed back the newly established Slovak border.[9]

General Maurice Janin and Eduard Beneš appealed once again to French premier Clemenceau for the Legion's quick evacuation home.[10] Thus far, only the most pressing medical cases had been allowed to leave. On the other hand,

Supreme Ruler Kolchak had become so hardened against the Legion that he was rumored to be actively working to prevent its evacuation. General Janin reported, "Kolchak in another diatribe against the Czechs, once more vows that he will place himself at the head of his troops and blood will flow."[11]

Colonel John Ward of the British Middlesex Regiment disagreed with General Janin's portrayal of Kolchak. Instead, Ward believed the supreme ruler to be nothing less than a genius. Ward excused Kolchak's public outbursts as evidence of the temperamental nature of a born leader. When ordered home, Ward left Russia and Siberia in the able hands of the one man he saw as Russia's savior and next tsar: Alexandr Kolchak. During farewells, Ward asked Kolchak if he thought all would turn out okay and Kolchak replied that he had no idea.

After deliberation on various perspectives, French premier Clemenceau announced his decision: all Slavic troops under Allied Command would remain to protect railway traffic and access in and out of Siberia. With this announcement, the YMCA and Red Cross bolstered their efforts to raise Legion morale. Chelyabinsk, Zlatoust, Ufa, Samara, Ekaterinburg, Kungur, Tumen, Tomsk, Myess, Shee, Shadrinsk, and Vladivostok housed legionnaires, prisoners of war, and Siberian troops. Stores of supplies, theaters, and club halls full of assembled equipment helped to feed, house and entertain the troops under the auspices of the YMCA. "The Russian club held numerous lectures, gave concerts, moving pictures shows, ran a canteen, provided religious services, health and patriotic lectures, and small vaudeville acts.... Many of the men who had been drafted into the new army had never seen a picture show before."[12]

Through efforts similar to those made by the Allied Railway Mission and the Russian Bureau, Inc., Herbert Hoover, who had been appointed head of the U.S. Food Administration by President Woodrow Wilson, siphoned off funds to maintain the Trans-Siberian and Chinese-Eastern railway systems. Hoover's efforts sent military, medical, and food supplies into the interior. Despite the more than $5 million worth of rolling stock and supplies provided to the Trans-Siberian Railway, the system of interconnected lines continued to atrophy one section at a time.

After visiting a Zlatoust hospital run by a Czech "Baroness," C. Alexander, a YMCA secretary reported,

> The word went around the hospital like fire, and the Matron and doctor had to ask the men to please stay in bed.... Upon leaving, the Doctor advised me that he expected ninety more men in from the front during the night.... Very early next morning their train came in. One long-legged, happy faced Czech said, "We have heard you were on the Byellie, but we could not find you there. They said you were in Ufa, again in Ufa we looked but they told us

that you were in Zlatoust, and we began to think that it was not true at all.' I met some of these men in the Invalid Home afterward, and they immediately recognized me, but I am ashamed to say, I could not recall their faces.[13]

Canadian and American troops also befriended many refugees. Stuart Ramsey Tompkins of the United States Army photographed lines of women and children as they waited along with abandoned pets for scraps of food. Every morning these refugees came to pick through anything thrown away by U.S. commissary cooks outside of the barracks. Children sometimes adopted units of the AEF as popular rumor spread that the Americans had the best leftovers.

It was about this time that the U.S. State Department sent General Graves and Ambassador Morris to Omsk on a fact-finding mission. The Division of Russian Affairs along with the State Department under DeWitt Clinton Poole encouraged the U.S. president to recognize Kolchak's regime. The State Department also advised Graves to provide Kolchak with any available supplies, munitions, and food for Omsk. Graves, on the other hand, thought that the people of Omsk hated Supreme Ruler Kolchak and his Stavka staff with good reason.[14]

Graves came to believe that the Allied intervention had been a fiasco from the beginning.[15] Bernard Baruch of the War Trade Board and Edward Hurley of the United States Shipping Board could use only well-established Red Cross channels to ensure arrival of materials at the front.[16] Worse still, constant famine and epidemics overwhelmed the Siberian countryside. Graves informed Allied Command that the American troops left in Siberia would be pulling back to Vladivostok.

General Janin found the Legion both efficient and professional in fulfilling security needs along the railway. Conversely, Kolchak no longer trusted the Czechs or the Slovaks. He demanded that the Legion return to the front to fight alongside his Siberian troops.

More than a year after Legion troops had been denied evacuation from the port at Vladivostok, Czechoslovak ships waited to take them home. By the end of May, a small contingent of legionnaires had been allowed to board the *Sheridan*. Alongside the Sheridan, the *Great Northern, Mobile, Rotterdam, Santa Clara*, and *Saxonia* took on supplies.

On May 29, 1919, as Kolchak's forces stormed Orenburg, American troops began to evacuate through Vladivostok following behind the *Sheridan*.[17] The *Archer* was one of only a few American ships packed full of road-weary Czechs and Slovaks. The *Archer* carried more than 1,900 legionnaires and nine Red Cross workers. It docked in Yokohama and Kobe while en route to San Francisco. Most of the American vessels carrying legionnaires headed for Pacific ports along the continental U.S. and Canadian coast. There troops would receive needed rest and health examinations before moving over land to the Atlantic coast. Unlike some of the American ships, the *Heffron* transported legionnaires across the Indian Ocean and up the Red Sea to Trieste, 300 miles south of Prague.[18]

Colonel Constant Cordier, Adjutant General of the United States, readied ships like the *Nanking* and the *Sheridan* for more legionnaires. On May 27, 1919, at 9:00 A.M., C. S. Hamilton advised the adjutant general of the *Sheridan*'s arrival in San Francisco. Military attaché to the Legion, Colonel Vladimír S. Hruban, stood by to translate. Legionnaires would be quartered at San Francisco's Presidio for medical attention. After recuperating, they would board Rio Grande Railroad cars on May 29, 1919, to travel through Salt Lake City, Denver, Chicago, and Pittsburgh until arriving at their destination in New York City.

As the *Sheridan* detachment moved through one large depot after another, the Czech and Slovak soldiers found themselves greeted by throngs of Americans. Many of the people who came to meet them were from Czech-American or Slovak-American communities, but still others had been reading about their progress through press accounts in local newspapers. The recovering legionnaires accepted gifts of donuts, oranges, coffee, and hugs. And while their host, the United States Army, worried over the trip's antiquated train cars, the Czechs and Slovaks considered the accommodations luxurious compared to the teplushkas they had just left behind in Siberia. The men of the *Sheridan* left Chicago at 8:30 on the evening of June 6. By lunchtime of the following day, they arrived in New York City.

In San Francisco, Omaha, Chicago, and Pittsburgh, the soldiers of the *Sheridan* had been given a tour organized by the Czecho-Slovak Alliance. At each of these layovers, dignitaries addressed the legionnaires to thank them individually for their bravery in Siberia. The Czechs and Slovaks could hardly believe the generosity and appreciation bestowed upon them throughout the United States. They had no idea that Carl Ackerman's accounts in the *New York Times* or Herman Bernstein's accounts in the *New York Herald* had made them all so famous.

One month after the *Sheridan* docked in San Francisco, the city of San Diego welcomed another unit of legionnaires. Allen Henry Wright stood dockside with many other Californians waving as the *Nanking*, a large vessel 443 feet long and 10,000 tons, pulled into port. Wright recorded the arrival of the *Nanking* through photographs and a written description:

> The steamer approached the pier, the soldiers on deck lined up against the rail and peering from portholes. An Army band played in blue jackets, Czech [and Slovak] national tunes. The men stood at attention, though men were crippled, leaning on crutches, canes or holding onto one another for support.

They sang the Bohemian national hymn, "Kde domov můj?" ("Where is My Home?"), the entire ship from stern to bow.[19]

Coincidentally, it was the Fourth of July, American Independence Day, an appropriate time for one democratic nation to welcome the crusaders of another. San Diego harbor flew the Czechoslovak red, white, and blue tricolors along with Old Glory. Miniature Czechoslovak flags adorned lapels and dresses, others flew overhead dockside, and hung from buildings adjacent to the harbor, anywhere visible to legionnaires aboard the *Nanking*.[20] As the *Nanking*, formerly the *Congress*, dropped anchor, the municipal fire whistle blasted.

The *Nanking* crew and passengers rejoiced at this seemingly surreal end to their 7,000-mile journey from Vladivostok. To the hearty cheers of "*Nazdar*" ("Welcome"), men aged 20 years to 70 made their way down the gangplank carrying their worldly possessions. One man even tucked a small puppy over his arm before leaving the ship. Allen Henry Wright took a picture of the mutt balancing on the exhausted-looking soldier's coat sleeve.[21]

C. J. Novotný, Josef Votava, Anton Pánek, Anton Jedlich, Major Wilde, and Senator Wright waved excitedly at the troops from amidst the crowd of San Diego and Los Angeles citizens gathered around. Many in the waiting crowd represented Czech-American and Slovak-American and other associations including the Czecho-Slovak Alliance, the Red Cross, and the War Camp Community Service.[22]

Signs around the port proclaimed "*Blaničtí Rytíři*" a seventeenth-century Bohemian rallying cry.[23] The captain of the *Nanking*, T. H. Dobson, his first officer B. K. Moreland and surgeon A. E. Dilley leaned against the railing watching the soldiers hobble off their vessel. Alongside them, diplomats and engineers from France and Canada, who had also sailed from Vladivostok on board the *Nanking*, waved from the deck.[24]

People enthusiastically enveloped the legionnaires while American Red Cross women presented food, pamphlets, and cigarettes. Major Vladimír Jirsa, the officer in charge, stepped forward and gestured to his men. The entire group of soldiers broke into song: "*Hej, Slováci*" ("Hail Slovakia"). Both the soldiers and the crowd surrounding them were deeply moved as tears wetted the cheeks of many. Afterward, the men again looked to Major Jirsa, who explained: "We could not express our feelings and tell you of our appreciation, so we sang it instead."[25]

The seriously wounded were then loaded into cars and sent ahead to Santa Fe Depot while those who were healthy enough marched behind their colleagues. Later, an informal reception was held for the legionnaires in the San Diego City Hall rotunda.[26] Afterward, trains arrived at Camp Kearny, where the *Nanking's* entire contingent went through medical examinations.

Troops showered and dressed in the first new clothes most had worn since leaving their homeland many years before. Overwhelmed by the care shown to his men, Major Jirsa tried to thank all of the attending staff members at Camp Kearny for their kindness.

Guests began to arrive at Camp Kearny in the late afternoon for a banquet given in the Legion's honor. Arrangements had even been made for Professor Josef H. Chopek, a visiting pianist from the Prague Conservatory, and his wife, a noted violinist, to play several well-known Czech and Slovak pieces for the men. As the soldiers rested after their meal, fireworks broke through the sky. Throughout the evening, the crowd listened by means of an interpreter to the Legion's stories from the Eastern Front, Russia and Siberia. Czechs and Slovaks explained how men fell on grenades rather than become prisoners of the Bolsheviks — so harsh would be their treatment at the hands of the Red Guard.[27] Though far from Siberia, everyone knew that the ordeal continued for tens of thousands of comrades.

At 10:10 A.M. on July 11, the first of the *Nanking* troops boarded trains at Camp Kearny. Their final destination in the United States would be Washington, D.C., and a historic meeting with the American president. Woodrow Wilson had requested the honor of meeting them.

Colonel Cordier was relieved when he received news that the first contingent from the *Nanking* had passed through New Orleans, Alabama, Georgia, and Virginia without incident. On the afternoon of July 11, a second train filled with more than 500 men left Camp Kearny under the leadership of

Bolshevik casualties on the Ussuri Front, not dated.

Colonel Guy I. Rowe of the 32nd U.S. Infantry. Rowe reported that he had been embarrassed by the dilapidated train compartments and was surprised when legionnaires thanked him profusely for their wonderful accommodations. They traveled aboard an ordinary train with one standard Pullman, 12 tourist cars, and three baggage cars — one used as a kitchen and another as a hospital car to house 12 sick and wounded men.[28] Unlike the first unit, this second train was delayed for repairs when cars broke down during the journey. The second group arrived in Washington, D.C., on July 16 at 9:00 A.M.

With half of the *Nanking* troops safe in Washington, D.C., Colonel Cordier turned his attention to the remaining men still waiting in San Diego. These last groups experienced difficulties on their journey across America. On July 28 at 12:05 P.M., the third contingent of more than 400 legionnaires departed San Diego with American and Legion officers under the command of Major Albert S. J. Tucker.[29] While pulling out of the St. Louis Depot, a Legion officer reported to Major Tucker that two strangers had been distributing pamphlets and harassing his men. Communist propaganda leaflets were discovered which greatly concerned Czech and Slovak soldiers, who begged Major Tucker to ensure this would not hinder their evacuation. Tucker forwarded the propaganda to the Army base in Norfolk with a report as the train proceeded east.

In Amarillo, Texas, Tucker halted his group to make accommodations for a Private Vleck of the Eighth Company who appeared to be suffering from appendicitis. Leaving Vleck in the care of Mrs. Nadden, an Amarillo Red Cross nurse, the train proceeded on its way to Norfolk, Virginia. The fourth and final unit would collect Private Vleck on its own way through Texas. This fourth train traveled with 11 coaches, one standard Pullman, one baggage car, and one kitchen car. It departed from Camp Kearny with the last of the legionnaires who had been on the *Nanking*. Four hundred and three Czech and Slovak officers had waited until the very end in order for their men to precede them. As the last of the *Nanking* legionnaires left San Diego station at 4:00 P.M. on July 28, they did so to tearful farewells. Eleven Red Cross nurses and doctors who had cared for them enthusiastically called out the few Czech or Slovak words they had learned from their patients.[30] This fourth contingent moved up the railroad line only a short distance before stopping to retrieve Private Frank Šimků of the Third Company, who had been hospitalized in San Bernardino, California, with malaria. From San Bernardino it traveled toward Texas where Private Fred Vleck awaited in Amarillo.

When a private by the name of František Polka was discovered wandering along the railroad tracks outside of Kyana, Indiana, arrangements had to be made to retrieve him as well. Private František Polka later described what had occurred on his earlier train trip to Norfolk: "At 2:00 A.M. I became sick on an earlier train trip, leaned from the train window to vomit, and the train lurched and I fell out."[31]

Private Polka of the Fourth Company had been treated at Camp Zachary's hospital in Louisville, Kentucky, for a crushed arm and finger, injuries sustained in the fall. Shortly after the last train retrieved him, the conductor discovered that Private Josef Kocourek had leapt from the hospital car. Private Kocourek suffered from battle fatigue and shell shock; he knew little of his present circumstances and even less of the English language. Kocourek must have been out in the countryside wandering lost and alone. After an exhaustive search, however, the fourth train was forced to proceed on to Washington, D.C. Asheville police promised to continue the manhunt for Kocourek. They searched for weeks but to no avail. Private Kocourek vanished into the American landscape never to be heard of again.[32]

Awaiting the passage of Legion trains, Americans stood in small groups along the roadbed if only to wave and yell "Nazdar." Where the legionnaires stopped, Americans gathered to gawk at the legendary Czech and Slovak fighters. Once the fourth and last contingent was on its way to meet with the president, Captain Malinka of Military Intelligence reviewed Major Tucker's Bolshevik propaganda pamphlets and passed them on to Edwin S. Ross, port intelligence officer, who reported that the materials were unsophisticated and of no real concern. Everyone agreed that the Legion troops had never been interested in the propaganda materials and were instead focused "on one thing — home!"[33]

As the Czechs and Slovaks gathered in Washington, D.C., a House subcommittee opened another inquiry into the evacuation of the Legion. Representative Woods of Indiana asked why these 4,000 Central Europeans traveled comfortably through the American countryside while 3,000 Americans waited in Vladivostok for vessels home. Secretary of War Baker explained that, for the most part, the Legion paid its own way and that "we have empty transports coming eastward."[34]

On the same day he appeared before this subcommittee, Baker also reviewed the *Nanking* legionnaires at the White House. The Czech and Slovak soldiers assembled in the rain as a Marine band dressed in crimson and white played from the White House portico. It was a drab, gray afternoon, but one that the waiting crowd would not easily forget. After battling through triumph and despair, these men deserved a big tribute. To meet with the United States president would only be a small expression of American support, but a symbol of friendship that would surely be a tribute to each of the men.

The legionnaires marched in formation through the West Gate of the White House and around the East Gate where they finally stopped at attention in front of the main porte cochere. Here President Wilson stood at attention surrounded by other officials of the United States, along with representatives of a Czecho-Slovak delegation. General March and Admiral Benson flanked the president, next to Secretaries Baker and Daniels.

> It was not only a most unique, but also one of the most touching ceremonies that have taken place at the White House during visits by foreign veterans. Previously, the President had reviewed the famous Blue Devils of France, the sprightly Italian *Bersaglieri*, who passed in the bright sunshine with flying colors, but today, there was something in the faces of the men who passed in review that made all who saw them, from the highest official down to the man in the crowd, feel that these men had gone through more tortures than those of war.
>
> Much of the tragedy of their experiences was written in the countenance of every man in the contingent, and yet they had a pride of bearing and a spirit of newly gained freedom that won them the admiration of the spectators.[35]

President Wilson walked forward to speak to the soldiers while at his side, Major Vladimír Jirsa, Legion company commander, joined Colonel Hruban, American military attaché, to help translate President Wilson's words for the men.

> Future generations will happily record the influence for good which you were privileged to exercise upon a large part of the population of the world, and will accord you the place which you have so courageously won. There is perhaps nowhere recorded a more brilliant record than the withdrawal of your forces in opposition to the armies of Germany and Austria, through a population at first hostile, or the march of your armies of thousands of miles across the great stretches of Siberia, all the while keeping in mind the necessity for order and organization.[36]

With these words, the Czechs and Slovaks gave three resounding cheers. The American president descended from his podium and, one by one, shook their hands.[37]

Few gathered that day realized that this American president had actually helped his friend, Thomas Masaryk, write the Czechoslovak national constitution. Few Americans knew how much this meeting meant to Woodrow Wilson as he continued to work for the establishment of the League of Nations. Few gathered together on this afternoon could have guessed how mistaken President Wilson's aspirations for these men would be.

The columns of Czechs and Slovaks turning in the rain and marching out of the White House gardens that day passed out of the pages of history and into oblivion. They were not remembered, their existence was swiftly forgotten in the minds of the American public. The world attention which once followed the Legion's 5,000 mile-plus progress with awe quickly became preoccupied by other events. Newspaper articles detailing the Legion's successes and remarkable persistence did not become legend. Instead it's story became filed away to yellow with age in archival collections across the world.

The Czechs and Slovaks who had arrived on the *Nanking* and who had traveled through the United States soon departed on board the *USS. Aeolus.* They arrived in Brest, France, on August 9, 1919, with 1,917 people on board, including seven females.

A vacuum developed within the Siberian army after Gajda resigned. Kolchak announced that General Dieterichs, formerly the Legion commander, had agreed to take over Gajda's vacancy. Dieterichs quickly discovered what Gajda already knew — promises of aid came easily to the supreme ruler, but action did not. General Dieterichs could not fight a war without guns or food; Kolchak's Western Front would soon be decimated.[38] By mid–July, Zlatoust fell to the Red Army; the following day, Ekaterinburg was overrun as well. Kolchak's hostility toward the Legion now boiled over as he blamed the Czechs and Slovaks for troop reverses at the front.

While General Dieterichs strategized without support from Omsk, the supreme ruler made plans to turn the counterrevolution into a holy war. Kolchak organized detachments called the Holy Cross and Yellow Banner to rally superstitious peasants against the leadership in Moscow. The Holy Cross and Yellow Banner, comprised of believers and priests, marched into battle with only banners and crosses to shield them. Attrition quickly drained the movement of its life's blood. What had started out as a hopeful front against Bolshevism had quickly turned into pandemonium and retribution.

Chapter Twelve

Foreign diplomats began pulling out of Omsk by August 1919. As the British made their exit under the Legion's protection, they did so knowing they were forsaking the men who had been their excuse for intervening in Siberia in the first place. In their wake, the British also abandoned the supreme ruler they had handpicked. Once the consulates emptied in Omsk, Red Army units threatened Kolchak's epicenter of government. By order of the United States Army, the Fifth and Sixth Czech and Slovak regiments dutifully moved into Omsk to protect traffic into and out of town.

As summer turned to autumn, Kolchak's circumstances soured dramatically. Of all the counterrevolutionary fronts, only Tomburg remained free of Red Army harassment. The fronts established earlier in the year were now barely surviving. Kolchak needed assistance, and the Czechs and Slovaks appeared to be the only rear guard in place to help.

General Deniken in southern Russia proclaimed his Cossack units victorious and the south Bolshevik-free. Though the *Copenhagen Dispatch* agreed with this assessment, Allied reconnaissance later countered Deniken's claims. So severe were the numbers of desertions within the White Army that officers ordered hospital wards to be searched in order to enlist soldiers with cases of typhus and famine. If a soldier could walk he could fight. As a result, disease spread unchecked throughout the ranks even as health facilities, staff, and medical supplies evaporated.[1]

The Russian civil war had drained Russian and Siberian resources, one of the most valuable of which was the Trans-Siberian Railway. Sabotage and neglect of the entire system threatened the only means of escape for refugees and soldiers alike. By autumn, personnel crucial to correct problems and keep the railroads working had given up to head east themselves. All along the Trans-Siberian line, people threaded their way through decaying boxcars, machinery, garbage, and bodies.[2]

Early in the Allied intervention, the Japanese Army had been assigned authority over all locomotives in the Pacific coastal theatre. It would oversee the cleaning and repair of each before returning them to the interior. Instead, locomotives began to disappear from the system. Upon investigation by Japan's own allies, missing engines were located in Vladivostok, being held under Japanese "care."[3] The Legion believed this was just another ploy to cause further chaos throughout Siberia in order to strengthen the Japanese incursion into the interior.

Recruitment posters depicting Bolshevik abuses stared out at refugees from depot walls, frightening and bewildering them. Depots became converted into rest stops, hospitals, or flop houses for the thousands of homeless refugees who headed to the Pacific coast ahead of the Red Guard. Bits of paper covered station walls, windows, and doorways, flapping in the icy wind as relatives and friends tried to inform one another of a destination, a meeting place, a safe house. These notes were seldom signed for fear local authorities might later use surnames to harass. No one could be trusted anymore, not even with an individual's name.

Fortunate travelers slept 12 to a room while others made do with whatever food, supplies, and rest they could find outdoors.[4] In the end, only the wolves grew fat.[5] Like Vladivostok and the other large urban centers of Siberia, Omsk quickly turned into a city of refugees. Kolchak generously opened all businesses and homes to them. Because there was no organized refugee effort on the part of the Omsk government, Ataman Semenov used the glut of human misery and the lack of locomotives to blackmail Czech and Slovak units.[6]

The Buriate people witnessed the entire saga from the hills surrounding the city. The world they knew was dying. Buriate herdsmen built shrines and sometimes invited legionnaires to pray with them. William Duncan remembered seeing them "guarding the shrine that kept bad spirits away; poles with rags attached. The wind blew these and the evil spirits would be afraid to come near."[7]

Throughout October, as temperatures began to drop, the streets of Omsk emptied completely except for Legion and White Army patrols.[8] Even though the Japanese hoarded locomotives under their control, teplushkas had to be used to move large numbers of refugees eastward. Packed boxcars transported families 500 miles to the east to temporary safety in Novo-Sibirsk. With so many thousands packed together, epidemics such as typhus and spotted fever began to run rampant. Omsk suffered so completely that the Legion referred to it as the "City of Death." The nickname stuck since it was so appropriate.

Along the steppe, dead winter grass and solitary tree stumps stood sentinel to stacks of corpses lining the track. With precious little time left for the living, the dead would remain unburied until spring. As the first snow of winter threatened, death tolls spiked into the tens of thousands from new waves of disease. Families abandoned those too weak to move. Travelers stripped the dead of boots, clothing, and supplies in order to keep dry, unaware

Kirgis befriend the Sixth Regiment, Petropavlovsk, not dated.

that typhus lice, hidden in the warm dark, continued breeding in furs and animal skins. From one city to the next, the dead shared their bedding and clothes with the dying and passed on contamination.[9] Since clean drinking water had become rare, bathing ceased altogether.

Defeated troops returning to Omsk merged into crowds of push carts crossing the Irtysh River. Pushing over the narrow bridge, everyone hurried the pace, realizing that once the Irtysh River froze solid the Red Guard would use it as a highway into the dying city. Legion units left behind to protect the rear noticed that silence had descended upon the Tartar and Buriate settlements nearby. Roadways no longer bustled with caravan traders and the familiar play of Buriate children had disappeared altogether. Yet Buriate camels and pack horses idled along city streets. When the legionnaires investigated, they discovered that disease had decimated nearby indigenous villages.

Indecisive, moody, and sleep deprived, Kolchak sat alone in his quarters in Omsk, while his Stavka ran the army and national policy. The supreme ruler, trapped in the throes of drug addiction, grew ever more haggard and unresponsive with each passing day. Only a year before while traveling through Japan on his way back to Siberia, the famous Russian admiral had been fed healthy doses of morphine by Japanese doctors. Kolchak had been unaware but by the time he had met Radola Gajda on that first train ride from Vladivostok to Omsk, the supreme ruler had already been transformed into a drug addict. Before his own evacuation of Omsk, French general Maurice Janin visited Kolchak one last time. Afterwards Janin submitted a detailed report to his superiors. Kolchak "was in a strange neurotic state. The allegations that he [Kolchak] has a cocaine addiction are probably true."[10]

Under General Janin's orders of November 6, 1919, the Legion's Sixth

Regiment prepared to leave Omsk for Vladivostok and home. Bolshevik activity had been sighted only 40 miles outside the city. Observing the Legion packing, the remaining citizens of Omsk panicked. Buildings fell silent, but remained open for scavengers and refugees following behind.

General Dieterichs, trying desperately to fill Gajda's shoes, realized that he faced far too many problems both in Omsk and at the front. Dieterichs called upon the supreme ruler. He would inform Kolchak that Omsk could survive only a few days more. The Red Army was less than 100 miles away.[11]

General Sakharov of Kolchak's Stavka command disagreed with Dieterichs' assessment and claimed that he could save Omsk. Dieterichs argued that Sakharov's strategy would prove too dangerous and ultimately fail in the end anyway. The citizens should evacuate immediately as the Legion was doing. Kolchak called General Dieterichs a coward and replaced him with General Sakharov. With little else to do, Dieterichs headed east. Hearing this news, General Janin wondered if General Sakharov could be the only White Russian left in all of Siberia who didn't know that utter defeat was imminent.

In a daze, Kolchak turned to the one leader still willing to fight: Ataman Semenov. In the current atmosphere of suspicion and betrayal, the two leaders found that they now had more to bind them together than keep them apart.[12] At the very least, they shared a common enemy.

Ataman Semenov ambushed supply trains, firing upon American Marines in an effort to extort money and weapons. On one occasion, the United States Army threatened to attack Chita in order to convince Japan of the severity of the situation. Marines had been captured and held hostage by Semenov. Only after the Japanese High Command interceded were the marines released and American troop trains allowed to proceed.[13] This and similar incidents convinced the United States that Masaryk's earlier warnings had proved correct: plans to intervene in Russian and Siberian affairs had been a disaster. The time had come to bring all the U.S. troops home.

At age 26, Grigori Semenov became a symbol to the United States Army of the untenable position it now held in Siberia. Frontoviks in Semenov's marauding bands added their expertise of explosives to terrorize the countryside at the very time that the Red Army rampaged eastward behind the evacuating Legion. Unstable and often shell-shocked, these ex-tsarist soldiers gathered together to test their capacity for violence.[14]

Over the months, stories coming from Semenov's camps grew ever more outrageous. On one occasion, Semenov was said to have traveled to Mukden, Japan, for a rest and to visit friends at the British Consulate. The Ataman's reputation preceded him. In Japan he held a kind of celebrity. Posing in his usual Napoleonic stance, with his hand inside his jacket and a lock of hair across his brow, Semenov amused his hosts by telling stories and quoting

Napoleon, his hero. Mimicking the French emperor gained Semenov instant recognition with the European socialites who saw him as a caricature.[15]

It was rumored that on an earlier trip, the "Ogre of Chita"[16] wined and dined with Mukden's upper crust while his troops back in Chita harassed and murdered untold numbers of innocents. One evening during Semenov's visit to Mukden, he became thrust into the center of a scandal. Although far from refined or handsome, he had earned himself a reputation with the ladies. Semenov had often been seen around Mukden in the company of a beautiful blond woman later identified as his wife. A British witness reported, "When the Ataman was leaving his hotel for the railway station, a woman said to be a notorious gypsy woman with whom the Ataman had for some time past been living in intimate relations, and who appears to have been discarded by him on his arrival in the Far East for his own wife, suddenly ran forward and addressing reproaches to him, swallowed some poison and immediately collapsed. She was removed to the Japanese hospital for treatment and appears to have survived."[17]

Masha Sharban, Semenov's mistress, would live through her self–induced poisoning to further her influence over the ataman. Their relationship hardly surprised anyone, but Semenov's devotion to her seemed out of character. Masha distanced herself and Semenov from his troops and his allies with her Semitic jokes and bawdy Yiddish songs. In return, Semenov's lavish presents to her caused fits amongst his own troops who were notoriously anti–Semitic.

The slaughtering of Jews, as demonstrated by the 1919 pogrom in Ekaterinburg in which 2,000 were murdered, was a common phenomenon in both Siberia and Russia. But the "Ogre of Chita" never attacked Jewish communities. Sharban, a dark-haired Jewish beauty and the widow of a rich Russian merchant, reportedly prevented him from victimizing her own people. As a result, Ataman Semenov forbade his men from attacking Jewish settlements. Untold numbers of Jews in and around Chita unknowingly owed their lives to Masha Sharban.

Too late, Kolchak realized that Gajda's original assessment of the conditions of the common folk in the villages and the White Army at the front had been accurate. The only way to win popular support was through land reform and democratization. Promises could no longer hold the war effort together. Gajda had left and Kolchak's reputation remained unsalvageable without him. Daily the supreme ruler's troops, newly outfitted in British uniforms, slipped across enemy lines to join the Red Army.

Action Franchise of Paris and the *Morning Post* of London both considered Allied demands on Kolchak to begin democratization efforts to be counterproductive. Whether this proved true or not, complete Allied recognition had been withheld until the supreme ruler conducted his promised elections.

Other Western newspapers echoed these sentiments. Kolchak ignored the requests. Instead, he surrounded his staff with the accoutrements of a tsar, separating the classes instead of uniting them.

When the Red Army penetrated into Mongol territory to capture enemy troops, Lenin announced to the West that local government officials had invited his army to proceed across the border. During this advance into Mongolia, the Red Army captured General Ungern Von Sternberg, one of Semenov's old cronies. The Mongolians, too few and too intimidated, never resisted Russian incursion.[18] The trampling of Mongolian sovereignty demonstrated Lenin's ferocity and served to warn Russia's neighbors. With a Red Army offensive planned for the new year, 1920, Kolchak's forces retreated from the front and by mid–autumn the Red Army had moved eastward with remarkable speed.

As all its plotting unraveled, Great Britain joined the United States in swallowing its pride by admitting the intervention had been a fiasco. Both countries began discussions to plan a final evacuation of the Legion. Secretary Lansing proposed the transfer of 10,000 troops per month beginning February 1, 1920. Lansing also ordered the last American troops to remain in Siberia until "the free passage of the Czechs [and Slovaks] to Vladivostok is assured."[19]

In the interim, American families began to welcome their expeditionary forces home. On November 8, 1919, the people of Pittsburgh celebrated the return of their own young men from the Western Front. At the end of several speeches, young children passed through the crowd asking for donations to help support men who returned home maimed or wounded. Newspapers filled with similar celebrations while columns running adjacent to the homecoming news depicted unimaginable horrors occurring throughout Siberia.[20]

On November 10, 1919, General Janin moved into crude quarters in Novo-Nikolaevsk. He had already been advised of General Dieterichs' departure and of the appointment of his successor, General Sakharov. Dieterichs' replacement had reportedly become "very pleased with himself, smiling and full of self–confidence" as he accepted the command of the Siberian army.[21] In answer to being handed over to yet another new commander, thousands more White Army troops deserted across the Manchurian border. When advised of the rising numbers of desertions, Kolchak reportedly remarked that it was a "mere temporary thing."[22]

Despite the supreme ruler's confidence, General Janin hurried to evacuate not only the rest of the Allied troops still in Vladivostok, but all Slavic soldiers acting as rear guard who continued to protect Siberia's train systems in the interior. Even prisoners of war, free for over a year, awaited repatriation to Austria, Germany, Hungary and Turkey. Instead, they had been forced to remain behind, helping the selfless Red Cross and YMCA stay one step ahead of the Red Army.

White Army troops in retreat described the brutal torture of the captured. Some 12,000 Bulgarians, Czechs, Poles, Rumanians, and Slovaks covered the retreat of Kolchak's White forces. If caught all knew what the Red Army held in store for them. It had been rumored that the most creative tortures would be reserved for the Legion.

The White movement that had once threatened to bring down both Lenin and Trotsky now suffered attrition due to the elements, illness, and desertion. The entire White Army, divided into four sections of between 40,000 to 70,000 soldiers, had fallen into a full-scale retreat.[23] If only to survive the elements, some White Army regulars who lagged behind volunteered to join the Bolsheviks.

Traveling on horseback became the only hope for thousands of refugees racing toward Vladivostok. Abandoned animals wandered city streets in wide-eyed terror, charging into buildings or idling in roadways. Horses from retreating armies were especially numerous. Fodder and hay had been reserved for starving people so when a rescued horse became lame, which happened often after walking on the endless ice, it became supper. Household dogs reverted to a feral state. All across Siberia they could be seen roaming back alleys in packs or huddling near the train tracks where they fought over bits of food. Starving, they became dangerous to both men and horses. Attacks on both by packs of dogs became quite common.

General Janin learned that Polish legionnaires considered turning their 4,000-horse cavalry west across European Russia and to head for home. The Poles had become convinced that the Red Army would allow them to pass through just to be rid of them. Janin warned Polish officers that such a journey would prove suicidal. The Soviet militia would surely kill them all if they traveled nearby. The Eighth Division of the White Army under General Kappels volunteered to protect rear areas to allow the legionnaires to pull out. Armed with this information, Janin persuaded Polish officers to travel alongside the Czech and Slovak Legion heading east toward the coast.

By the second week of November, Kolchak, still resentful of the Czechs and Slovaks, asked Allied commanders for protection. White forces had begun fleeing over the frozen Irtysh River and the supreme ruler intended to follow suit. Allied Command conceded to his request.

Kolchak handed over command of the Siberian army to General Sakharov.[24] Sakharov's immediate plans to attack the Red Army began with overestimating his troop numbers. Aware of their fate, masses of deserting soldiers fled down the railroad — a railroad still being guarded by Czech and Slovak units. Panic erupted up and down the Trans-Siberian line when troops thought to be holding back the Red Army were seen instead joining the horde of refugees heading toward Vladivostok. Siberian civil order ceased to exist.

By November 15, Omsk fell under siege. Left to prove himself to a city in crisis, General Sakharov would be found wanting.[25] For hours, the Red Army battered the city from the opposite bank of the Irtysh River. Sakharov's men fought valiantly but the shelling proved too debilitating. No matter how often Sakharov contacted the Allies, neither the British nor the Americans responded with reinforcements.[26] They had already set sail for home.

Kolchak's Stavka held seven trains in reserve with the entire Russian treasury on board.[27] Realizing this, the Red Guard announced that it would never permit Russia's gold reserve to leave the region.[28] A humbled Kolchak now requested that the Czechs and Slovaks escort him to safety. Though furious, General Janin reluctantly agreed to the supreme ruler's request. The legionnaires found themselves in charge of a leader they despised and a gold hoard they believed belonged to the Russian people. Newspapers reported that "the Russian treasury was transported in 29 freight cars. The train commandant and officials of the State Bank occupied a passenger coach in its middle connected with the others by telephone and having escorts at either end."[29]

Kolchak's entourage left Omsk with artillery fire exploding in the distance. Over 200 refugee trains had to be detoured for the supreme ruler and the Russian treasury to pass by.[30] Kolchak's entourage continued to Tartarska, Kastul, and Chuym, while refugees watched from sidings in their doomed boxcars. Nearly all of these travelers would be captured by the Red Army in a matter of hours.

Omsk, the "City of Death," fell to the Soviets in less than two days. Numerous wooden structures in Omsk caught fire like matchsticks. In less than a day over half of the city had burned to the ground.[31] General Sakharov's futile efforts had cost more than 40,000 men.

By the end of November, Kolchak's army of over 800,000 had shrunk to fewer than 20,000 soldiers. Only fuel from Suchan continued to keep Kolchak's trains moving. Desperate and nearly hysterical, Kolchak appointed Ataman Semenov as commander of Siberian forces east of Lake Baikal.[32]

Consul General Harris and 25 American Red Cross representatives visited Kolchak's train to inform him that he was speeding toward a city filling with revolutionary fervor. Workers and peasants who had marched through the streets chanting slogans were now rioting. Except for Kolchak's rear guard, only the Legion remained east of Achinsk. The Czech and Slovak Sixth Regiment and the Polish Legion stood between the Red Army and Kolchak's trains; if they faltered, the supreme ruler would face immediate capture.

On December 9 Minister Pepelayev demanded Kolchak dismiss the incompetent General Sakharov from his post of commander in chief. General Vojcechovsky was asked to take over the post but refused. Unwisely, General

Kappels, a heroic officer of great dedication to Russia, accepted the title of Commander and Chief of Staff of the Siberian forces.[33]

With such insane levels of danger, even the YMCA secretaries evacuated their posts in the interior. YMCA superiors advised Americans to remain in their boxcars and out of any direct line of fire, and to accompany Czech and Slovak troops in their evacuation. One secretary, reportedly bored and curious, stepped outside to see what the commotion around his train was all about.

> He and a Czech guard watched two Social Revolutionists run out of the station, during a lull in the firing, with a stretcher to pick up one of the many wounded lying about. The soldiers started for the entrance with a poor wretch when there was a particularly loud boom from cannon across the river and without further adieu they dropped the helpless man and ran for shelter ... and then the Czech guard who had been watching, suddenly dropped — dead from a stray bullet."[34]

The fall of Omsk spotlighted not only Kolchak's failings, but also the misguided Allied intervention. Stories from the city during and after its evacuation recapped the horror. The Red militia found ten White Army generals and more than 100 officers in Omsk. Ransacking homes and businesses, the Soviets also located huge numbers of black market goods hidden in the warehouse district. Kolchak's Stavka had been selling stacks of stockpiled materials for personal profit throughout the entire reorganization period of the Omsk government.[35] Thousands of uniforms, boots, and thick wool coats sorely missed at the front had been in storage all along and now came under Red Army control.

A shortage of coal and engines deepened along the Irkutsk section of railway. Polish soldiers vocally opposed Kolchak's squandering of coal reserves necessary for the safety of others. The Poles also turned on the Legion, blaming them for their own situation.[36] Kolchak eagerly joined in with criticism against the Czechs and Slovaks; he complained "Czechs [and Slovaks] are stopping all trains in Siberia with the exception of those under Czech detachment escorts. Today my locomotive was seized and the chief officer of my escort arrested."[37]

Kerensky, former president of Russia's Provisional Government, visited the Russian Embassy in Washington, D.C., where he heard of Kolchak's comments. Kerensky became indignant, pointing the finger at Kolchak and the Allies for the implosion of Siberia. He told the American press that only the Legion had acted above reproach throughout the entire intervention period. The Legion, Kerensky reminded readers, had become scapegoats for the Allies, who should have been ashamed of the role they had played in abandoning the Czechs and Slovaks to the will of Kolchak's failed government. Kerensky added that he believed that the Legion remained true to its original mission, something posterity could not say for either the counterrevolution or the Allies. The Allies immediately countered Kerensky's fury in the press.

As if to prove these editorials wrong, Bolshevik success across Siberia swamped the media. Kolchak's army disintegrated. White Russians fled across the Mongolian and Chinese borderlands or joined the Red Army. With no army to buffer it, the entire Siberian nation seemed to be on the move heading toward the Pacific coast. In one convulsive attempt to secure safety, a river of people traveled alongside the train tracks next to speeding trains crammed full of those lucky enough to find standing room on board or hold on to the sides of boxcars. The counterrevolution did not receive any new support from these refugees. An enormous number of those fleeing were running away from war and brutality, not toward a White Russian dream of past glories.

For weeks rumors circulated that Vladivostok's harbor teemed with Allied ships waiting to transport refugees to safety. As trains passed through depots, people surged forward, crushing children into open doorways and knocking each other under the wheels. Even as the Soviets battled in the area of Irkutsk, people prayed to board trains heading to Vladivostok.[38] Trains heading eastward were already overcrowded with fleeing soldiers and many of these would never find their way to the coast. Along one lone stretch of railway that connected Taiga to Krasnoyarsk, boxcars and locomotives had been discovered frozen shut, their wheels stuck firm to the tracks. After prying the doors open, soldiers discovered that the travelers sealed inside had piled against the doorways trying to escape. Instead of transporting refugees to safety, these trains became frozen tombs.

The Sixth Regiment and the last of the Red Cross received reports that up the line, hospital trains sat on sidings, also deserted by Siberian engineers. Locked inside these boxcars, sick and wounded troops had also been allowed to freeze to death.[39] The British and French reported that the soldiers' bodies they discovered had been mauled by animals.[40] Though familiar with death, British and French troops stood by in shock as bodies of civilians and soldiers were once again bundled together alongside the railroad bed for future disposal.[41] One British officer later wrote, "Officers and men who passed through the worst horrors of [the war in] France were not left unaffected by these sights, yet the [Siberian] crowd did not appear to be affected by anything but curiosity.... The only coffin I saw was in the Polish church at Novo-Niko-laevsk, and the only shrouds I saw were those wrapped around dead children."[42] These "wood piles," as the Siberians referred to them, ran nearly the entire length of the Trans-Siberian Railway.[43]

In the United States, America's role in the Siberian tragedy began to come to light. The public was not pleased with what it learned. The *New York Times* reported that not only had the Czechs and Slovaks been sacrificed to expeditionary zeal, but the Allied troops sent to protect democracy and end violence in Siberia had actually made matters worse. The *New York Times* warned the Wilson administration that it would forever share guilt for atrocities committed under Kolchak's regime since Wilson had been loosely allied with the supreme ruler. In order to shrug off some of this blame, the United States Congress distanced itself from anything having to do with Russia or Siberia.

In the closing days of 1919, Thomas Masaryk had traveled to the Russian Far East to order that all legionnaires be sent home.[44] Dr. Václav Girsa and Bohdan Pavlů, original members of the first Družina and the Czech-Slovak National Council, met with President Masaryk in Vladivostok to facilitate these evacuations. Both Girsa and Pavlů had deserted the trenches on the Eastern Front to join the Russian army. They witnessed the Legion's first journey across Siberia during the summer of 1918. They had been on hand for the Perm and Chelyabinsk uprisings and the triumph of the Czechs and Slovaks uniting the entire Trans-Siberian line through the Baikal Mountains. They had felt the betrayal of the Allies when the Legion was ordered to return to the interior in order to establish a doomed second front. Girsa and Pavlů had shared the hopes for Kolchak's Siberian front and commiserated on a personal level over the perversion of this esteemed Russian explorer and war hero. Now on the eve of their own evacuation, Girsa and Pavlů reflected on their unintentional participation in abuses against the Siberian populace.

While preparing to leave for Prague, Girsa and Pavlů composed a letter to Woodrow Wilson, president of the United States. In clear and simple terms they explained that as representatives of the Legion in Siberia, they believed that the Allied nations had willfully misled the Czech and Slovak troops. Girsa and Pavlů argued that the Legion had been used as a shield for a war criminal and his corrupt Stavka staff which was at this very moment absconding with the Russian treasury. Composed in warranted frustration, the letter read,

> In protecting the Railroad and maintaining order in the country, our army is forced to act contrary to its convictions.... Under the protection of the Czecho-Slovak bayonets, the local military authorities commit acts which stupefy the entire civilized world.
> The burning of villages, the murder of peaceable Russian inhabitants by the hundreds, the shooting without trial of democratic men under suspicion only of political disloyalty, are everyday facts, and the responsibility for them before the court of the world falls on us, because, having an armed force, we have not prevented these injustices.
> This passivity is the direct result of our neutrality and an intervention in Russian internal affairs, and it is thanks to this that in maintaining it with an absolute loyalty we become, in spite of ourselves, accomplices to the crime.[45]

The letter from Girsa and Pavlů found a resting place at the bottom of a file marked Military Intelligence, its contents too embarrassing to be released to either the U.S. public or its allies. After Girsa and Pavlů left Siberia, newspapers diverted their attention from the intervention and coverage of the Legion faded away.

Evacuation of the Legion began in earnest over two years after it had originally been promised. Nonetheless, the Fifth and Sixth Legion regiments remained stranded on the western side of Lake Baikal to guard the Russian treasury and its former supreme ruler. As soon as Omsk had fallen, communication lines went dead — neighboring communities ghostly still.[46] Reports from the interior simply ended.

Ataman Grigori Semenov, at last a recognized military leader, understood too late that he had lost his sole military ally. He contacted General Syrový, vainly begging the Legion to stay to help fight partisans gathering near Chita, and to keep the Trans-Siberian line running still longer. Syrový refused. Kolchak's seven trains took only five days to travel the 500 miles from Omsk to Novo-Sibirsk, but to the west, the Red Army steadfastly gained ground while continuing to overwhelm thousands of refugees along the way.

Legion officials waiting in Vladivostok wondered how the Fifth and Sixth regiments could outpace the Soviets before evacuation ships would be forced to depart. For thousands of legionnaires, relief would prove too little too late. Again the *New York Times* reported:

> Their participation in the Russian civil war was accidental; they had no personal interest in Siberia, and they wanted to go back to their own country, where they were badly needed. Their government wanted them to come home and was willing to repay the Allied governments for the expense of bringing them back; but we would not let them go because they were essential to the Allied position in Siberia. America would not send troops; England, France, and Italy could not. So the Czechs were made to stay.[47]

Legion General Syrový and French General Janin bitterly orchestrated the supreme ruler's withdrawal. The Fifth Regiment, garrisoned along with the Poles at Novo-Sibirsk, provided a shield for the Sixth Regiment to pull back behind them. The Sixth Regiment then waited east of Novo-Sibirsk in Mariinsk and Achinsk where partisan bands threatened to attack the railway line. Here the Sixth Regiment covered the retreat of the Fifth Regiment and the Polish troops pulling behind. Utilizing this leapfrog strategy, legionnaires evacuated while maintaining control of their immediate surroundings. Territory west of the line fell under Soviet control almost immediately after the Fifth and Sixth regiments moved through.

By the time Kolchak reached Novo-Sibirsk, several Stavka ministers had deserted their posts. General Gajda's resignation had been the first in a series of losses for Kolchak.[48] Once leaving Omsk, Gajda continued to receive reports concerning Kolchak's situation. General Dieterichs' own experience only served to validate Gajda's initial belief that the Stavka would bring down Kolchak's government. Neither General Dieterichs nor Gajda found solace in knowing his assessments had been proven correct. Both men were disgusted to learn that the infamous General Sakharov had exchanged his Siberian uniform for a British uniform and fled to safety across the Chinese border.[49]

Gajda had arrived in Vladivostok to news of an Omsk engulfed in flames and a retreating supreme ruler lost deep in drug addiction who was just now evacuating eastward ahead of certain death. Saddened by these developments, Gajda settled his train at the edge of Vladivostok Harbor where his broněviky the Orlík (Falcon) flew the green and white colors of Siberia.

Immediately after his arrival, White Army officers began to call on him for guidance. General Rozanov, a sadistic ex-tsarist officer whom General Gajda had often denounced, was now stationed in Vladivostok in charge of the White Army barracks. Rozanov's mistreatment of his own men had become so volatile that even the Allied Command censured him on several occasions.[50] White Russian officers told Gajda of brutality and murder taking place in Rozanov's barracks. Gajda empathized but remained aloof, seldom leaving his train. After losing everything by involving himself in Russian disputes, Gajda was now a general without an army and a man without a country. Despite all he had fought for, Czech and Slovak officials had also distanced themselves from him. To many of the White officers approaching him for help, Gajda appeared hardened and unemotional.

General Gajda's popularity with these White officers had not gone unnoticed and his presence in Vladivostok caused concern for both Rozanov and the Japanese. General Rozanov had become well known, especially in Japanese circles where his favor had been curried. They hoped to remove Gajda as quickly as possible, evacuating him on the earliest possible ship. With Gajda out of the way, the Japanese wanted to collaborate with Rozanov.

In an unprecedented move, more than 160 of Rozanov's old guard took to the streets of the city in protest against his treatment of men in the barracks under his command. They were soon joined by another 1,500 laborers also holding grievances against Rozanov. Soon another 500 Russian officers left White Army barracks to protest their treatment at the hands of Rozanov's staff.[51]

Within 48 hours, street fighting erupted, focused in and around the east end of the city between the railroad depot and the port. During this anarchy, Allied officials hid behind locked gates waiting for more detailed information. Though they detested Rozanov, none cared to become entangled in the internal squabbles of the counterrevolutionaries. Only the Japanese Army reported in force and this to assist Rozanov.

Rumors circulated that upon hearing of Japanese interference, Gajda threw his considerable influence behind the other side. Hearing rifle fire from central Vladivostok, the Legion, garrisoned on an island in the harbor, gathered in force to help their censured colleague. They rushed to the island shoreline only to discover that boats normally stationed there had all disappeared into the night, effectively marooning the legionnaires.[52]

What was left of the entire garrison, intimidated by Rozanov, pushed Gajda and a small band of expert shots in retreat toward the Vladivostok railway station. Other White officers who fought alongside Gajda were able to flee to sanctuary in American headquarters. Against the mandate of his president's *Aide Memoire*, Graves accepted responsibility for safekeeping these deserters from General Rozanov's wrath. Rozanov's forces surrounded the American compound while Gajda and his band fled to the rear of the train depot, where they were picked off one by one by sniper fire.

In the early morning darkness, the streets surrounding the depot fell silent. Legion General Čeček and General Klecanda awoke to officers of General Rozanov's staff insisting they accompany them to White Army headquarters in Vladivostok. On the dock, all of the ferry boats had magically reappeared.

At White Army headquarters, Čeček and Klecanda were hustled past wounded troops and into Rozanov's offices. Without speaking, the furious Russian general had Čeček and Klecanda led down a series of narrow corridors to the rear of the barracks. In a small dark room, its door slightly ajar, the two Legion generals were presented with a man shackled to a chair, beaten black and blue, his face distended and swollen with welts and bruises, blood caked throughout his gouged scalp.

Čeček and Klecanda entered the room to have a closer look.[53] The Russian officer standing nearby pointed at his captive and announced, "You Czecho-Slovaks have done a great service to Russia. She thanks you and she pays you!"[54] In chains, Radola Gajda looked more like an animal than the leader of a city in revolt. Lifting his face, he smiled at his two old friends. Gajda was unchained and released before Rozanov had a change of heart. Under guard, Čeček and Klecanda drove through the city to deposit Gajda on board the British transport ship *Suffolk*. There Gajda remained under protective guard until the *Suffolk* sailed to safety in Western Europe.

As the Entente nations pulled their men out, Japanese leaders announced that Japan intended to not only remain behind but to send even more troops into Siberia. General Rozanov publicly thanked the Japanese for helping in the capture of Gajda and putting an end the Vladivostok revolt. Although Admiral Kawahara demurred to Rozanov's public statement, it was widely rumored that the Japanese had removed the Legion's ferry boats from the harbor, which effectively marooned them to their island barracks and prevented interference in the affair.

From on board the *Suffolk*, Gajda openly disputed Rozanov's proclamation that the revolt he led had been Communist-inspired. "Its supporters were of Russian democratic classes and its leaders [were] members of the Tsar's Duma, three figures of Kerensky's government and many young Russian officers."[55] As 1920 dawned, Gajda and tens of thousands of other legionnaires evacuated. Once they had gone, the entire city of Vladivostok became a closed security port — no traffic allowed in or out without Moscow's approval.

Many of the legionnaires were forever scarred by their experiences in this strange and beautiful land but perhaps none more so than Gajda. The brutality of war and the many friends lost to it changed him forever. Gajda would never distance himself from the reputation he had earned while in Siberia — a reputation both earned and ruined there.

Along with the burning of Omsk and the exodus of tens of thousands currently traveling toward Vladivostok, the story of Gajda's failed revolt became headlines in the Western press. The supreme ruler, once the Allies' hope for Russia and Siberia, became bogged down somewhere along the Trans-Siberian Railway while the Americans and their allies left their memories of this land behind them.[56]

Chapter Thirteen

Early in September 1919, Consul General Harris of the American Mission in Irkutsk had cabled authorities at home that the "Czechs have 7,000 Japanese rifles, but no ammunition."[1] Slovak-American associations across the United States had lobbied "to bolster the morale" of the legionnaires in Ekaterinburg and Chelyabinsk by moving more American troops to nearby positions, but the Americans were already leaving.[2] Consul General Harris had hoped to make it to Nikolaevsk to assess the deteriorating situation on the railroad but by the time his cables received any attention in Washington, D.C., Petropavlovsk, 200 miles west of Omsk, had already fallen under full Red Army control. A few weeks later, Harris' communications became more frantic in tone. By November he advised his superiors in Washington that he would be evacuating along with Japanese ambassador Kato, British general Alfred Knox, and French general Maurice Janin with the Legion situation still unresolved.

At the Czechoslovak National Assembly in Prague, relatives of legionnaires still guarding the Trans-Siberian Railway demonstrated for their immediate evacuation.[3] Once protected by the Legion, the railway line east of Ufa running through Ekaterinburg, Chelyabinsk, and Irkutsk had already become evacuated. This defensive move prompted Kolchak to publicly accuse the Czechs and Slovaks of harboring Bolshevik tendencies.

Dr. Girsa and Mr. Pavlů immediately admonished Kolchak that the Legion's rear guard, isolated and vulnerable, remained behind simply to protect him. Russian and Siberian railway personnel along the entire Trans-Siberian line had been leaving their posts for months. Presently only the Czechs and Slovaks assured that the final escape route to the Pacific coast remained open for the swelling tide of humanity clogging roads and trains heading eastward.

The Allied Command had promised to leave a force of more than 64,000 troops behind in Siberia if the supreme ruler and his *Stavka* staff could restore a viable Siberian front. Pavlů and Girsa admonished the Kolchak camp for remaining unresponsive to the offer. Instead, the Allies departed Siberia, leaving the beleaguered Legion behind to fight the advancing Red Army in order to give the supreme ruler time to make his escape.

By December 1919, American diplomats to the peace conference in Versailles announced that at least 72,000 Slavic troops still remained in Vladivostok waiting to be evacuated. Great Britain and the United States volunteered to share the evacuation of 36,000 troops each immediately.[4] As the last of the Red Cross arrived in Irkutsk from the interior of the Russian Far East, it reported that legionnaires had begun to fall behind on their escape eastward. "The Czech trains had broken down with their engines frozen up." Abandoning these trains, the Legion took to the rails on foot while tearing up track behind as they fled ahead of the Red Army.[5]

When Trotsky's units closed in, the Legion stopped and turned to meet its pursuers. The Czechs and Slovaks agreed to leave Siberia if the enemy would provide a neutral zone between each front of 67 miles (100 versts). Later, Allies and the White Army officers, safe and warm back in Vladivostok, would consider this offer treasonous.

By the new year, Japanese officials in Vladivostok once again complicated matters by confiscating over 8,000 boxcars. They announced that engines would be held "in reserve." The Legion's position along the Trans-Siberian Railway served as a buffer between mercenaries like Ataman Semenov, working for the Japanese and the Red Guard.[6] But once Legion officers realized that the Japanese had begun to slow their progress, they held onto rolling stock when possible in order to ensure that trains returned to the rear and not into Japanese hands.[7] Unfortunately, this brought the Legion into direct conflict with other groups also en route to Vladivostok who had been unaware of Japanese activity. Poles and Rumanians began to accuse the Czechs and Slovaks of hoarding locomotives to save themselves.

In the first days of January 1920, the remaining White Army fronts began to collapse in upon themselves, scattering retreating units across the frozen countryside. One British officer noted that the "position now is that all Russian echelons from the front eastward are at a standstill and consequently are being captured by Reds at a rate of 10 to 20 a day."[8]

Russian and Siberian families had witnessed just about every horror imaginable.[9] For many who escaped to begin life again in Western Europe or America, the last days of 1919 and the beginning of 1920 would remain frozen forever in their memory. Many families traveled along with retreating White Russian troops. Russian wives followed their men, remaining behind the lines to help feed and comfort them. As an American soldier observed:

> In this work an immensely important part was done by the women whose heavy lot it was to accompany their husbands.... In the Izhevsk division, for instance, there were about 250 women and children. Most of these families joined their husbands in the icy march.... They were of inestimable help, taking upon themselves the difficult labor of feeding the fighters and caring for

the sick and wounded. It would be difficult to estimate the number of men what owe their lives to their never tiring and careful hands.[10]

Parallel to the railroad tracks, refugees traveled two sleighs abreast. Often when artillery bombarded the line, these sleighs became heaps of twisted wood and metal that blocked the roadbed. Hardened by both civil war and unbelievable scenes of carnage along the route eastward, refugees trudged past victim after victim with little or no reaction.

Throughout January 1920, 40,000 legionnaires remained marooned in Irkutsk. Worse still, rumor had it that Polish and Serbian units trailed even farther behind. Later, it is believed, the Red Army's Fifth Rifle Division caught up with these stragglers and annihilated them. The Reds then turned their attention toward Rumanian units that fled in a panic from a similar fate.

Remnants of Kolchak's forces sat in Irkutsk under Legion protection. Americans who also remained behind in Vladivostok cabled up the line for everyone to hurry: "The problem was to get out and to get out fast."[11] Like a house of cards, the Russian Far East had begun to cave in on itself.

With huge numbers of refugees congregating in Vladivostok, the entire city began to resemble Omsk just before it collapsed. Omsk had doubled and then tripled in population. Vladivostok's population had already doubled and would soon triple. Along with the tens of thousands of refugees clogging the port city, disease and famine settled into the city as unwelcomed roomers. As each new transport ship left carrying ecstatic Allied troops home, masses of Russians, Siberians, and foreign troops crowded the docks begging for transit. The lucky ones who survived the trek found at the end of their journey to Vladivostok that no one waited to help them escape. Hope stopped at the docks as transport ship after transport ship disappeared over the horizon.

In the meantime, the Red Army rampaged eastward through the Siberian countryside, gobbling up villages and murdering thousands. Reports of wild bloodletting circulated throughout the land. Only a few Russians with extraordinary connections to the world outside were able to find a place on board Allied transport ships. Many in the tsarist upperclass had left months before. They headed directly to Japan carrying jewelry and valuables with them. Throughout the last months of 1919, the international press had reported that the best hotels in Tokyo were clogged with these unlikely refugees. Often ex-tsarists lived off contacts or family possessions, but funds were beginning to run out by 1920.[12]

Other families who fled eastward were part of the more than 20,000 Jewish refugees forced to leave European Russia during new cycles of pogroms. Once in Vladivostok, the luckier ones contacted a relative, perhaps even one living in the United States — anyone who could send them money to travel overseas. A few American military troops remained behind in order to guard sections of line near Suchan. This was allowed since they had kept earlier promises with partisans in the region to end atrocities. Because of this agreement and the neutrality of local American units, small amounts of fuel continued to supply the Trans-Siberian Railway. Even so, the supreme ruler's entourage had become stalled, slowing all the other transport trains following behind.

With severe shortages in fuel and vehicles, the Legion restricted access to its trains. The Allies finally announced that they would grant Czech and Slovak troops first priority over other units heading east. In chaos, people traveling alongside the Legion trains began to lose faith and fight for carts, carriages, horses, anything to help them continue moving. General Syrový, commander of the Legion, reported to his superior, General Janin, that many of the remaining locomotives in use on the Trans-Siberian had begun to seize up in January's freezing temperatures. Syrový worried that travelers could easily become a mob and overwhelm his units still protecting the supreme ruler's entourage. General Syrový had already intercepted reports that White Army deserters joining striking miners in the Suchan mining region had begun to attack troop trains and evacuating families.

All of these issues only served to further demoralize the Legion, whose responsibility it was to safeguard the railway system. Worse still, Kolchak was rumored to be "half mad with anger, and drinking heavily."[13] Major Husák had been stationed at Nizhne-Udiinsk to oversee the supreme ruler with a Legion storm battalion comprised of 1,300 men. The supreme ruler reportedly waited in his boxcar — a total recluse with only Anna Timirev at his side. Husák advised Timirev that more than 30,000 miners on the Trans-Siberian Railway up ahead called for Aleksandr Kolchak's head.[14]

Generals Janin and Syrový had been telegraphing Paris for instructions concerning the supreme leader's position. No answer had been forthcoming. As far as Syrový and Husák knew, Kolchak and his Legion guard were completely isolated and on their own. Kolchak voiced concerns that the Red Army, moving swiftly up the line, would overtake his position. Husák sent a further series of telegrams back and forth to Syrový and Janin, aware that Kolchak's concerns could easily prove true. "Was it possible to evacuate Kolchak by horseback through the woods and across the Mongolian border?" The forests surrounding the Trans-Siberian line were crawling with partisans and frontoviks, both heavily armed and interested in capturing the supreme ruler and his gold reserve. In addition, Husák was informed that winter snowdrifts would surely slow travel or, at worst, kill the horses. Kolchak would be safest where he sat in his cars on board the railway line until the situation with the Czeremchova miners up ahead in Suchan could be resolved.[15]

Kolchak argued at length with Husák, finally accusing him of holding

Timirev and himself hostage. General Zankievitch, a former Russian supporter of the Legion, interceded on Major Husák's behalf, settling Kolchak's fears long enough to allow Husák to telegraph the Allies again for assistance. These telegrams also went unanswered.

In secret, Kolchak then began to contact Ataman Semenov. Semenov never liked Kolchak but the supreme ruler now traveled with the Russian treasury — a prize too large for any ataman to ignore. Semenov agreed to do whatever Kolchak ordered. Together they came up with a plan, one that made no tactical sense even to Semenov. In the interest of gaining millions, the ataman agreed with anything Kolchak suggested. The tunnels of Lake Baikal would once again be the target for demolition. One huge blast of dynamite could seal Husák's Czechs and Slovaks on the wrong side of the Baikal Mountain Range. It mattered little to the deranged supreme ruler that he would suffer the same fate and surely be captured by the approaching Red Army.

For the second time, Legion telegraph operators intercepted crucial communiqués that threatened the entire area — this time between Kolchak and Semenov. Under Legion orders Kolchak's trains inched along toward Irkutsk while General Syrový made arrangements to seize all river steamers. Under Semenov's orders, General Nicolio Bogomolete fired on American troops stationed near the city depot in Verchne-Udiinsk. Kolchak waited inside his boxcar for word from Ataman Semenov, unaware that Syrový had launched a sneak attack against General Skipitrov, who headed Cossacks working under Semenov in the field. During Syrový's engagement, more than 1,300 of Semenov's men were captured along with his infamous broněviky, the Destroyer.[16]

The supreme ruler's plan had not only failed but now his relationship with Semenov became common knowledge amongst what was left of loyal White Army units. Soon afterward, members of Kolchak's entourage began to drift away. In no time only 60 out of an original 600 officers had not left Kolchak.[17] The Czechs and Slovaks under orders to guard the supreme ruler were now his only hope. They had slowed their own evacuation to protect a man who was willing to kill them all, and for what? Hardened toward the supreme ruler's fate, though he had once been a heroic figure to them all, Legion rear guardsman resolved to abandon him if he was found conniving against them again.

The Legion moved trains quickly from one siding to the next, maneuvering through congestion, but any consistent advancement had become all but impossible. Czech and Slovak soldiers, unhappy with their cargo, also resented the Russian treasury that slowed down their pace. Though no great fans of the old Romanov regime, legionnaires agreed that the gold they protected belonged to the Russian people. The Legion wanted to make sure no one, not the Japanese, not even Kolchak, removed it from Siberia.[18]

Lieutenant Colonel Číla, commander of the Tenth Regiment, ordered an accounting of the gold bars.[19] Each gold brick weighed more than 32 pounds, and the entire treasury in the Legion's care had been rumored to be worth more than 651 million rubles. It consisted of gold, silver, platinum and paper currency. Legion troops, living on the treasury train, had been assigned to travel with it and never to leave it out of their sight. General Janin's orders to Syrový concerning the treasury had been the same as those concerning Kolchak's protection. Janin wanted the Legion to do its best and to know that he would be there to back them.

By the time the Czeremchova miners' strike had been settled, Kolchak's entourage had sat in Nizhne-Udiinsk for such a long time that Irkutsk began to resemble Omsk before it fell into Bolshevik hands. On January 4, 1920, Kolchak sent word to Allied Command that he had changed his mind and now wanted to turn the Russian treasury over to their care. His change of heart proved too little too late. The Allied consulates in Irkutsk had already closed their doors and moved on.

While entering Irkutsk, Kolchak learned that the former Irkutsk Government, once friendly toward the supreme ruler, had fled, following American and French delegations to the Pacific coast. On January 7, 1920, Irkutsk became a city under the leadership of the Political Center. Kolchak would have to rely upon its discretion. The Political Center united in one final goal — to end White and Red fanaticism rampant in the country. The new government of Irkutsk, made up of Kerensky followers, nonparty people and workers from *zemstvos* (municipal labor unions), had all been persecuted by Kolchak's Omsk regime at one time or another.

On January 11, 1920, more disturbing news filtered in to the Fifth and Sixth Legion rear guard. Along with many of Kolchak's White Army generals, 13 boxes of gold from the Russian treasury had been discovered missing. Worse still, Nikolsk-Ussuriesk had fallen to the Reds, leaving Soviet militia free to attack Irkutsk next.[20] News that the Poles holding part of this rear guard had been captured did not concern the supreme ruler but greatly distressed the Legion.

Bedraggled White Army units led by General Kappels, an army of more than 10,000 men, were said to be struggling toward Irkutsk, holding off the Red Guard as they retreated. With food and horses scarce, these soldiers marched through the forests. By January 14, only this last group under Kappels and the Czechs and Slovaks protected Kolchak from capture. Irkutsk remained under Japanese control as Kolchak's train, protected by the Legion, stopped to rest in the depot. Japanese troops moved into position to surround it. Legion Command had heard rumors that the Japanese planned to sell Kolchak to the approaching Red Guard in order to confiscate the Russian treasury.

Unsure what the other would do next, Legion and Japanese troops faced one another across their gun barrels.

Kolchak contacted Ataman Semenov one last time to ask for help. Once again Semenov and Kolchak devised a scheme to ensure the supreme ruler's safe passage. Thirty-one leaders of the Political Center were taken hostage in Irkutsk. Known as the *Angara* hostages, these kidnapped leaders were taken during the night and placed on board the icebreaker *Angara*. Semenov ordered the vessel to sail out to the middle of Lake Baikal where his crew would wait for further instructions.

Dismayed, the Allied Command demanded the release of all 31 hostages and warned Kolchak that this time he had gone too far. The supreme ruler promised that the hostages would be released after he had left Siberia a free man. In effect, Kolchak tied his fate to that of the *Angara* hostages. Beyond Irkutsk, the Soviets waited to see how the situation would play itself out.

At first, nothing was heard from the kidnapped leaders. Kolchak continued to assure that each would be kept safe even though he really had no idea where they had been taken. Originally, the supreme ruler's men guarded them. Unknown to Kolchak, however, Semenov had already replaced the supreme ruler's guards with his own. When Semenov's men took over, the supreme ruler's fate was sealed.

> Among them were two former members of the Constituent Assembly, Pavel Milhailov and Boris Markov, who had taken part in the anti–Bolshevik movement in Siberia since 1918. The sentry posted by Kolchak's officers over these people was originally drawn from his own troops. But Lieutenant Skipailov, one of the most sadistic of the officers who later followed Baron Von Ungern-Sternberg into Mongolia, arranged to have a sentry from Semenov's forces substituted for the original. With the ground thus cleared, Skipailov ordered the hostages, 30 men and one woman, placed aboard the ice-breaker *Angara* on the morning of January 6, 1920, and taken out onto Lake Baikal. Here they were severely beaten over the head with a heavy wooden stick used for knocking the ice crust from boards and thrown into the lake.[21]

The hostages had already been murdered when Kolchak assured the Allies of their safety. When news of the gruesome murders finally broke, crowds gathered in Irkutsk demanding Kolchak's head. All around the city, troops loyal to the Political Center gathered to attack his entourage. Even General Dieterichs demanded that Kolchak be shot for this, his latest antic.[22]

From the west bank of the Angara River, Captain Krásná, commander of the Irkutsk Legion and his adjutant, Lieutenant Gustav Bečvář, crossed town to military headquarters. They had been telegraphing superiors for instructions concerning Kolchak all week. Dr. Blahoš, in contact with General Janin up the line, begged the Allies to release the Czechs and Slovaks from their current duty. The Legion wanted nothing more to do with Kolchak or the gold reserves. Telegrams flowed back and forth in a flurry as street fighting erupted in Irkutsk.

> Here we are in the midst of enemies; the Japanese, moreover, are an uncertain quantity and Semenov is a menace. The Czechs and others are exposed over 2,000 kilometers to the assaults of the Reds, who have forced the Poles to capitulate. The rear guard fights under difficult conditions; there is a deficiency of locomotives and of coal. They [the White Russians] have been massacring to their heart's content around Lake Baikal, and have flung 31 hostages into the water, while hordes of Semenov continue to loot and murder.[23]

From January 17 to the 21, Semenov stationed his men in the town of Trotiskosavsk near Irkutsk. While he was waiting for orders from Kolchak, his men entertained themselves by massacring innocents. On January 17, a firing squad shot a group of Trotiskosavsk citizens. The next day, more prisoners were hung in the town square. By the third day, Semenov decided to poison others. On the fourth day, he burned many at the stake. The brutality continued until no citizens of Trotiskosavsk remained.[24] Meanwhile, all around Semenov territory fell to the Red Guard.

As the Trotiskosavsk incident proceeded, General Kappels and his floundering White Army troops served as a buffer between the Bolsheviks and the supreme commander in Irkutsk. On January 20, Kappels entered what was left of Nizhne-Udiinsk, set on fire by the enemy. Kappels, suffering from frostbite in both legs, remained determined to lead his men to safety. Of the many White officers once typical in the old tsarist army corps, General Kappels had a stellar record. He had been considered by some to be the best Russian officer ever fielded. He had always been dearly loved by his troops as was General Vojcechovsky, whose regiment remained in the vicinity of Kappel's.

In Nizhne-Udiinsk, Major Husák waited with a garrison of Czech and Slovak troops for orders from Allied Command to intervene in the *Angara* hostage incident. The only Allies in the immediate area were the Japanese, and they acted solely for their own aggrandizement.[25] Reports of locomotives that had run out of coal clogging tunnel entrances forced the Legion to move into a heightened state of alert. The Allies had handled the entire affair so poorly that Legion Command complained bitterly of betrayal. Though Kolchak's train flew the colors of France, Britain, Japan, and Canada, only the Czechs and Slovaks remained nearby to guarantee him. All others were safe on ships heading for home.

The 39 tunnels became clogged with locomotives as mobs took to the streets in Irkutsk, demanding Kolchak be arrested. For the supreme ruler and the Fifth and Sixth Czech and Slovak regiments, time had run out.[26] Kappels' unit, reportedly moving toward Irkutsk, remained too far away to help. Semenov launched an attack on areas surrounding the 39 tunnels, but Legion intelligence reported that the Ataman and his men were clearly interested in the Russian treasury, not in saving the supreme ruler.

The Political Center Party of Irkutsk demanded that the Legion's Fifth and Sixth regiments release Kolchak and the gold into their care before Semenov or the Red Army attacked. The Political Center announced that it would allow the Legion to proceed to Vladivostok but not Kolchak. Legionnaires had also been informed that Lenin recently banned all forms of corporal punishment. Kolchak might be imprisoned but would not physically be harmed in the care of the Irkutsk government. The Czechs and Slovaks, believing that the supreme ruler should be tried for his criminal activities, had never been interested in his execution. Legionnaires believed the Political Center Party in control of Irkutsk to be more reasonable and moderate than many political factions ruling towns and cities throughout Siberia. The Political Center Party had also been known to be anti–Bolshevik, so Kolchak would be safe in their hands.

General Janin and General Syrový discussed alternatives and finally telegraphed Paris for further instructions. Janin waited but no answer arrived from Allied Command. The Japanese, knowing full well what the Legion had to do, offered to take care of Kolchak and the gold. Legion Command refused. The Czechs and Slovaks saw no difference between the Japanese and Semenov. After all, Semenov was in the pay of the Japanese.

In Irkutsk, Legion officers Krásná and Bečvář waited for orders from French general Janin, not knowing that Janin awaited instructions from Paris. Paris had obviously decided not to reply. Mob violence increased in Irkutsk until finally, well after nightfall, Janin and Syrový telegraphed an answer to Krasna and Bečvář from headquarters in Verchne-Udiinsk.

> "It was nearly midnight," Bečvář wrote later, "Miserably, I tramped through the darkness, challenged several times by the guards." Kolchak was quartered in a corridor carriage.... "I will announce you to the Admiral," said the adjutant.... Bečvář said the Czechs [and Slovaks] had received orders to hand him over to the Russians at dawn.[27]

Kolchak and Bečvář discussed assurances made by the government in Irkutsk, the Allies, and even Moscow. Even though the Legion hated what Kolchak's regime had stood for, Bečvář found himself deeply upset over his orders. The supreme ruler, strangely in control and at peace for the first time in weeks, politely asked Bečvář to once again contact General Syrový. Bečvář found Kolchak agreeable and respectful despite his current circumstances. This time the supreme ruler wanted to communicate directly with Syrový. Gustav Bečvář agreed to do what he could.

Kolchak now stood apart from the others in his entourage. Once again in control, he seemed more the Russian war hero who had earned world respect than a madman addicted to morphine. Bečvář returned to headquarters to send yet another telegram to Syrový and Janin. Time slipped by and still no reply came.[28] Finally, Bečvář returned to the supreme ruler's car. Kolchak's staff asked for news but Bečvář lowered his eyes and shook his head sideways. Kolchak and General Zankievitch stood by. Gustav Bečvář, once the college student who was to be executed by his Hungarian officer on the Eastern Front just before deserting, thought about the momentous situation that had led him to this place.

> "It is too late," Bečvář spoke slowly, the words sticking in his throat.... "I think I should tell you, sir, that there are rumors in the station that the Japanese may interfere and take you into their train before dawn...."
> [Kolchak replied,] "You are not misleading me? If there is no hope at all, there is something I could do, you know, rather than let myself be handed over to the Bolsheviks."
> Bečvář could only repeat his words. Kolchak considered, then thanked him formally, shook hands, and said goodbye.[29]

Kolchak no longer looked the hero who had arrived in Siberia months before. He was emaciated and drawn, but memories of this last meeting left Bečvář in awe. Bečvář gained new respect for the man and understood why he had once been one of Russia's most impressive war heroes.

Miners from the countryside entered Irkutsk and joined in the street violence. All through the night, Bečvář hoped that the Japanese might do something kind. Instead, at dawn, soldiers from a Legion guard, dressed in their best uniforms, marched into the Irkutsk station. Admiral Kolchak, Prime Minister Pepelayev, and Madame Timirev were dressed and waiting.[30] At the other end of the tracks the treasury was turned over to six Political Center delegates.

Kolchak and others warned Anna Timirev to stay in her compartment but she refused. Bečvář saw the supreme ruler, Minister Pepelayev, and Madame Timirev emerge from their train. On the far bank of the Angara River a car and a truck waited with engines idling, exhaust billowing above the snow. Bečvář remembered that it was a cold dreary morning. Fifteen minutes after driving away from the train depot, Kolchak and his two companions had been deposited at a long rectangular building in the northeast end of Irkutsk.[31] The supreme ruler was housed in the infirmary of the Irkutsk jail with Timirev and Pepelayev in cells next to his room. The doors to their quarters were never locked, allowing the three to see each other at will. Furnishings, though sparse, were clean and comfortable. All efforts had been made to guard Kolchak in a suitable atmosphere for one of Russia's once-great war heroes.

Premier Millerand of France telegraphed General Janin, demanding an immediate explanation. With a groundswell of Allied disapproval arriving in Paris from the Entente Powers, Millerand ordered Kolchak's release.[32] The Political Center Party of Irkutsk refused. The French blamed General Janin for Kolchak's situation. Notification of the supreme ruler's arrest spread quickly. Back in the Irkutsk depot, Bečvář and Krásná smuggled General Zankievitch, who feared reprisals, out of the city.

General Janin's explanations and descriptions of continued attempts to get clarification hour after hour from his superiors in Paris did little to help his cause. Even though they had desperately tried for clarification, Syrový and Janin became responsible for Kolchak's arrest. Both would be accused of incompetence.

The Stevens Mission notified General Graves of President Wilson's orders for all Americans left in Siberia to evacuate immediately. However, promises made to the remaining Rumanians, Czechs and Slovaks, and what was left of the Polish Legion, had to be kept. Director of American Army Transport Services, General Frank L. Hines, took charge of evacuating the Central Europeans. Hines feverishly worked to get each echelon into position at Vladivostok Harbor. The 9,000 Americans still in Siberia had orders to leave by the end of February. Still, Hines announced that the Legion evacuation remained his top priority.[33] The British promised to send two extra transport vessels to help in the Hines effort. The efficient and yet panicked tone of these communiqués carried with them an undercurrent of American and British guilt for leaving the Legion so long in the interior. The end had finally come for both the Siberian government and for the intervention and everyone involved knew it.

General Kappels' officers, nearing Irkutsk, reported that their leader was near death from frostbite that continued to climb up through his body. General Kappels allowed a Legion doctor to examine him but then refused further help from the Czechs and Slovaks. Kappels had been advised to enter a hospital immediately but remained behind. He led his army toward the Baikal region with the Soviets in pursuit. On January 27, 1920, General Kappels died, leaving General Vojcechovsky, the former Legion commander, in charge of the last White Army unit west of Irkutsk. The Fifth and Sixth Legion regiments, feeling both wronged and frustrated, took control of Kappels' body and transferred it to Chita for a hero's burial with full military honors.

Irkutsk resembled Omsk before it fell to the Bolsheviks. When Vojcechovsky's army approached the outskirts of the city, communications ended between Verchne-Udiinsk and Vladivostok. Nightmare images once again crowded the streets. One British officer reported piles of naked, frozen and gnawed bodies of men, women, and children being stacked at every station.

The Legion once again became blamed by refugees and the Japanese for engines disappearing from trains. Rumors spread that the Czechs and Slovaks left the sick and dying to perish around Irkutsk. The people of Irkutsk, however, regarded the legionnaires as acting responsibly. They saw the supreme ruler's arrest in a totally different light. Supreme Ruler Kolchak had been responsible for kidnapping and murdering their leaders, and the people of Irkutsk demanded justice.

By the end of January 1920, Kolchak's situation had worsened.[34] Red army units following Vojcechovsky's army surrounded the entire Baikal region. Almost overnight, the Political Center of Irkutsk stepped down and evacuated toward Verchne-Udiinsk, hurrying ahead of the last legionnaires guarding the railroad line.[35] In its absence, the Soviet Military Revolutionary Party overwhelmed Irkutsk.

Under orders from Moscow, the new government of Irkutsk placed Kolchak under arrest and ordered an investigation to begin. Vice-Chairman Popov, a well-educated attorney, acted as interrogator for the state. Popov and Chairman Chudnovsky, both ardent Bolsheviks, questioned Kolchak's distant past as well as the Omsk regime. When it came to specific events, especially those regarding atrocities and the *Angara* hostage incident, both interrogators deferred to the capable Menshevik attorney, Aleksandr Nikolayevich Alekseevsky. After all of the effort the party had expended to catch Kolchak, the atmosphere surrounding his trial became peculiarly controlled. Observers noted, "They were surprised, and it seems faintly awed, by the trim figure who underwent dispassionately their brief, almost apologetic inspections…. The Supreme Commander dictator inspector they had expected [instead] reminded them all of the earlier days when he had been a world-reputed admiral and explorer of great renown and presence."[36]

Kolchak answered their questions, which often centered around his troops' brutality toward peasants in and around Omsk.[37] The supreme ruler appeared disturbed and surprised by descriptions of abuse as though he had not known of these incidents. The amount of pilfering in the Stavka ranks also obviously stunned him. Though he continued to apologize for his lack of specific knowledge, Kolchak answered all questions put before him.

Siberia disintegrated into mass chaos so acutely that people had little time to dwell on the investigation and trial ongoing in Irkutsk. On January 31, 1920, a revolt once again erupted in Vladivostok led by White officers against General Rozanov. This time it succeeded with a Bolshevik, Conrad Lazo, Czechs and Slovaks, and Siberian Social Revolutionaries uniting to force General Rozanov's removal.

Ataman Semenov, now posing as Admiral Kolchak's greatest supporter, challenged General Janin to a duel, while coining slogans such as "Have Janin's blood."[38] In a country with little else, slogans had become very popular. The Legion did its part to clarify reports, but the atamans and their sponsors, the Japanese, continued to confuse the press by spreading misinformation and self-serving propaganda. General Skipitrov, who had ordered the *Angara* hostages murdered in the first place, had been reportedly murdered himself— a report that turned out to be accurate. In addition, General Rozanov, the infamous commandant of Vladivostok's White Army headquarters, escaped aboard a Japanese vessel dressed as a woman. Unfortunately, this report turned out to be true.[39]

By the end of January, the *Tokyo Dispatch* reported to the world that Kolchak had escaped from Siberia and now resided happily in Manchuria. He had not. In Irkutsk, the supreme ruler's interrogation continued uninterrupted, growing more intense with each passing day. Meanwhile, Generals Janin and Syrový worked diligently to explain their orders regarding Kolchak, but criticism mounted against them anyway.[40] Contrary to popular understanding, General Janin repeated that he had tried on various occasions to get directives from his superiors in Paris. He never received any answers. Street fighting and the threat of Japanese units against the Legion's Fifth and Sixth regiments in Irkutsk hastened the decision to turn Kolchak over to the Political Center. "We handed over to the Political Center, Admiral Kolchak, who like every Russian citizen is subject to trial by court of law for his actions. Admiral Kolchak could not rely upon receiving sanctuary with the Czecho-Slovaks, against whom he committed a criminal offense giving his orders to Semenov to prevent by all possible means our movement to the east, and not even to stop at the destruction of bridges and tunnels."[41] To this General Syrový added his own statement: "In spite of difficulties and dangers threatening our evacuation, we actually protected Kolchak for longer than we could afford to."[42]

Though unfairly accused by their own Entente leadership, the legionnaires were not surprised by the hypocrisy shown to them or to their generals. No matter how often or to whom they tried to explain misconceptions concerning Kolchak's situation, the press accused Janin, Syrový and the Legion of failing in their duty. As Kolchak's interrogation went on, the Czech and Slovak rear guard continued to hurry through the Baikal Mountains, often on foot, protecting the track as they had promised while Allied Command blamed them for continued chaos in Siberia.

Vojcechovsky fled with his army in the only direction now open to them — toward Irkutsk. As his bedraggled White Army reached the outskirts of town, Revkom committee members became convinced that Vojcechovsky meant to free Kolchak and the Russian treasury. It seemed a repeat of the Ekaterinburg situation only months before, when Vojcechovsky hurried toward Ekaterinburg and hastened the death of Tsar Nicholas and his family.

On February 6, 1920, Kolchak entered the most sensitive phase of his trial. Alekseevsky asked about specific incidents while citing proof that each one had been the responsibility of the supreme ruler. For the first time Kolchak became upset. In dismay, he ended his testimony with this statement:

> The village of Stepnoi-Badzhei was burned down by the insurgents themselves. Taseevo was a fortified point which it was permissible to destroy in war. I must say that such cases were very infrequent on the large Western Front [the Ural front]. In that front there were also two or three cases of villages being burned down in fighting. I recently had a conversation with a member of the Revolutionary Committee. He asked me whether or not I knew about the atrocities perpetrated by the single units. I said that I did not know that such were the general rule but that I would admit it did happen in certain cases. Thereupon he said to me: "When I came to one village with the insurgents, I found several persons with ears and noses cut off by your troops." I replied, "I do not know definitely of any such troops. I admit that such a case was possible." He continued, "I reacted to it in such a way that I cut off the foot of one prisoner, tied it to him with a string and in such a shape let him go to your side, eye for eye, tooth for tooth...." To this I could only say to him, "Next time, possibly people, one seeing one of their own with a foot hacked off, will burn down a village and massacre its people.... This is usually done in war and in a struggle.[43]

Kolchak returned to his cell on the evening of February 6. At dawn on the following morning, February 7, 1920, Kolchak and his minister Pepelayev were awakened at dawn. They were told to dress warmly and led outside. Pepelayev began to panic but Kolchak stood erect as charges and punishments were read aloud by REVKOM members.[44] The two men were then marched away. It was still quite dark outside, but Anna Timirev, alone in her cell, could hear their boots crunching across the snow. The two men walked to a tributary of the Angara River nearby. A hole had been cut into the ice. Outside the city, General Vojcechovsky decided to turn his troops away from Irkutsk for fear of attack by local militia. Kolchak's last chance faded in the distance with them.

Pepelayev was pale and several times looked as though he might pass out. Kolchak refused a blindfold.[45] Trembling, Minister Pepelayev asked a guard to help tie his blindfold in place. Madame Timirev stood waiting next to her cell window. She knew what would happen next. And then she heard a volley of gunshots and after a moment another. It was all over. The two bodies were then dragged over the slope of ice down to the gaping hole. There, each man was pushed separately through the opening and under the surface of the icy river.

Later, Madame Timirev would be released to proceed to Vladivostok. Kolchak's long journey had finally come to an end. News of the executions spread quickly. The Legion once again took the brunt of accusations that followed. The Legion newspaper *Československý deník* tried in vain to answer all of these but no one really listened. They had already made up their minds.

> The Revolutionary Committee [REVKOM] was aware that the Soviet government [in Moscow] had issued a decree abolishing the death penalty.... We who protested against the murders at Omsk and the terror wielded by the Kolchak government protest today, unpopular though this may be. Moral principles and justice admit of no exceptions. He that violates one is responsible for further acts of violence. Blood cannot be washed away by blood.[46]

As remnants of the White Army retreated around Irkutsk, the last of the Czech and Slovak troops remaining behind began to negotiate for their own passage through to the Pacific coast.[47] By mid–March, the tsar's treasury and all of central Siberia fell to the Red Army.

Chapter Fourteen

Aleksandr Kolchak's government in Omsk, initially hailed by Allied leaders and the peasantry as the hope for a new Siberia, spurned the people it was meant to save. Kolchak's army officers, among some of the least courageous and most brutal military men of the era, had devastated any chance for popular support. During his trial, Kolchak said of his Omsk regime, "In the Army, decay; in the Staff, ignorance and incompetence; in the Government, moral rot, disagreement and intrigues of ambitious egotists; in the country, uprisings and anarchy; in public life, panic, self–seeking, bribes and all sorts of scoundrelisms."[1] By the time of his death, greedy subordinates and morphine addiction had reduced the supreme ruler to a tragic shell of the formerly revered leader. American ambassador Morris summed Kolchak up as "an honest and courageous man of limited experiences in public affairs, of narrow views and small administrative ability."[2] The demise of Kolchak and the Omsk government ushered in a reorganization of the Russian Far East. Immediately following his fall, the government in Vladivostok, relieved also of Generals Rozanov and Skipitrov, thanked the United States for its neutrality.

While Kolchak stood trial, one of Lenin's loyal men, Krasnoshchekov, sat in an Irkutsk jail wondering whether the Whites would hang or shoot him. Krasnoshchekov, though decidedly Bolshevik, yearned for a slow and peaceful conversion to Communism for Siberia. What concerned him and many others most was the Japanese. As fate would have it, the Red Army reached Irkutsk in time to rescue Krasnoshchekov, after which he received approval from Lenin to set up a separate national government in Siberia. The Far East Republic was born, not yet fully Communist but certainly anti–Japanese.[3]

In February 1920 the Red Army moved north against Allied forces in Archangelsk and Murmansk to end Allied intervention. After months of interfering in Siberian disputes in Archangelsk, an American lieutenant wrote: "Not a soldier knew, not even vaguely, why he had fought, or where he was going now, nor why his comrades were left behind beneath the wooden crosses."[4]

One month after Kolchak's execution, the Czech and Slovak Legion's Fifth and Sixth regiments reached the outskirts of Vladivostok. American Expeditionary Forces had already neared final stages in their own evacuation by then. Cables of commiseration continued to flow into Legion Command over the Kolchak debacle. Former premier Alexander Kerensky, visiting Prague two days before news broke of Kolchak's execution, reminded the world not to blame the Legion for Allied incompetence. Kerensky sought to gain the support of not only the Czechs and Slovaks, but also the Poles, Rumanians, and the people of other newly organized Central European states.[5] Kerensky, the failed leader of the Provisional Government under the Mensheviks, hoped to mobilize a new military effort against the Bolsheviks.

On several occasions the possibility of mutiny within the Czech and Slovak ranks ran high as the Allied Command received reports of soldiers openly sympathizing with Bolshevik forces in light of the hostility felt toward White Russian officers. To some extent this would have mirrored earlier mutinies within Latvian, Rumanian, Polish, and other ranks also disheartened by Allied promises and miserable treatment at the hands of corrupt White Russian officers.[6]

Eduard Beneš, speaking on behalf of the fledgling Czechoslovak nation, thanked Kerensky but stood behind Czechoslovakia's noninterference policy concerning Russia. Beneš added that the leadership of Prague and Bratislava wanted its troops to return to their homeland where they could help protect Czechoslovak borders so that the nation could finally live in peace.

Following the executions of Pepelayev and Kolchak, General Janin received orders to return home to Paris. In April 1920, General Dieterichs requested a last meeting with Janin in order to deposit a small wooden chest in Janin's care. Dieterichs and a companion, Mr. Guilliar, warned the French general that they were being followed and that he should keep the chest concealed and under diplomatic seal while crossing the Indian Ocean and on toward France.

When General Janin reached the port in Marseille, no official courier received him. Surprised, Janin traveled discreetly to his villa in Grenoble to hide the chest before moving on to Army headquarters in Paris. Janin assumed orders to head the French Military Mission in Prague would await him. Instead, this request was categorically denied; the general was informed in no uncertain terms that an inquiry into the entire Kolchak affair would soon begin in Paris.

Confused and humiliated, Janin convinced himself that the wooden chest and its contents would earn him the respect he so rightly deserved. After retrieving the box, Janin called upon the Russian Grand Duke living in Paris as a member of a large Russian expatriate population of White Russians. The wooden chest, still under diplomatic seal, had survived through summers and winters, overland and over sea. Finally, its mysterious contents had reached the rightful owner: Tsar Nicholas Romanov II's closest living relative.

Janin presented the chest to the grand duke and watched in excitement as he opened it. "Besides the dossier of documents and photographs, the wooden box contained 'about 30 fragments of bone, a little human fat which had dripped off logs on which the bodies were burned, some hair, and an amputated finger which expert knowledge [American military forensics] identified as one of the Empress's ring fingers, charred remains of jewelry, a small iron icon, scraps of clothing and a shoe, such small metal accessories as buttons, belts, bits of blood-stained carpet, revolver bullets, etc.'"[7] General Janin explained that there were no teeth found because the ruling household heads had been decapitated and removed by a German agent, a Mr. Apfelbaum, after their execution.

The speechless grand duke sat horrified before the open box. Finally able to speak, he demanded that the chest be removed from his sight and sent back to Russia immediately. Janin tried to explain that when these articles had been recovered in Ekaterinburg, an inquiry in Harbin identified them as belonging to the tsar and his family. The grand duke refused the chest and ended the meeting.

Bitterly, General Janin made arrangements for the chest to return to Russia. He could think of only one ex-tsarist officer still in command of units fighting against the Bolsheviks. General Wrangel, who was fighting in Crimea, was in the midst of a calamitous evacuation. Janin sent the chest to Wrangel's field command anyway.

Janin never received the recognition he thought due him. French Command laid blame for Kolchak's execution and the fall of Irkutsk solely on Janin's command. Though there would never be an official reprimand, Janin's military career slipped silently into oblivion along with his knowledge of the chest's whereabouts.

General Radola Gajda, on the other hand, arrived in Paris not only a free man but a famous one. A *Petit Parisian* newspaper correspondent met the young ex-legionnaire at the docks to interview him. Gajda, once a leader of thousands, recounted his frustrations, especially concerning Kolchak's personal history and military blunders. Gajda said that despite the Siberian people's need for land reform and a constituent assembly, Kolchak failed to provide either. Gajda went on to describe his inability to continue in the capacity of commander of the Siberian army when the White officers he represented behaved more cruelly than the Red Army he fought against.

Within a week of the publication of *Petit Parisian*'s interview with Gajda, Kolchak was executed. Gajda was stunned; despite all else, Kolchak had been a mentor and friend. Gajda remained in Paris where he entered the Military High School Staff College. His work at the academy excelled even as reports of his famous retreat began to surface in the press. "It has been said that the accomplishment of this withdrawal without disaster will be acclaimed by strategists of the future as one of the finest examples of military genius in history."[8] Ironically, in the end, Gajda had secured the military expertise that Kolchak had accused him of lacking.

Every White Army defeat meant that the Red Army grew ever stronger. After the fall of Omsk, the Soviets adapted to popular thinking and took advantage of the supreme ruler's failed legacy. For a short period, local partisans won the hearts of the peasants. Once White Russian elements had been eliminated, the Red Guard began to brutalize the Siberian population.[9]

On February 12, 1920, the *San Francisco Chronicle* reported that local shipping had been diverted from Vladivostok Harbor to Shanghai. American sources announced that Vladivostok would fall to the Bolsheviks at any moment.

On April 1, 1920, General Graves departed from Vladivostok to the Japanese styling of "Hard Times Come Again No More." With the last transport ship pulling away from Vladivostok Harbor, all vestiges of order in the city ended. For the tens of thousands left behind, the suffering had only just begun. Much like Omsk and Irkutsk before, Vladivostok spun into the throes of complete chaos. Thousands of refugees filled its broad avenues, sleeping in alleyways and begging one another for food. Like so many before them, most would succumb to epidemics that ravaged the countryside. From November 1919 to April 1920, over 60,000 men, women, and children died from typhus in Novonikolaevsk alone.[10]

Throughout 1919 and into 1920, as Siberia fell to the Red Army, Austrian, German, and Hungarian ex-POWs had been filtering into International Huts run by the YMCA. Many were without food or warm clothing. The YMCA fed them and gave them shelter while arranging for their evacuation. By April 1920 German transports working with the German War Prisoners Department began to evacuate these POWs home. The *Mount Vernon* repatriated more than 4,000 legionnaires in addition to more than 700 POWs from Germany and Hungary who had formerly been employed by the American army. Fifteen hundred prisoners of war awaited the *Scharnhorst*. It arrived so late that the waiting soldiers had been forced out into the elements and nearly froze to death until the International Hut opened nearby to assist them. Thousands had already been evacuated but many others would be left behind to face the Red Army.

American troops and charities left via Vladivostok on April 24, 1920.[11] Allied Command finally decided to leave Russia and Siberia to sort out disputes on their own. American newspapers reported mounting numbers of dead as destruction spread across the Russian Far East. Though the United States government offered humanitarian aid to both Moscow and elements of the counterrevolution, strict military adherence to Wilson's *Aide Memoire* remained. By the time the Allies fled through Vladivostok, the majority of high-ranking White Army officers and officials had already evacuated. Tens of thousands of White troops fled with their families toward the Pacific coast as the Red Army stormed eastward. It was the fate of the common soldier to remain behind to face Bolshevik retribution. Once in a while stories broke in the Western press summing up the ordinary soldier's fate.[12]

In the Crimean Peninsula, as well as in the northern regions of Siberia, the White Army persisted despite its inevitable demise. The Transbaikalia fell completely under Soviet militia control by October 1920 as the Red Army spread southeast into the Southern Maritime Provinces.[13] Here along the Pacific coast and to the south in the Crimea, remnants of the British and American navies undertook several unofficial yet heroic efforts to save marooned White Russians.[14] Despite unsanctioned evacuations, thousands upon thousands perished from disease, starvation, and murder.

In the south, Bolshevik forces crossed the Sea of Azov, while simultaneously bombarding the city of Odessa. Deniken's White Army retreated south as he proceeded to Yalta.[15] Later, Deniken discovered that more than 16,000 of his own men caught along the Caucasus front had frozen to death.[16] Baron Wrangel took over Deniken's counterrevolutionary forces and evacuated them from the area. Troops not fleeing by sea had to find their way to Mongolia and Sinkiang over land.[17]

The Russian Far East provinces had become too dangerous for most refugees. The route of the White Russians became so brutal that hysterical families could be seen fleeing with their belongings in tow all across the region. Only the Japanese remained behind, magnanimously announcing that they would step into the vacuum left by Kolchak's regime. Almost immediately, thousands of Japanese troops arrived in Vladivostok Harbor.

In an effort to impress the Japanese, the Socialist Revolutionary Government (SRG) began arresting its former friends and associates.[18] Though the SRG once supported Radola Gajda's effort to oust White Russian general Rozanov, by April 1920 it began rounding up anyone formerly involved with the Legion. The SRG even arrested Comrade Lazo, a Communist leader who had supported Gajda in the Vladivostok revolt. Prisoners were jailed and quickly executed but the SRG had more creative plans for Comrade Lazo. It threw him alive into a steam engine.[19]

By autumn of 1920, the last counterrevolutionary offense had been launched and failed. Survivors would spend the following years dodging the wrath of Red military units that burned crops and murdered the citizenry. Over the next decade, the Red Army hunted down and executed the vast majority of counterrevolutionaries left in hiding.

In the meantime, the Japanese leadership optimistically entered a third and final phase of intervention. Even as the relationship with the Americans began to falter, Japan hoped to manipulate the futures of both Russia and Siberia.[20] Tenaciously, the Japanese held their position alone in the Russian Far East for two more years. In time, however, even the Japanese government realized what Thomas Masaryk had warned of and the Allies finally admitted: Siberia had become a hopeless morass of violence, political intrigue, and chaos — impossible to manage in its present state.

Though Lloyd George called the Czech and Slovak takeover of the Trans-Siberian Railway "one of the greatest epics in history," the entire incident soon became relegated to the back pages of newspapers.[21] The *Mount Vernon* left Vladivostok with 3,372 men, 58 women, and 22 children on board at the end of May 1920. Another 699 Austrian and German prisoners of war on board were being repatriated, accompanied by 60 American troops to keep the peace. There was significant anger among Czechs and Slovaks when they learned that Central Power POWs had places to sleep while 700 legionnaires did not.[22] In addition, Czech and Slovak soldiers on board suffered from lack of water. The *Mount Vernon* finally docked in Norfolk, Virginia, on June 12, 1920. Also in June 1920, ships carrying additional legionnaires docked in Vancouver, Canada, where the Red Cross and Canadian Army greeted them. Only a few citizens accompanied these officials, since Canadian newspapers

Legion evacuates on the America I, *Vladivostok Harbor, not dated (courtesy Military Historical Archives, Prague).*

carried scant information on the arrival of the *Ixion*, the *Protesilaus*, and the *M.S. Dollar*. As in the United States, these echelons traveled by train across the Canadian wilderness to the east coast.

On June 22, 1920, the *Vancouver Sun* reported that around 3,400 men who traveled on board the *M.S. Dollar* had disembarked in Vancouver. "A thousand men dressed in red trousers and fur trimmed *kepes* kept in perfect time to the tune of four bands accompanying the troops. One of the bands had a huge brown bear drawing a drum cart and a Siberian pony.... Behind the troops marched two orphan boys who had been adopted by Czecho-Slovak soldiers."[23]

Passenger vessels *Czaritsa*, *Valencia*, *Minekahanda*, and *Belgic* carried hundreds of legionnaires to the west coast of Canada. All along their overland journey by train, people in small towns turned out to offer refreshments and a hearty handshake to the Legion troops.[24] The Czechoslovak Seventh Regimental band, directed by Dr. Charles Hummel, played for locals, followed by a symphony orchestra from the Ninth Regiment whenever possible. Throughout the United States similar scenes occurred.

After consulting the British government, the Canadian government's Department of Labor announced that it wanted these heroes to work for a "short period of time on railroad construction."[25] This seemed such a great idea that the British Foreign Office saw the possibility of impressing Austrian, Hungarian, Rumanian, and Polish soldiers into similar labor crews throughout Great Britain. The Czech and Slovak Legion not only found this "stunningly insensitive" but also insulting since the entire idea seemed to disguise an effort to ensnare legionnaires and other Slavic soldiers into work crews as slave labor. Both the British and Canadian governments backpedaled from this bright idea when Legion officials pointed out that all of the troops mentioned had been promised evacuation years before. In July 1920, the last of the Legion passing through Canada departed via Halifax and headed off toward Trieste.

By December 1920, the remaining organized Czech and Slovak units left Vladivostok. After wandering through the Russian Far East for over two years, the Legion was finally forced to pay its own way home. For the tens of thousands of legionnaires who returned to their beloved homeland, the state of Czechoslovakia under Thomas Masaryk's leadership proved a dream unimaginable before the war. Even so, over half of the original Legion soldiers had not survived to see it. They were instead buried across Siberia in provinces and towns their families would probably never hear about. Soldiers who were not on board these last convoys had to be left to fend for themselves. No one really knew if there were stragglers or not, and the fate of Czechs and Slovaks captured earlier by the Red Army also remained in question.

Altogether some 70,000 men returned home to the free state of

Legion artillery troops inside a broněviky, *1918.*

Czechoslovakia. Legionnaires often returned to their homeland accompanied by women and children. Many tried to find a life of normalcy but the experience of living on teplushkas in Siberia haunted them. Though the world had soon forgotten, ex-legionnaires could not erase images of death and destruction from their minds. Most suffered from the constant memory that over half of their number had never made it back. They had been left behind in graves that spread the entire length of the Trans-Siberian Railway.

Drawing on the Legion's expertise, Masaryk's government placed the legionnaires who returned in positions of leadership. They became the founding fathers upon which the new state of Czechoslovakia relied. Lying in the heart of Central Europe, the fledgling nation would pay dearly for its geographical position in the coming years, and many former legionnaires would be the first to suffer.

In 1922 František Truhlář, the young engineering student from Kolín, wrote to inform his family that he was still alive in Siberia. He had managed a lumber mill in the interior of Siberia as a prisoner. The Red Cross had just visited him. František sent his letter through the Red Cross, advising his family members in Bohemia that he would finally be becoming home. They had not heard from him in years and all assumed he had died in the war. But he was indeed alive and had finally been released from a Cossack labor camp. Back home in Bohemia, the Truhlář family had given up hope of ever seeing František again. When the letter arrived they were overjoyed. They made plans for his arrival and waited for his return. The wait stretched on month after month, leaving them with the feeling of déjà vu. Weeks turned into months and months into years. František never made it home.

The Truhlářs comforted themselves with the only photograph they had of František — a dashing mustachioed youth dressed in a crisp Hapsburg uniform, arms folded across his chest as he stared smartly back into the camera. The picture was taken in 1914, only days before František departed for the Eastern Front. This photograph, transported from Kolín, Bohemia, to the United States, had a place of honor on the mantel of his sister's home in Peru, Illinois. She raised her children as Americans but kept alive the sorrowful legend of Uncle František Truhlář and his mysterious absence. Had František died from the elements or illness trying to get home? Had he been executed? Why was he in Siberia in the first place? Hadn't he been sent to fight for the Hapsburgs' against the Russians on the Eastern Front?

In 1992, after the wall that divided East from West fell, William Jerry Vlastnik and his wife Billie Ann left Peru, Illinois, on their first trip to Czechoslovakia. He had promised his mother that he would visit her original village of Horní Chvatliny. It sat in the rolling green hills of Bohemia. William and Billy were on a mission to keep a promise they had made to William's mother over many years. If ever given the opportunity, William and Billie Ann promised to search for "a vestige" of Uncle František Truhlář. William's mother had always meant to solve the mystery of her youngest brother's disappearance, but immigration to the United States had taken her and her children far away from his fate. Complicating matters even more, after the Nazi occupation came the Communists and, as for tens of thousands of other Slavic families, contact with relations in their homeland village ended.

Since Bill's mother had become too old to keep up her search, it fell to him. Any trace of the dashing young man whose photograph sat on the family mantelpiece in Illinois

Uncle František Truhlář, engineer in uniform just before leaving for the Eastern Front, 1914 (courtesy William Vlastnik).

would make his mother happy. For years Bill had stared at the face of the young mustachioed soldier in his new Hapsburg uniform taken in the city of Olomouc on the eve of his deployment.

With a heavy heart Bill Vlastnik and his wife, Billie, returned to Illinois in the summer of 1992 to inform Bill's mother that no trace of František Truhlář could be found in the Czech Republic. Family papers and records in the village of Horní Chvatliny, along with documents in the provincial capital, had all come up empty. Even the village memorial of World War I dead that sat in the town square lacked the name of František Truhlář. Though the memorial had several other names that Bill's mother recognized, her little brother's had never been listed among them.

František Truhlář, the handsome young engineering student, disappeared into the wilds of Siberia and all traces of his short life ended there. Only the photograph taken days before František left for the Eastern Front remained to prove he had ever existed, that and the undying loyalty of a sister now fragile with age. On hearing this news, Bill Vlastnik's mother grew despondent.

Seeing her reaction, Bill became even more determined to learn something about his uncle. When his mother died in 1994, Bill continued his search anyway. He returned to Horní Chvatliny to revisit relatives, rummage through area cemeteries visiting veteran's graves and war memorials, and even comb through records in the state archives. By the end of summer, the Vlastniks still hadn't discovered anything. Weeks of searching had only deepened their frustration. Nothing was left of Uncle František's service record, his war effort — nothing of the man at all.

Bill and Billie Vlastnik finally prepared to return to Illinois empty-handed. On the morning of their flight, the Vlastniks drove to Prague with a cousin who had helped them in their failed search. All three sat quietly, deep in thought, watching the scenery as it passed outside the car window. The hills of Bohemia, hues of blues and greens, rolled along, birch groves thick in the distance. Suddenly Bill ordered his cousin to turn down a dirt road up ahead. Bill had never noticed it before. Bill's cousin argued with him, worrying that the Vlastniks might miss their flight home. After all, he knew the back road led to a dilapidated little farming community. Nothing would come of this detour — nothing but a waste of time. But Bill remained resolute as the car turned down the side road and over the hillside beyond. After a mile or two, a small village appeared in the distance.

The Vlastniks entered the village from the main road, where cottages fronted a town square, like so many they had visited in vain. At its center sat yet another war memorial. They could see that it was dilapidated, chipped and weed infested. The three travelers parked and went to search one last time. An inscription dedicated the memorial to local men who had been killed in World War I on the Eastern Front. Their names were inscribed beneath faded oval impressions where ceramic photos of each man had once sat. Every image had long ago fallen away to shatter on the thick memorial base below.

Running his fingers across the filthy letters on one side of the colonnade, Bill read, František Truhlář. Here, hidden away in a little farming community unfamiliar to the Truhlář family, Bill and Billie finally discovered recognition of František. Weeds had grown high around the memorial's base, tangling against its filthy colonnade, pitted and dirty with age. Bill could see white chips of ceramic speckling the ground below.

As Billie watched in surprise, Bill dropped down on one knee and began to scratch through the earth, pulling up shards of broken ceramic placards — pieces of portraits left buried through decades of neglect. Just as Bill began to straighten, he felt a larger shard give way. The object came loose — a flat oblong shard about five inches in length and coated with dirt. Bill stood up, turned the object in his hand and began rubbing away the grime. As he cleared away the only ceramic portrait that had not been destroyed with age, the face of a young man became revealed. It was the image of a soldier standing erect — a dashing young man in a new crisp uniform with his arms folded in front of himself and a slight smile playing on his lips. Uncle František stared out at Bill. Uncle František — the very same photograph that Bill Vlastnik had admired all of his life, the picture of a young engineering student taken in 1914, only days before he left for the Eastern Front.

This was the only ceramic oval to survive after decades, buried in the soot during the Masaryk government, the Nazi occupation, and throughout all the decades of Communist rule. Bill Vlastnik could now return home. He had kept his promise.[26]

Epilogue

Over the ensuing years, as arguments in the press began to cool, authorities directed their attention toward growing concerns over the world economy. Entente interests in Siberia and, to a large extent, Russia, ended. For decades afterwards, the leadership in Moscow resented both Western Europe and the United States for their military interference. After all, the declared aim of the Allied intervention to evacuate the Czech and Slovak Legion had been miserably neglected and unfulfilled. With this in mind, the Moscow leadership felt vindicated in its paranoia against the Allies. Not only had the intervention poisoned East and West relations, but the scandal over the Allied betrayal of the Legion caused the entire incident to be quickly swept under the rug. Allied governments refrained from further reflection on the intervention fiasco, its meaning, or its legacy.[1]

After the Czech and Slovak evacuation from Vladivostok, Moscow quickly consolidated Red army positions in order to finally control lands stretching from western Russia east to the Pacific Ocean. The Red Army spread across the Russian Far East, hunting down foreign troops. Swiss, American, English, and French soldiers, to name only a few, disappeared into the wilderness forever. Others died of malnutrition and illness in labor camps over the following decades.[2] For generations Siberians and Russians would pay for the Allied intervention as the Red Guard meted out wave upon wave of retribution to anyone who had befriended a foreigner.

Locals, hoping to outlast the government in Moscow, returned to eking out a living in forests or hiding in isolated rural valleys across the hinterland. In the Amur region, guerrilla warfare against the Red Army continued on for years. Kamchatka experienced several skirmishes, but the last of the larger counterrevolutionary efforts ended in 1923 in the Yakutsk Province.[3] White Russian partisans led an especially effective revolt in the Commander Islands, but even that fell by 1924. Little is known of civilian revolts that may have continued in the interior during the 1920s and 1930s. Information regarding the ongoing situation in Siberia had been effectively silenced by Stalin's regime. Soviet historians controlled the dissemination of information in the distant provinces, and history under Communism became an effort at reinvention rather than objective reporting.[4]

As the 1920s passed and all of Europe slipped further into economic crisis, anarchy and Communist-inspired unrest plagued the struggling nations of Central Europe. Though more stable than most of the new nations, Czechoslovakia suffered as ethnic rivalry erupted periodically along its borders.

Both the *Detroit Free Press* and the *San Francisco Chronicle* had continued to follow the Japanese intervention through 1922. Both newspapers applauded Japanese efforts in the Russian Far East, often calling for the United States to remain closely allied "to our friends across the Pacific."[5] In direct opposition to their sentiment, however, the *New York Evening Post* and the *Springfield Republican* voiced the opinion that Japan had begun to travel down an imperialistic path that would one day lead to America's front door.

Intervention in Siberia proved not only to be a political and military failure, but also a business disaster. While many American businesses pulled out when Kerensky's Provisional Government lost power to the Bolsheviks, others believed that a White Russian defeat could only be temporary. They continued investing in both Russia and Siberia even under Soviet control. By the time Stalin settled into the top position at the head of the Communist Party, American firms still doing business throughout Siberia had lost everything. The International Harvester Company, for example, never recouped more than $13 million it invested during the intervention period. Gone were the tens of millions in investment dollars made by Park, Davis and Company, Victor Talking Machines, Westinghouse Electric, and New York Air Brake.

In the aftermath of the intervention, it appeared that nothing survived the taint of Allied contact in Russia or Siberia. Herman Bernstein of the *New York Herald* and Carl Ackerman of the *New York Times*, who had both traveled extensively with the Legion, had become authorities on the intervention period in Siberia. In time, however, even their accounts became suspect. YMCA efforts, once lauded as selfless, came under attack as well. In an official congressional inquiry the YMCA was accused of inflating canteen prices while working in the Siberian interior.[6] Eventually the Association would be exonerated but not before its reputation had been damaged in the press.

Impassioned opinions concerning Russia, Siberia, and even Central Europe quickly lead to controversy. Even so, Aleksandr Kolchak, at first portrayed as a victim and then a monster, quickly became forgotten. Counter-revolutionary officers who escaped Russia and Siberia scoffed at simplistic portrayals of the White Russian front. Many accused the Allies of naively intervening in matters they knew nothing about. Even worse, they accused Allied Command of making promises it never intended to keep.

On hearing of Kolchak's death, General Mikhail Konstantinovich

Dieterichs, once Legion Commander, said farewell to the Czechs and Slovaks and retired to Harbin. Later, the last vestiges of the Siberian Autonomous Movement implored him to work to reestablish Siberian stability. Dieterichs agreed, even though it was obvious that such an effort would be short-lived. By October 1922, as ruler of the Priamur Government, Dieterichs bade farewell to the first Japanese troops to finally evacuate for home.[7] Dieterichs hung on month after month, until forced to surrender in February 1922. Later, he was glad to hear that the Japanese government would return the North Sakhalin Islands to Russia as a final gesture of friendship. Even so, by 1925 any remnant of Japanese contact with Siberia had been eradicated by the Red Guard.

Many former legionnaires entered politics in order to help the Masaryk government run towns and cities across the new state of Czechoslovakia. Others returned to pick up their prewar lives as farmers, laborers, teachers, artisans, engineers, and businessmen. Still others emigrated to the United States or Canada — countries that had showed them kindness and friendship during their evacuation homeward.

Most of the legionnaires who emigrated settled in Illinois, Iowa, Minnesota, Nebraska, Pennsylvania, and Texas. Some took up mining and factory work, occupations common in the industrializing regions of the Východoslovenské, Eastern Slovakia. Czechs, on the other hand, often remained in the skilled trades of larger urban areas in the industrial midwestern and mid–Atlantic states. Whether they remained in the homeland or emigrated overseas, many who had experienced the intervention period became tainted by it.

General Graves spent his life touring, writing and lecturing to the American public about his experiences in Siberia. Grave's adherence to President Wilson's *Aide Memoire,* though mandated, plagued him forever after. As the head of the American Expeditionary Force, Graves' dutiful obedience to his president's orders had left him unable to react to situations as they arose in Siberia. Graves came to believe that the *Aide Memoire* had doomed the AEF from the outset by compromising U.S. moral authority in the field. He later wrote that "innate inconsistencies of the *Aide Memoire* were such that they could be interpreted differently by different army officers and diplomats. Short of the President, there was no one to say what these phrases meant and throughout the entire period, when they were interpreted differently, it proved impossible to secure from the White House any clarification."[8]

There were others who prospered in the aftermath of the failed Allied intervention. Throughout the months following the Legion's evacuation, Ataman Grigori Semenov tormented the lands around Lake Baikal. By April 1921, as the Japanese pulled back along the Pacific coast of Siberia, Semenov was reportedly moving his troops to Peking. Little was then heard about his whereabouts for quite awhile.

One day walking down a street in San Francisco, General Graves passed a familiar looking face. *Grigori Semenov!* The former American Expeditionary Force commander reported the presence of this merciless ataman to Colonel Charles Morrow. Together they tracked down Semenov and charged him with war crimes. Graves hoped for a public trial and sentencing in an American courtroom, but the best Morrow and he could manage was a hearing before the Senate Committee on Education and Labor.

Morrow produced evidence connecting Semenov to over 100,000 murders. In addition, Graves testified that he had personal knowledge of the Trotiskosavsk incident in which Semenov's men spent over five days murdering trainloads of citizens for their own personal amusement.[9] Though most of these charges had been proven true, Semenov could not be held by the United States government. Instead, he was censured and expelled to Manchuria, where once again the ataman came under the employ of the Japanese.

It appeared to Graves and Morrow that the world had forgotten this once infamous scoundrel. After his censure and release by the United States, Moscow tracked Semenov's activities. Under the watchful eye of the Soviet Cheka, Semenov and Kalmikov finally became liabilities to their Japanese hosts.[10] Even so, Semenov remained comfortable in his new homeland of China where he brazenly victimized locals.

Soviet officials finally grabbed Semenov's old friend, Von Sternberg, in Mongolia and returned him to Siberia where he faced a court-martial and firing squad.[11] Ataman Semenov made himself scarce in Manchuria until the beginning of World War II when he once again became connected to atrocities committed while in the pay of the Japanese. Eventually, Soviet troops tracked his location and sent a contingent of Red Army soldiers across the border, where they surrounded him. Along with seven other counterrevolutionaries of the civil war era, Grigori Semenov was escorted to Moscow.

This time, the Military Collegium of the Supreme Court of the U.S.S.R. summoned Japanese and Allied witnesses, along with hundreds of Semenov's Siberian victims. Semenov was accused of counter-revolutionary activity in 1917 — a charge often employed throughout the Stalinist era. All of the accused were found guilty. As a result, five of Semenov's White Russian cohorts were executed by firing squad, but much to the approval of thousands of Russians, Siberians, Europeans and Americans, Ataman Grigori Semenov's execution became a solitary affair. He was hung by the neck alone and with little ceremony. No one applauded Semenov's demise more than veterans of the Legion and General Graves.

On Clay Street in San Francisco's trendy Pacific Heights neighborhood, members of the *Kaut Compana Club* gathered twice a month. Membership was exclusive — commissioned ex-tsarist naval officers only. Most members fled Russia and Siberia before 1920, many leaving through Vladivostok, sailing through the Philippines on the way to the United States. Working aboard merchant ships or taking other jobs near the sea, they all stayed on to become naturalized American citizens. One officer reported, "We talk about our old building falling to pieces ... like we are falling to pieces. Russia was lost for us a long time ago."[12]

Also feeling lost and abandoned were the men who served under General Graves in his American Expeditionary Force. After returning to the United States they discovered that Congress refused to recognize them as a legitimate military unit. They would be denied military service benefits. Harry Hoskins and other American servicemen formerly stationed either in or near Murmansk, Archangelsk, or Vladivostok returned home to find their service considered an embarrassment. The fact that more than 100 soldiers returned with Siberian wives strained matters even more.[13]

Conversely, General Radola Gajda returned to Czechoslovakia from France a national hero. President Thomas Masaryk gratefully promoted him to command an army unit in the city of Košice in southern Slovakia. Gajda immediately set to work renovating the town, overseeing the building of an open-air bath, tennis courts, football fields, cafes, and gardens. The revitalization of Košice became a stunning example to the rest of the country, once again earning Gajda national honors. After his work in Košice, Gajda was promoted to one of the highest military posts in the nation as divisional commander in Prague.

Though Gajda's successes kept him busy, he became restless, moody and haunted by his Siberian experiences. He cast about for something to give his life meaning. In Siberia, he had once studied Bolshevism, wondering if its message of equality and brotherhood would serve the peasantry. In Omsk he found that Marxist rhetoric proved hollow, its economic philosophy flawed. Under the Omsk regime, General Gajda experienced firsthand the effects of dictatorship. Kolchak, a national hero and personal friend to Gajda, had become brittle — ruined by addiction and the sycophants surrounding him. In the end, Gajda witnessed his friend, Kolchak, abuse both the White Russian army and the Siberian masses in his role as the supreme ruler and dictator of Omsk.

Throughout the 1920s, Gajda's search for answers seemed to lead him to dead ends. Even President Thomas Masaryk's dream of democracy, struggling under the weight of world economic stagnation and ethnic rivalries on Czechoslovakia's borders, appeared moribund. And then just as he began to give up, Gajda discovered a new political philosophy that offered to unite all peoples under the umbrella of the state. It seemed a vibrant economic direction-- a theory offering to answer the needs of the poor. Could this be the solution for the impoverished peoples of Central Europe, Russia and Siberia? Gajda threw himself into Czechoslovak Fascism with renewed vigor. In an unpredictable move he even headed an effort to overthrow Masaryk, who he thought unable to answer the problems of a world depression. By 1926, the coup a failure and his intentions discovered, Gajda was forced into retirement after two months in prison.

In 1929 Gajda renewed his efforts in Czechoslovak politics when he ran for the National Assembly. This time he succeeded, becoming a member of the far right Stříbrného Liga.[14] Again, intrigue forced Masaryk's government to arrest the once heroic officer. As one of Czechoslovakia's highest-ranking military figures and a man famous for saving tens of thousands of Siberian peasants in 1919, Gajda now faced trial for treason. Though acquitted, by the 1930s Gajda disappeared from public view, his reputation in ruins.[15]

When the Nazis entered Czechoslovakia in 1938, Gajda came face to face with the true character of Fascism. Too late he realized his terrible error. The German Fascists who now brutalized his country rounded up former legionnaires and threw them into camps — Gajda included. After the end of World War II, the nation he had once served left him in prison — a risk to the new government under Eduard Beneš.

By 1945, Gajda shared a cell with another ex-Legion general, Jan Syrový, an accused Nazi collaborator. In April 1920, Syrový left Vladivostok with Ataman Semenov's guns trained on his back. Semenov was furious that under orders from French General Maurice Janin, Syrový had turned over the Russian treasury to the Red Army.

When Britain and Germany signed the Munich Agreement in 1938, Syrový became appointed Minister of War by a Czechoslovak government occupied by the Germans. Jan Masaryk, the dead president's famous son, along with Eduard Beneš, acting president of Czechoslovakia, had already fled to Britain in 1938, where they governed Czechoslovakia in absentia. Syrový stayed on in Prague where he was named premier of a nonpolitical cabinet following the Munich *Diktat*.

By October 1938, Slovakia and Ruthenia won autonomous status under Nazi authority. Many republicans in Thomas Masaryk's and then Eduard Beneš' government who had been legionnaires in Siberia fled into exile or joined the resistance.[16] Many others who remained behind were tracked down, imprisoned, and then executed by Nazi authorities. Syrový, on the other hand, remained untouched in his official role. Some believed that Jan Syrový ruled in order to protect his occupied homeland as best he could and to protect its citizenry from the occupying Germans. Many disagreed.

In the 1950s, the Communist government pardoned Gajda and left Syrový in prison where he died in 1953 — yet another Legion officer with a defiled reputation. After release from prison, Gajda's public life ended and his name joined Legion history in the archives of yellowing newspapers. He, like Kolchak, quickly became forgotten.

After the Berlin Wall fell, a lawyer representing the Gajda family contacted the Hoover Institute at Stanford University in Palo Alto, California. The family hoped to give the archives a leather-bound photo album belonging to Gajda from his days in Siberia. Rumor has it that family members worried the album would fall into Czechoslovak government hands and be destroyed because of Radola's failed reputation. Today, the album sits in the Hoover Library stacks, deep in the bowels of the archive. It is covered in semiprecious stones, intricate original artwork of steep mountain valleys and battle scenes. Presented to their young leader by the Sixth Regiment, the photo album was dedicated to the young colonel, Radola Gajda, from his beloved men, legionnaires who believed that he had saved their lives.

Mary Andrejka grew up in Chicago hearing fantastic tales about how her father, Josef Halama, had disappeared into the vast recesses of the Russian Far East as a young soldier. For years Halama's wife, Marie, waited for him to return, but news never came. In time, as other husbands had long since returned from the war on the Eastern Front, Marie gave up hope. Realizing that her husband, Josef, had died "out there" somewhere, Marie worked the fields on their farm in Bohemia, raising her children alone.

One early evening Marie was working in the garden next to the family farmhouse. She straightened to rest her back, wiping sweat from her forehead, and glanced off into the distance. Across the hillside opposite a solitary traveler approached. Squinting against the dying sunshine at the silhouetted figure, she noted something peculiarly familiar in his stride. Marie's children playing nearby watched openmouthed as their mother dropped her hoe and ran screaming toward the hill. For a moment the Halama children were terrified. They watched as their mother became the second figure on the hill. The two figures faced one another, running. They paused a few paces apart and then the two embraced.

Josef Halama had been walking home for years. As atrocities mounted and friends died while waiting to evacuate for home, Halama and four cohorts left their teplushka on the Trans-Siberian Railway and began to head south. As legionnaires they lived in constant fear of being caught and executed by the Austrians, Germans, Hungarians, and of course the Russians. Even though the war had ended, life-threatening struggles continued to plague their little group.

In the end, only Halama survived to tell the harrowing journey they experienced. The group had turned south, hiding from the Bolsheviks, the Germans, even the White Russians — walking nights sometimes with no idea in which direction they had traveled. They forged rivers, crossed deserts, scaled mountains, enduring the summer heat or winter cold. One thing remained constant — home.

Halama's memories of the simple farmhouse and the image of his wife and children fed his desire to live. It brought him safely to Bohemia.[17] Later, Marie and Joseph Halama quit farming and immigrated to the Cicero/Berwyn area of Chicago, a large colony of Czech-Americans in Illinois. Here they joined relatives who had preceded them.

Other Czech-American and Slovak-American families heard similar stories of soldier relatives lost in the Siberian wilds. Still others, like Stefanie Maejer, whose quote begins this book, had family and friends who just wanted to become "Americans." They didn't want to hear about being Czechs or Slovaks anymore, let alone about the odyssey of the Legion in a faraway frozen land. Unlike Stefanie Maejer's family, however, Josef Halama's children, especially his daughter, Mary, grew up hearing tales about life in their homeland. But it was always Josef's adventures as a young soldier in Siberia that held his daughter's attention. Mary Andrejka kept photographs of her father in uniform, marveling at his courageous journey home.

After her father passed away, Mary began to ask other Czech-Americans in the Chicago area if they knew why he had been so far from home in the first place. After all, the war was fought to the west in Russia and Ukraine. No one seemed to believe that Mary's father walked all that way from the Trans-Siberian Railway deep in the interior of far-away Siberia. Americans never heard about a Czech or Slovak army that survived in the Russian Far East by fighting and living on trains. After many years of being treated as though her father had been a liar and Mary too gullible, she quit sharing her father's story.

And then the Berlin Wall fell. Czechs and Slovaks traveled freely to the West. Stories from the homeland, long ago suppressed, began to emerge. Mary decided to attend a Czech and Slovak genealogical conference in Chicago. In a large hall she attended a lecture by a military historian on the Vienna Archives. In her lap she had photographs of her father dressed in the uniform of the Legion. She met other people with similar photographs. Unbelievably, among them Mary Andrejka made the acquaintance of three other people who lived in or around the Chicago area whose soldier relatives had walked home from Siberia. Like Mary these families did not know what had brought their legionnaires to Siberia in the first place. It was the beginning of a long journey into the past for them as they pieced together the remarkable story of the Legion and their loved ones. They continue to meet to share research and to realize that the unfolding story of the Legion has been both remarkable and hidden.

In the fall of 1997, Mr. Michael Egan with the Commonwealth Graves Commission had been sent to identify and conserve United States military gravesites in the Churkin Russian Naval Cemetery in Vladivostok, Siberia. There, Egan found American Expeditionary Force gravesites in terrible disrepair. In even worse shape, however, were gravestones nearby. In time, Egan also restored Canadian graves, yet he had no authority to work on the many Slavic gravesites that he also identified. Money and manpower to clean and restore them did not exist. Egan was so concerned by their condition that he began to write letters asking for help.

One of his letters made its way to Mary Andrejka, whose father had walked home from Siberia. In it, Egan said, "Both sites [U.S and Canadian] are] overgrown with brush, with a significant number of headstones either missing or knocked over. The Commonwealth War Graves Commission has performed restoration work on the Allied site, but to my knowledge, no one has done anything to the Czech [and Slovak] site."[18] Thousands of abandoned troops like the Czechs, Poles, Rumanians, and Slovaks had relatives who waited for them at home. Thousands were never heard from again — lost in the overwhelming violence of World War I. Most are buried along the steppe in towns with names their families would never recognize.[19] Like Mary Andrejka, Stephanie Maejers, and Bill Vlastnik, there are thousands of families looking for a remnant, a grave, a clue to solve a similar mystery and to end a family's sorrow. Time is against them.[20]

Chapter Notes

Prologue

1. Jay Winter and Blaine Baggett, *The Great War and the Shaping of the 20th Century* (New York: Penguin, 1996), 49.

2. Vladimir Dedijer, *The Road to Sarajevo* (New York: Simon & Schuster, 1966), 15–16.

3. Gordon Brook-Shepherd, *Archduke of Sarajevo: The Romance and Tragedy of Franz Ferdinand of Austria* (Boston: Little, Brown, 1989), 45.

4. C. A. Macartney, *The Habsburg Empire, 1790–1918* (New York: Macmillan, 1969) 814.

5. Jean Berenger, *A History of the Habsburg Empire, 1273–1700*, trans. by C. A. Simpson (New York: Longman, 1994), 24–25.

6. Francis Dvornik, *The Slavs of European History and Civilization* (New Brunswick, NJ: Rutgers University Press, 1962), 126.

7. *Ibid.*, 442.

8. Victor S. Mamatey, *Rise of the Habsburg Empire; 1526–1815* (New York: Holt, Rinehart and Winston, 1971), 15.

9. A. J. P. Taylor, *The Hapsburg Monarchy, 1809–1918* (London: Hamish Hamilton Press, 1951), 238.

Chapter One

1. Zbyněk Zeman, *The Masaryks: The Making of Czechoslovakia* (London: Weidenfeld and Nicholson, 1976), 18.

2. In the introduction to Thomas Masaryk's book *The Making of a State,* Hapsburg expert and British newspaper reporter Henry Wickham Steed discusses Masaryk's character strengths and his immense influence upon those who read his writings in both philosophy and sociology. See Thomas Masaryk, *The Making of a State: Memories and Observations, 1914–1918* (New York: Frederick Stokes, 1927), xvii.

3. Zeman, 18.

4. Brook-Shepherd, 127.

5. Alan Palmer, *The Lands Between* (New York: Macmillan, 1969), 77.

6. Even so, most of the Reichstag remained true to the emperor in Vienna. Neo-Slav policies had become a confused hodgepodge of unsuccessful fronts before the war. After the assassination of the archduke, Karel Kramář wrote, "We have no wish to leave the Monarchy ... though we are Slavs through and through and feel great sympathy for our brothers, we do not want to follow a policy leading to subversion or which would result in the borders of the empire being altered." For further information see John Bradley, *The Czechoslovak Legion in Russia, 1914–1920* (New York: Columbia University Press, 1991), 25.

7. Karel Čapek, *Talks with T.G. Masaryk,* Michael Henry Heim, trans. Dora Round (New Haven, CT: Catbird Press, 1995), 117.

8. Indeed, universal suffrage had been introduced as early as 1907 in the Czech lands. For more information see Daniel Edward Miller, "Antonín Švehla and the Czechoslovak Republican Party, 1918–1933" (Ph.D. diss., University of Pittsburgh, 1989), 417.

9. Robert A. Kahn, *Dynasty, Politics, and Culture, Selected Essays,* ed. Stanley B. Winters (Boulder: Social Science Monographs, 1991), 201.

10. Peter P. Yurchak, *The Slovaks: Their History and Traditions* (Whiting, IN: Obrana Press, 1947), 198–199. See also Vladimír Zuberec, "Milan Rastislav Štefánik in the History of the Slovak Nation and Czechoslovakia," *Czech Life Magazine,* 1992, 4–5.

11. Zuberec, 4–5.

12. Betty Unterberger, *The United States, Revolutionary Russia, and the Rise of Czechoslovakia* (Chapel Hill: University of North Carolina Press, 1989), 10–11.

13. Interestingly, Radola Gajda was at the Serbian front during the same period. On October 20, 1917, France bestowed the rank of officer in the French Foreign Legion, its highest honor, on Štefánik. Yurchak, 198–199.

14. Zuberec, 5.

15. Robert H. Ferrell, *Woodrow Wilson and World War I, 1917–1921* (New York: Harper and Row, 1985), 126.

16. Bradley, 27–28.

17. *Ibid.*, 29.

18. Palmer, 123–124.

19. In the last months of the war, Štefánik was seriously handicapped with constant pain. After surgery failed to correct his wounds and suffering from a variety of other health issues, he came under the care of a series of associates who accompanied him in Legion recruitment efforts. Milan Getting accommodated Štefánik while traveling throughout the United States. Štefánik never regained his health, living in immense pain during the final years of his life. See Yurchak, 202.

20. Emanuel Poche, *Portrait of Prague* (London: Hamlyn, 1969), 8.

21. Zuberec, 5–6.

22. Stanley Washburn, *On the Russian Front in World War I: Memoirs of an American War Correspondent* (New York: Robert Speller and Sons, 1982), 31.

23. In the first months of training, Prague's 28th Regiment gained notoriety by demonstrating en masse against the Austrian war effort. Later, after fighting courageously at the front in their Hapsburg uniforms, the 28th Regiment once again became the focus of attention by deserting across the Eastern Front in formation. Gordon Cremonesi, *The Russian Army in World War I* (London: Gordon Cremonesi, 1975), 155.

24. William Keyes, "We Are and We Shall Be: Puppetry and Czecho-Slovak Politics 1860–1990," *Pittsburgh History: A Magazine of the City and its Region* (Summer 1992: 82).

25. Gustav Bečvář, *The Lost Legion* (London: Standley Paul, 1939), 19.

26. Unterberger, *The United States, Revolutionary Russia and the Rise of Czechoslovakia*, 4.

27. Bradley, 28–29.

28. Clarence A. Manning, *The Siberian Fiasco* (New York: Library Publishers, 1952), 43.

29. Elizabeth Wiskemann, *Czechs and Germans: A Study of the Historic Provinces of Bohemia and Moravia* (Oxford: Oxford University Press, 1938), 74–78.

30. In the second half of the nineteenth century, thousands of Czechs and Slovaks immigrated to the United States and Russia. Tsar Nicholas II found these immigrants to be skilled workmen, often better trained and educated than Russians. As a result, Czechs gained preferential treatment by employers who hired them to work on state projects like the Trans-Siberian Railway. As minorities, Czechs and Slovaks often lived together in the larger urban centers in both Russia and the United States. Russia's historical ties appealed to Slavs but the United States represented a new beginning with all the freedoms imaginable. Emanuel Voska and Will Irwin, *Spy and Counterspy* (New York: Doubleday, Doran, 1940), 15.

31. *The Slovaks and the Pittsburgh Pact* [brochure], Pittsburgh, Bohemia Hill Sokol Lodge #4 Committee (Chicago: Tykla Brothers Press, 1918), 14–15.

32. Kenneth D. Miller, *The Czecho-Slovaks in America* (New York: George H. Doran, 1922), 79–80.

33. Yurchak, 199–200.

34. "The Czechoslovak Volunteers: History of Whiting, Indiana, " *Nase rodina: Journal of the Czech and Slovak Genealogical Society International, 7*, no. 1 (April 1993): 23–24.

35. After the Battle of White Mountain in November 1620, many celebrated Czech aristocrats, religious leaders, and intellectuals fled to the New World by way of Saxony and Western Europe. As a result, many Czech musicians, educators, and artists later enriched their adopted homeland rather than contributing their expertise to the land of their ancestors. See Josef Martínek, *One Hundred Years of the CSA: The History of the Czechoslovak Society of America, 1854–1954*, trans. R. A. Gorman (Cicero, IL: Cicero-Berwyn Press, 1985), 258–261.

36. Following September 1914, New Yorkers and Chicagoans held conferences and organized a variety of groups (one later becoming the *České národní družení*, "Bohemian National Alliance") to collect funds and materials for the war effort. Women knitted in auxiliaries, penny pinched, and strategized in their local organizations to collect funds and recruit for relief work. In time their efforts brought in millions of dollars. For more information see Martínek, 267–268.

37. *Ibid.*, 275.

38. *Ibid.*, 270–271.

39. Vienna believed Prague to be a cesspool of conspirators and every Czech- or Slovak-American traveling there a spy. In some cases, they were correct. Emmanuel V. Voska worked for the Czech Mafie before America entered the war. Afterwards, he became a member of the American Military Intelligence Division of the United States Army, employing strategy learned under the Mafie. Martinek, 266–270.

40. Zeman, 85.

41. Dr. Alice Masaryk shared a cell in prison with a spy working for the Mafie, Mila Jarušková, a governess in the employ of German Ambassador von Berstorff's household. German agents were known to frequent the Berstorff home where Mila Jarušková took detailed notes of conversations before turning them over to the Allies. Once captured, Jarušková became imprisoned in Prague where she befriended Alice Masaryk. For more information see Voska and Irwin, 59.

42. Following the assassination of Archduke Franz Ferdinand in Sarajevo on June 28, 1914, an intricate web of alliances began to pull nations on the side of Austria-Hungary and

those on the side of Serbia into a war stance. Mobilization of one alliance member forced the mobilization of another until each faced a true world war. Most, however, assumed that initial skirmishes would end quickly and peace would be restored. Nothing was further from the truth.

43. Peter Fleming, *The Fate of Admiral Kolchak* (New York: Harcourt Brace and World, Inc. 1963), 59.

44. Washburn, 31.

45. Henry Wickham Steed, *Through Thirty Years* (Garden City, NY: Doubleday, 1925) 125.

46. In *Čas*, Masaryk had to examine options carefully, often subsuming his contempt for corrupt Russian staff officers in order to support the Russian troops' efforts on the Eastern Front. Masaryk, 11–12.

47. George Nekrasov, *North of Galipoli: The Black Sea Fleet at War, 1914–1917* (Boulder, CO: East European Monographs, 1992), 97.

48. For an excellent description of Admiral Kolchak's background including his years as an explorer, see M. I. Smirnov, "Admiral Kolchak," *The Slavonic and East European Review* (January 1933): 377.

49. Benson Bobrick, *East of the Sun* (New York: Poseidon Press, 1992), 399–400.

50. Fleming, 54.

51. Fleming, 95.

52. Edwin P. Hoyt, *The Army Without a Country* (New York: Macmillan, 1967), 177.

53. Bertram D. Wolfe, *Three Who Made a Revolution: A Biographical History* (New York: Stein and Day, 1984), 65.

54. *Ibid.*, 64.

55. *Ibid.*, 182.

56. *Ibid.*, 209.

57. *Ibid.*, 128.

Chapter Two

1. Vladimír Klecanda, "Operations of the Czechoslovak Army in Russia During the Period 1917–1920," trans. by Jerry V. Matyka, *Journal of Military Science* (1921): 1.

2. *Ibid.*, i–ii.

3. Bradley, 42.

4. In a later German study of the Third Regiment, formed in 1917, 60 percent of Družina volunteers proved to be university students, while 20 percent had already graduated. This should have been known to the Russian High Command since the Czech colonies of Petrograd, Moscow, Kiev, and Warsaw consisted mainly of professionals. Bradley, 40–41.

5. Emmett Hoskins to home, 1917, p. 14, Emmett Hoskins Collection, Hoover Institution Archives.

6. Bradley, 53–54. Emphasis here is my own.

7. Klecanda, 5.

8. Mass surrenders were rare, however, though later the estimated number of Slavs said to be deserting became routinely inflated by the Austrian High Command in order to cover up its own incompetence. Bradley, 30–31.

9. *Ibid.*, 42–44.

10. Henry Baerlein, *The March of the Seventy Thousand* (London: Leonard Parsons, 1926), 31.

11. Bečvář, 29.

12. Early in 1914, Wickham Steed and Emanuel Voska, two associates of Thomas Masaryk's in the West, met with Britain's Lord Kirchener. Kirchener confided in them that, "The French under-estimated the power of the German armies. We'll lose Paris, probably. We'll win in the end, though three years at least, maybe four. And if your people stand by, I'll do all I can to help you when we make peace." Voska, 14–15. By September 1914 the German forces on the Western Front had already crossed the Marne and had Paris in their sights. Lord Kirchner's remarks forced many in the Allied Command to readjust their thinking concerning how long the war would last. See also John A. White, *The Siberian Intervention* (Princeton, NJ: Princeton University Press, 1950), 9.

13. Harry Hoskins, "The Story of an Expedition," p. 9–10, Box 1, Harry Hoskins Collection, Hoover Institute Archives.

14. Bradley, 31–32.

15. *Ibid.*, 20–21.

16. Bečvář, 42.

17. Nekrasov, 120.

18. Emphasis is my own.

19. Emphasis is my own.

20. Bradley, 36–38.

21. A private from Prague, Skelnička would one day immigrate to the state of Nebraska in the U.S., where he often revisited his camp experience. In his oral interview with Mr. Joseph Swoboda, archivist for the Nebraska Czech Heritage Project at the University of Nebraska at Lincoln, Skelnička related personal memories of the prisoner of war camps and his travels with the Czechoslovak Legion. Joseph Skelnička, interview by Joseph Swoboda, April 29, 1977, tape #1, Nebraska Czech Heritage Project University of Nebraska at Lincoln.

22. Skelnička planned to visit the young man's mother after the war to tell her the circumstances of her son's death and the depth of his humanity. Decades later, Skelnička remained haunted by the inability to recall this young Samaritan's name. Delirium and the incredulity of his journey suppressed it and many other painful memories in Skelnička's consciousness. Skelnička, interview.

23. Bradley, 45.

24. Robert Paul Browder and Alexander F.

Kerensky, eds., *The Russian Provincial Government, 1917, Documents,* Vol. 1, Palo Alto, CA: Hoover Institution Publications, 17.

25. Siberia, twice the size of Canada, is a land rich in natural resources. Large numbers of fur-bearing animals, and plentiful timber, gold, platinum, coal, and iron resources made it one of the most desirable territories to develop at the turn of the nineteenth century. Wild boar, tiger, deer, wolf, and bear were prevalent as well as small game like pheasant.

Most areas, including the cities, had no running water, paved roads, or electricity. The Russian ruble, the denomination used by the turn of the century, normally exchanged at 50¢ to the dollar. By mid-war, however, it would plunge to 32,000¢ per dollar. For further information see Hoskins, "The Story of an Expedition," pp. 2, 5, Part 3, Box #1, Harry Hoskins Collection.

26. George Frederick Wright, *Asiatic Russia* (New York: McClure, Phillips, and Company, 1902), 2:388–394.

27. Violet Conolly. *Siberia Today and Tomorrow* (New York: Taplinger, 1976), 15, 16.

28. Emphasis is my own.

29. For an explanation of the Russian and Siberian "mir" tradition among the Raskolnik*s* see George Fredrick Wright, *Asiatic Russian,* vol. 2 (New York: McClure, Phillips, 1902), 296–317.

30. *Ibid.,* 299–301.

31. White, 34.

32. "Siberia and Eastern Russia," 22–26, Military Intelligence Division, Classified Documemts, United States War Department National Archives.

33. *Ibid.,* 24–25.

34. White, 47.

35. Though enthusiasm over the Trans-Siberian Railway ran high especially with technical and design personnel, politically it had been a cause for great concern. Russians believed that the Koreans needed to be equally as enthusiastic. Without Korea, Japan and China would feel threatened. On the other hand, western diplomatic circles knew that any efforts to approach Korea on the part of Russia would ignite Japanese anger. For further information see Walter La Feber, *The New Empire: An Interpretation of American Expansion, 1860–1898* (Ithaca, NY: Cornell University Press, 1963), 57, 382–383.

36. Roland S. Morris, *A Railway Three Nations Want* (San Francisco: St. Francis Reunion Committee Booklet, 1922), 1–4.

37. Wright, 316.

38. Hoskins, p.2, Part 3, Box #5, Harry Hoskins Collection.

Chapter Three

1. Due to a shortage of rifles among the Russian troops, many soldiers had to be sent into battle with no weapons at all. These troops were under orders to follow behind, pickingup the guns of wounded and dead comrades. *Ibid.,* Box #1, 10.

2. Bradley, 56.

3. Tatiana Browning and Kyril Fitzlyon, *Before the Revolution* (Woodstock, NY: The Overlook Press, 1978), 15.

4. Robert D. Warth, *Nicholas II: The Life and Reign of Russia's Last Monarch* (London: Praeger, 1997), 229.

5. Browder and Kerensky, 1:106.

6. Mark Steinberg and Vladimír M. Khrustalev, *The Fall of the Romanovs: Political Dreams and Personal Struggles in a Time of Revolution* (New Haven, CT: Yale University Press, 1995), 102.

7. Nekrasov, 116.

8. *Ibid.,* 121.

9. Washburn, 299.

10. Morris, 1–4.

11. Browder and Kerensky 2:1,045.

12. Bradley, 55–56.

13. Palmer, 136, 138–139.

14. Bradley, 60–62.

15. Morris, 1–4.

16. Nicholas Svidine, *Cossack Gold: The Secret of the White Army Treasure,* trans. Leonard Mayhew (Boston: Little, Brown, 1973), 15.

17. Ference Imrey, *Through Blood and Ice* (New York: E. P. Dutton 1930), 52–53.

18. Under such circumstances it was remarkable how well the Trans-Siberian line worked even in the darkest moments of Kerensky's war effort. See Hoskins, p. 1, Emmett Hoskins Collection.

19. *Ibid.,* 10.

20. Ward Rutherford, *The Russian Army in World War I* (London: Gordon Cremonesi, 1975), 253.

21. U.S. Department of State, *F.R. Lansing Papers, 1914–1920, vol.2* Papers Relating to the Foreign Relations of the United States, (Washington, DC: Government Printing Office, 1940), 343.

22. Early in the war, Masaryk and Štefánik concentrated their efforts on enlisting the support of Czech and Slovak POWs. Later, they gathered together a highly visible contingent within the Russian ranks in order to influence the Provisional Government's treatment of former Hapsburg troops. With the Bolshevik Revolution, these efforts had been left in upheaval. Bradley, 50–52.

23. Baerlein, 92–93.

24. Bradley, 70–71.

25. Richard Goldhurst, *The Midnight War* (New York: McGraw-Hill, 1978), 87–88. Emphasis is mine.

26. Bradley, 58–59.

27. *Ibid.*, 58–59.

28. Vaněk, Otakar, Volta Holeček, and Rudolf Medek. *Za svobodu: obrázkova kronika československého revolučního hnutí na Rusi 1914–1920* (Prague: Nakladem Pamatniku odboje, 1929) 4.

29. Baerlein, 104.

30. This evacuation has been summarized in a few accounts but details are vague as to how the First and Second divisions and others farther to the rear boarded trains, fed themselves, and lived on in horrific conditions during the first critical days on the railway. John Bradley mentions that villages near Bakhmach were pillaged, raided "like Mongol expeditions," but little hard evidence is given. It seems obvious, if not inevitable, that the Legion resorted to the same methods other armies in the area used to acquire shelter and food, which included stealing, but one wonders how accurate these accounts are or whether the possibility remains that either Bolshevik or German accounts of the march later colored these events of the evacuation. It is hoped that an accurate accounting of Czech and Slovak "requisitions" while in Siberia will answer the question. See Bradley, 74–75.

31. "The Czecho-Slovak Incident" translated by Voska file #1, 1b, Ernest Lloyd Harris Collection, Hoover Institution Archives.

32. "Famine in the Ukraine," *New York Times,* April 18, 1918, 4.

33. Emil Lengyel, *Siberia* (Garden City, NY: Garden City, 1943), 212–213.

34. Stephen M. Berk, "The Coup D' Etat" p. 187 Hoover Institution Archives.

35. "Muscovites Representative Are Ready to Put 3,000,000 Men in Field to Defend Their Claims to Real Democracy: Kaiser Refuses to Hold Negotiations," *San Francisco Chronicle,* January 4, 1918, 1.

36. George F. Kennan, *Russia and the West under Lenin and Stalin* (Boston: Little Brown, 1961), 39.

37. Later, during peace negotiations in Versailles, the Brest-Litovsk Treaty became a blueprint and example of German and Austrian "fair treatment." Many historians now believe that Germany sealed its own postwar fate with the French by treating Russia so criminally at Brest-Litovsk. Leonid I. Strakhovsky, *The Origins of American Intervention in North Russia, 1918* (Princeton, NJ: Princeton University Press, 1937), 3–4.

38. *Ibid.*, 130–131.

39. Emphasis is mine.

40. "Admiral Kolchak," *Saturday Evening Post,* July 3, 1920, 8.

41. William Duncan, "Letters Home," p.1, Verkeodinsk, Siberia, August 26, 1918 Hoover Institution Archives.

42. Bradley, 79–80.

43. "The Czecho-Slovak Incident," Box 2 file 1. pp. 2–3 Ernest Lloyd Harris Collection. Hoover Institution Archives, Stanford University, File #1, Box #2, 2–3.

44. A German occupation of Irkutsk would have gained the military control of the regional railway, allowing German troops to push into Manchuria. If this were to have occurred it would have broadened the war effort considerably. Bradley, 88–91.

45. Lansing Papers, 358.

46. For more information see Christopher Lasch, "American Intervention in Siberia: A Reinterpretation," *Political Science Quarterly,* 77, no. 2 (Jun 1962): 218–219.

47. White, 112.

48. Ernest Lloyd Harris Collection, 2–3.

49. Baerlein, 104.

50. Telegram from Ernest Lloyd Harris, Esq., American Consul General, Irkutsk, Siberia, to the American Consulate, Moscow, Russia, June 25, 1918. pp. 1–2.

51. Emmett Hoskins, 5.

52. Bradley, 59–60.

53. *Ibid.*, 79–80.

54. "The Czech Revolt," *Times* (London), 2 Jul 1919, 5.

55. "Claims of the Czechs," *New York Times,* 5 March 5, 1918, 10.

56. Zeman, 113.

57. Berk, 177–178.

58. David Kelley, *The Czech Fascist Movement, 1922–1942* (Boulder, CO: East European Monographs, 1995), 27–28.

59. Bradley, 82–83.

60. Manning, 46.

61. Later, after the war, Gajda returned to the fledgling nation of Czechoslovakia, having flirted with Bolshevism and Socialism. He now openly professed the new political ideology of Czech Fascism. As a political insider, Gajda evolved from the commander in chief of the Czechoslovak Army to leading a coup d'état against Thomas Masaryk's government. This incident landed Gajda in jail and branded him a political scoundrel in the eyes of those who had once idolized him. Even so, Gajda's efforts on behalf of the Russian peasantry and his own men while in Siberia should not be ignored. No matter what his rationale, Gajda became responsible for saving tens of thousands of lives and for standing up against the abuses of both the Red Army and of Kolchak's *Stavka* staff headquartered in Omsk. For more information see Kelley, 27–28.

62. Letter from Strombach, Head of Penza

Soviet, to Czechoslovak Communist Party Headquarters, Moscow, April 3,1918. Quoted in Vaněk,
Holeček, and Medek, 66–68.
   63. Victor M. Fic, *The Collapse of American
Policy in Russia and Siberia, 1918* (Boulder,
Co:East European Monographs, 1995), 8–9.
   64. Later Communist writers such as Vavrak
admitted that "recruitment efforts" had been
poorly timed, serving only to anger the Legion
rather than gain the interest of individual members. Bradley, 83.

Chapter Four

   1. White, 15.
   2. James William Morely, *The Japanese
Thrust into Siberia, 1918* (New York: Columbia
University Press, 1957), 244.
   3. See the testimony of Raymond Robins,
U.S. Congress, Committee on the Judiciary,
*Brewing and Liquor Interests and German and
Bolshevik Propaganda*, 66th Cong., 1st sess., 1919,
vol. 3, 820–821.
   4. James Bunyan, *Intervention, Civil War,
and Communism in Russia, April–Decmber, 1918:
Documents and Materials* (Baltimore: John Hopkins Univeristy Press, 1976), 88.
   5. Betty Unterberger, *America's Siberian
Expedition, 1918–1920* (Durham, North Carolina: Duke University Press, 1956), 92.
   6. Steven Potach, "The Role of the
Czechoslovak Legion in Allied Policy toward
Russia, 1918" (graduate seminar paper, History
Department, University of Minnesota, Minneapolis, MN, June 1975).
   7. White, 246–249.
   8. "Siberian Outlook Not Encouraging,"
Pittsburgh Post, May 31, 1918, 2.
   9. *Ibid.*
   10. Gen. William S. Graves, *America's Siberian Adventure* (New York: Jonathan Cape and
Harrison Smith, 1931), 45.
   11. Berk, 167.
   12. Baerlein, 134–135.
   13. Bradley, 85–86.
   14. National Archives, United States War
Department: General Staff, Military Intelligence
Division. Military Reference Branch Classified
Documents, Special Staff Records, 1917 to 1921,
#164 to 212. United States Army Military Intel-
ligence Records, #165, note #4, 2.
   15. Bradley, 85.
   16. Bradley, 85–86.
   17. Fic, 8.
   18. Hoyt, 90.
   19. "Vexation of Central Power: Russia's
Czech Troops," *Times* London, June 13, 1918, 5.
   20. Bradley, 85–86.
   21. White, 246–249.

   22. Bradley, 85–87.
   23. Fic, 9.
   24. If not for suspicions planted by the Germans in the minds of Lenin and Trotsky, the
Legion might well have made it through to
Vladivostok without war. The situation in
Chelyabinsk proved to both the Legion and the
Bolsheviks that only fighting would provide
them their aims. See Baerlein, 113.
   25. *Ibid.*, 159.
   26. Captain Radola Gajda, Commander of
the Sixth and Seventh regiments, had already
prepared a plan of action advising that all cities
along the railway were to be disarmed and each
Bolshevik unit confronted. Bolshevik forces were
to be shot on the spot if incidents of sabotage
occurred. Village and city hostages could be
taken but had to be treated decently. His plan
of action predated the Chelyabinsk incident by
over two weeks and was not allowed to be
enacted by the Odbočka. Captain Radola Gajda,
Plan of Action, Order number 38/1 (3 May 1918),
Novonikolayevsk, Siberia.
   27. Bobrick, 393–395.
   28. While these confrontations were occurring along the Trans-Siberian Railway, Thomas
Masaryk traveled throughout the United States
meeting Czech-American and Slovak-American
community leaders in places like Chicago,
Cleveland, and Pittsburgh. From May 29 to 31,
he took part in talks in Pittsburgh hoping to
obtain recognition for a plan to unite the Slovak
people with the Czechs in an independent
autonomous state. The Austro-Hungarian
Empire had already become so weakened that
discussions for a federated state to evolve from
the former empire proved hopeless. German
dominance of the region eclipsed federated status in Hapsburg areas of the empire at war's end.
For more information see, "Czech Leader is
Coming to Recruit Army," *Pittsburgh Daily Dispatch,* May 31, 1918, 3, 14.
   29. William Duncan, "Letters Home," May
26,1918, Quarterly Reports 1918, William Duncan Collection.
   30. Historians have developed theories that
supported their own school of thought rather
than dispassionately studying the facts. For
many legionnaires who took part in the odyssey
of the Czechs and Slovaks across Siberia during
this period, a German conspiracy lay at the root
of all of their misfortune. Soviet historians, on
the other hand, blamed the Allies and the White
Army for provoking a clash that pitted the
Legion against the Moscow leadership. During
the Cold War, émigré historians used the Legion
as an example of farsighted anti–Bolshevik
efforts to crusade against Lenin and Trotsky
which began as far back as the summer of 1918.
Czech and Slovak Communist historians, ignor-

ing their own archival evidence, simply echoed Moscow's theories of imperialistic adventurism. Ideological prejudice colored each and every theory throughout the following decades in historical scholarship on all sides. Inevitably the entire incident became relegated to the back pages of newspapers and historical research. See Bradley, 87–88.

31. "The Czecho-Slovak Incident." File #1, Box #1, 4–5, Ernest Lloyd Harris Collection.

32. Unfortunately, Radola Gajda's reputation was very quickly to falter. Lengyel, 218.

33. Ernest Lloyd Harris, "Telegram to Moscow Consulate," June 25, 1918, 8, Ernest Lloyd Harris Collection, Box #1.

34. United States War Department: General Staff, Military Intelligence Division. Military Reference Branch Classified Documents, Special Staff Records, 1917 to 1921, #164 to 212. United States Army Military Intelligence Records, #165, chapter 1, note #3, 1918.

35. Gajda also sent orders to his echelon officers. Order No. 38/1 ordered the aviation and engineering units not to "execute any backward movement except to give armed assistance." He also ordered that weapons be distributed and immediate reconnaissance of each train's vicinity, especially the railway station up the line, be taken. Gajda mandated that every train under his command be equipped with at least one machine gun on the ready and that "not more than one quarter of the total men for each train could leave their train to visit any city at any given time." This order also informed commanding officers of the disintegrating situation up and down the railroad lines. Unterberger, *The United States*, 185–187.

36. Paul Dotsenko, *The Struggle for a Democracy in Siberia, 1917–1920* (Palo Alto, CA: Hoover Institution Press, 1983), 30.

37. Vaněk, Holeček, and Medek, 7.

38. The uprising of the Czecho-Slovak Legion as seen from a variety of perspectives by historians is highly controversial. Kratochvil's *Cest revoluce* maligns Gajda for acting against his own Chelyabinsk Congress by refusing to negotiate with the Bolshevik militia at Novonikolayevsk rather than choosing to attack. The Soviet newspaper *Izvestia* covered the first Soviet report of the Czechoslovak revolt on May 29, 1918. Coverage of the uprising in Czech, Slovak, and Russian reports would remain diametrically opposed to one another afterward. *Izvestia*, no. 107 (371), May 29, 1918.

39. Interestingly, Trotsky's Order #115 was made under the instructions of Moscow in Lenin's name. Later, Soviet historians ignored Trotsky's role in the incident once he had fallen out of favor with Communist Party membership. Unterberger, *The United States*, 176–177.

40. Manning, 49.

41. Baerlein, 110.

42. Manning, 49.

43. Skelnička interview April 29, 1977, Tape #62.

44. David R. Francis, United States ambassador to Russia, reported to Washington in May 1918 that Count Mirbach and his agents seemed to dictate to the Soviet government in Moscow. Francis intimated that if hard proof could be found that Lenin was under the pay of Germany then the Allies had good reason to reestablish a second front. Lasch, 219–220.

45. Baerlein, 135.

46. Wright, 348.

Chapter Five

1. Klecanda, 15

2. Dieterichs had been cooperating with the Bolsheviks with relative ease in the Pacific Province while awaiting Allied transport ships. Cooperation was not only prudent but helped Dieterichs secure the port from any future Bolshevik intrigue. A contingent of legionnaires already in Vladivostok had been hampered from giving help to Legion troops in the field. For further information concerning General Dieterichs and the precarious position he and his troops faced encamped by the port of Vladivostok, see White, 252–253.

3. The Moscow leadership had confiscated documents from the Bureau of the Czecho-Slovak National Council's Moscow office after the uprising in May, 1918. Dr. Maxa's correspondence with Paris asking allied leadership to recognize the independence of Czech and Slovak peoples was seen by Lenin as proof that Count Mirbach had been correct — the Legion must be in league with capitalist centers of power. A cable also in Lenin's possession from Masaryk ordering Dr. Maxa to begin an uprising in Siberia was later proven to be a fabrication. Fic, *Revolutionary War for Independence*, 458–459.

4. Most of Semenov's men cared only for gaining quick riches from the war developing in their homeland. Stanley K. Hornbeck Papers, "American Expeditionary Forces in Siberia," Hoover Institution Archives.

5. Bobrick, 403.

6. Because of its extensive experience in the Spanish-American War as well as continuing work on the Western Front, the YMCA had become very adept at establishing volunteer centers in the field. The *Krasnaya Retchka* and the *Spaskow* prisoner of war camps had been established in Siberia in order to feed and clothe German and Austrian captives. Volunteers from the Red Cross and the YMCA spread overland to

contact orphans and widows in order to provide help. The YMCA often sold items such as cigarettes, matches, candy, tobacco, soap, fruit, and coffee. Kenneth Andrew Steuer, "The Pursuit of an 'Unparalleled Opportunity': The American YMCA and Prisoner-of-War Diplomacy Among the Central Power Nations During World War I, 1914–1923," PhD diss. University of Minnesota, 1998, footnote #17, 456–457.

7. Telegram to Moscow Consulate from Irkutsk Consulate, Ernest Lloyd Harris Collection, Box #1, June 25, 1918, 3–6.

8. Bečvář, 127–128.

9. Svidine, 20–21.

10. William Duncan. *Letters Home, 1918.*

11. Svidine, 19–22.

12. Hoyt, 139.

13. Hoyt, 140.

14. *The New York Times Current History of the European War,* vol.16, 105.

15. Hoyt, 141–142.

16. Victor Mamatey, "Dissolution of Austria-Hungary" *Journal of Central European Affairs* (10 Oct 1950), 256–70. The only Mamatey reference is *The Rise and Fall of the Habsburg Empire.*

17. William Duncan recalled witnessing the execution of several men who were taken out and shot by the Legion after subduing the town of Barrabinsk. One was an engineer from the Trans-Siberian Railway who had admitted shooting a Czech in the back. Another had been a commissar in Barrabinsk who had been responsible for the mutilation of a Czech officer. Another was a Hungarian caught running into the forest and another Duncan was unable to find any rationale for executing. On the other hand, Duncan also wrote relatives back home of an incident in which three legionnaires fleeing a force of Bolsheviks had stopped at the house of a doctor, who bandaged their wounds. When the Bolsheviks later found out about help given to the enemy by this local doctor, his hands were cut off and as Duncan describes, "the last sight my eyes beheld as we pulled out from that village was the house of the doctor in flames." Letter Home from William Duncan, Barrabinsk, Siberia, June 9, 1918, 1.

18. Fic, *Revolutionary War for Independence,* 318.

19. Emmett Hoskins Collection, 15.

20. *Ibid.,* 14.

21. Bobrick, 398.

22. On its way to Russia, the Root Mission had neglected to stop first in Japan. This perceived slight convinced the Japanese of the mission's sinister and hidden agenda. The United States government flatly denied having any motives other than those publicly announced, but the Japanese continued to believe that the opposite was true. All American railway commissions, diplomatic delegations, and humanitarian groups were henceforth seen by the Japanese as a cover for secret aggression planned with Russian approval and against Japan. For more information concerning the strained relations between Japan and the United States during the intervention into Siberia, see *The New York Times Current History of the European War,* vol. 16, 110–111.

23. George Kennan felt that eastern Siberia could be kept from both Japanese and German influence by American forces. These U.S. forces had to act as a buffer between the Russian people and all foreign elements now inside Siberia. A central issue in Kennan's intervention theory had become the independence of eastern Siberia. George F. Kennan, "Can We Help Russia?," *America Faces Russia: Russian-American Relations From Early Times to Our Day,* ed. Thomas Bailey (Ithaca: Cornell University Press, 1950), 126.

24. George F. Kennan, "American Troops in Russia: The True Record," *Atlantic Monthly,* vol. 203 (January 1959).

25. Lansing to Wilson, June 23, 1918 in *F. R. Lansing Papers,* 364.

26. Hoyt, 135.

27. The summer of 1918 had proven to the Bolsheviks that they were fighting a strong and wily enemy. The cities in western Russia were suffering from hunger and mob violence and Jurenev's message captures the feeling of impending doom. Most Soviet leaders held the belief that the Czechs were intent upon overthrowing Bolshevism. General Gajda, in his *Moje paměti (My Memoirs),* Prague 1920, believed Russia was still too weak to field a national army of any consequence. The Germans, waiting in the west, would surely overwhelm them given time. For more information concerning the fall of Simbirsk and the summer engagements of the Czechs along the Ussuri and Volga fronts, see Klecanda, 14–16.

28. "Count Von Mirbach Assassinated by Two Unknown Men in Russian Office," *San Francisco Chronicle,* July 7, 1918, 1.

29. "Bolsheviki Suppress Uprising in Moscow with Sanguinary Violence," *The San Francisco Chronicle,* July 9, 1918, 1.

30. "Hundreds of Officers Executed by Lenin," *New York Times,* August 22, 1918, 3.

31. Graves, 44–45.

32. Geoffrey Hudson, "The Far East at the End of the First World War," *Contemporary History Journal,* vol.4, no. 2 (April 1969):176–177.

33. This remark, coming from the commanding officer of the United States Army Expeditionary Force, seems in itself peculiar. General Graves left San Francisco with direct orders from President Woodrow Wilson to "help the Czechs

in any way possible." The marooned legionnaires were, in fact, the official reason that American troops had been sent to Siberia. Or were they? It would appear that all of the Allied nations had ulterior motives, motives other than their officially stated goals for sending troops to the Russian Far East provinces of Siberia. General Graves obviously questioned the Slavic troop evacuation plans being used as an excuse by the Allied Command for other hidden agendas. Graves, 44–45.

Chapter Six

1. Nekrasov, 124.
2. Elena Varneck and H. H. Fisher, *The Testimony of Kolchak and Other Siberian Materials* (Palo Alto, CA: Stanford University Press; London: H. Milford, Oxford University Press, 1935), 52.
3. Svidine, 15.
4. Fleming, 100.
5. Hoyt, 177.
6. A. Balawyder, "The Czecho-Slovak Legion Crosses Canada, 1920," *The East European Quarterly*, vol. 6, no. 2, 190–191.
7. "Mr. Skelnička appears to have been lucky since his accommodations were only one half as crowded as other echelon trains which usually carried over forty men per boxcar. His memory of the months spent traveling in the *teplushka* seemed to be colored by periods of boredom and a confusing blur of fighting the enemy." Skelnička interview, Tape #62, part II.
8. Hoyt, 189.
9. Bobrick, 398–399.
10. This became especially important when marching during the summer of 1918. On foot with the legionnaires, William Duncan timed their progress and was astonished that even with such poor boots and no socks, the Legion covered nearly six *versts* (1.067 km) an hour. Letter home, William Duncan Collection, July 18, 1918.
11. Jaroslav J. Verner, "The Mail Goes Through: A Siberian Trip Report," *The Czechoslovak Specialist*, vol. 57, no. 2 (March/April 1999): 1.
12. *Ibid.*, 17.
13. Letters Home, William Duncan Collection, June 14, 1918.
14. Radola Gajda married in Siberia without divorcing a first wife waiting at home in Slovakia. Legionnaires were also discovering that White Russian officers traveled in comfort with wives and mistresses. During periods of little resistance along the railway, women and children had been welcomed but as harassment and violence increased, additional travelers drained resources and became a dangerous distraction

for the men fighting. White Russian officers were known to leave their troops during battle in order to protect wives and family members in the rear. Several died trying to reach trains carrying relatives. Fleming, 149–150.
15. Bobrick, 399.
16. George S. Phelps, "The YMCA with the AEF in Siberia" (unpublished manuscript). YMCA Collection, Hoover Institution Archives, Box #57, 1, 1918.
17. William Duncan, *Letters Home*, 1918.
18. Skelnička interview, tape #62, part II.
19. The fact that London newspapers reported that over 500,000 war prisoners in Siberia were spread across the Trans-Siberian Railway also impressed the Allied Supreme Command in Paris. See "Crisis Reached in Russia as Former German Captives Win Control of Irkutsk Affairs," *San Francisco Chronicle*, July 21, 1918, 5.
20. Letter home, William Duncan Collection, 1918.
21. "Czecho-Slovaks Routed by Bolshevik Forces in Attacks on Several Towns," *San Francisco Chronicle*, July 12, 1918, 2.
22. Phelps, 1.
23. *Ibid.*, 1.
24. Skelnička interview, tape #62, part II.
25. "Vladivostok Falls to Czecho-Slovaks After Disarming," *San Francisco Chronicle*, July 5, 1918, 2.
26. Čápek, 270.
27. *Ibid.*, 272.
28. William F. Miller, "Unit's Last Man Now 92; Old Soldier helped Czechoslovakia," *Cleveland Plain Dealer*, October 24, 1988, 1-B, 5-B.
29. Munitions, rifles, armored vehicles, truck parts, field guns, lathes, barbed wire, Sumatran rubber, rope from the Philippines, farming equipment, ship and airplane parts, sugar from Cuba, and even jute from India all sat on sidings along the Trans-Siberian Railway or stacked in warehouses dockside in Vladivostok waiting to be distributed to the troops and people of western Russia and Siberia. This fact alone gave the Allies reason to prompt General Dieterichs to protect Vladivostok from the Soviets. See Bobrick, 396.
30. Military Intelligence Division. *General Description and Introductory Information.* "Siberia and Eastern Russia," part I, Military Monograph Subsection, M.I.2., Hoover Institution Archives.
31. White, 260.
32. "Heavy Demands on Red Cross Forecast," *San Francisco Chronicle*, August 24, 1918, 2.
33. Berk, 185–186.
34. Baerlein, 167–171.
35. *Ibid.*, 166–167.
36. Vaněk, Holeček, and Medek, 260.

37. Bečvář, 137.
38. Baerlein, 167–171.
39. Hoyt, 132–133.
40. Letters Home, William Duncan Collection, 24 Jul 1918.

Chapter Seven

1. Ivan Narodny, "Mr. and Mrs. Nicholas Romanoff Humble Citizens in Exile," *San Francisco Chronicle*, April 7, 1917, 1.
2. Unfortunately, inaccurate stories of the Romanovs' whereabouts surfaced throughout June and July 1918. One such report had the entire family escaping on a steamer from Murmansk. This report supposedly came from a Russian eyewitness who traveled on board the very same ship where he reported seeing the royal family. See "Former Czar's Family Flees Safely from Murman Coast," *San Francisco Chronicle*, July 4, 1918, 1.
3. As late as mid–July 1918, the Western press awaited this show trial, reporting from time to time that Nicholas II would be turned over to his cousin, Britain's King George V. Reports also described daring escapes to freedom in the north — all inaccurate. See "Agree to Give up Czechs," *New York Times*, July 3, 1918, 1.
4. "Duke Michael of Russia Proclaimed Czar; Marching against Moscow," *San Francisco Chronicle*, July 4, 1918, 1.
5. Bobrick, 385.
6. "Russian Wireless Statement Gives Details of Former Ruler's Execution for Alleged Conspiracy; Ex-Empress and Son Sent Away for Safety," *San Francisco Chronicle*, July 21, 1918, 1.
7. Harry Hoskins, 11.
8. Fleming, 86.
9. Fleming, 85–87.
10. Emmett Hoskins, Box 1, 2–3.
11. Fleming, 88.
12. Vaněk, Holeček, and Medek, 8–9.
13. Emphasis is mine.
14. Bradley, 100.
15. The Imperial Gold Reserve was estimated at the time to be worth over 330 million dollars [USD]. Bobrick, 395.
16. Baerlein, 188–190.
17. Bradley, 102.
18. In his letters home, William Duncan, with the YMCA, exclaims, "I am witnessing scenes everyday that *The New York Times* sure would give all the space to in the Sunday Supplement if I could only produce the negatives. It is a shame to be in such a position and without photographic ammunition." William Duncan, *Letters Home*, 1918.
19. Hoyt, 148.
20. Klecanda, 15.

21. "Baikal Tunnel Blown Up," *New York Times*, August 21, 1918, 3.
22. In dispatch #106, Alphonse Guinne announced that Captain Ivankin from the second Novo-Nikolaevsk Regiment was identified early in the summer as one soldier who helped to keep the Baikal tunnels secure. Ivankin was awarded the Cross of the Legion of Honor as recommended by Colonel Kadlec and General Gajda in a telegram from Sludanka. Unfortunately, Gajda could not keep the last tunnel from again being attacked later that summer. See the Evatsia Collection. "Telegram from the Czecho-Slovak Army to other echelons along the Trans-Siberian Railway," #106, Hoover Institution Archives.
23. Klecanda, 15.
24. Bradley, 92–95.
25. This description comes from the *New York Times* correspondent, Carl W. Ackerman, who traveled with the Legion throughout the summer of 1918, sending dispatches and reports home to his editor for the American public to follow the Czech and Slovak advance toward Vladivostok. Later Ackerman's reports were compiled in his *Source Records of the Great War*. For information about the Baikal advance see vol. 6, "Siberian Independence Proclaimed," 231.
26. Fleming, 126.
27. General Alfred Knox became an open supporter of Admiral Kolchak, convinced that this was perhaps the one man who could put Russia and a second front back together again. Lengyel, 221.
28. Incredibly, during a dinner in Krasnoyarsk, General Knox, a guest of the English vice-consul, announced to all in attendance that he believed Siberia was not ready for democracy. Instead the region needed a dictator, preferably General Gajda or Admiral Kolchak. Dotsenko, 52.
29. Fleming, 126.
30. Berk, 184.
31. Varneck and Fisher, 151.
32. *Times* (London), June 12, 1918, 6.
33. "Japan Ready for Joint Intervention in Siberia," *San Francisco Chronicle*, July 23, 1918, 1–2.
34. "Czecho-Slovak Army Declared Hope of Russia," *San Francisco Chronicle*, July 20, 1918, 4.
35. In July 1918, Kerensky, who had fled west when the Menshevik government fell, was invited to the U.S. by Socialists to discuss the effects of Bolshevism in Russia. Rumors of Allied intentions surfaced openly in the press. By December 23, 1918, an official but secret agreement was signed between France and Great Britain. See "Kaiser's Force in Siberia Smashed," *San Francisco Chronicle*, July 14, 1918, 1.

36. White, 240–241.

37. William Sydney Graves, born in Mount Calm, Texas, on March 27, 1865, was the son of a Baptist minister. He graduated from West Point in 1889 and spent ten years in the Seventh Infantry, which played a major role in the Spanish-American War. Later, Graves became assigned to the general staff, first as its secretary and then as an assistant to the chief. By 1918, he had been promoted to major general and given command of the American Twentieth Infantry Division. Secretary of War Baker met with Graves on August 2, 1918, to place the command of the American Expeditionary Forces (AEF) in his able hands. Unfortunately for William Graves, he had never been informed of President Wilson's intentions in Siberia. The quagmire of political intrigue and violence involving both the Bolsheviks and America's allies left the situation in which the AEF found itself ambiguous at best. Graves and his men floundered as a neutral force, caught between factions and without any clear directives from their commander in chief. White, 426.

38. Department of State, *Papers Relating to the Foreign Relations of the United States, 1918, The World War.* (Washington, D.C.: Government Printing Office, 1933), 15. See also: William Appleton Williams, *The Tragedy of American Diplomacy* (New York: Dell, 1959), 94–95, 116–117.

39. The problem of Bolshevik social revolution underscored the naivete of the Wilson government, which conversely affected the ability of the United States to confront the Soviet government in any meaningful way for decades afterward. Gabriel Kolko, *Main Currents in Modern American History* (New York: Harper & Row, 1976), 59–62.

40. Graves, 67.

41. Hidden within this telegram is the assumption that the effort of the Czechs and Slovaks was somehow to help the Allied war effort and that the Allied Command should take advantage of their success. Telegram to the Secretary of State, Washington, D.C., from Harris, Irkutsk Consulate, July 29, 1918, Ernest Lloyd Harris Collection.

42. Graves, 66.

43. Bečvář, 155–156.

Chapter Eight

1. This stanza is taken from a poem written by Colonel Rudolf Medek of the Legion while on board one of the teplushkas. Colonel Medek would later chronicle his experiences while in Siberia in his 1929 memoir, *The Czech Anabasis Across Russia and Siberia.* Rudolf Medek's *"Lvi*

Srdce" "Lion Hearts" can be found in Baerlein, 122.

2. In the fall of 1918, General Knox organized and ran an officers' school in Vladivostok. He hoped that one day this academy would provide Russia with a new officer corps, one trained in British strategy. Balawyder, "The Czecho-Slovak Legion Crosses Canada," *The East European Quarterly* 4, no. 2 (April 1920):178–180

3. Manning, 149.

4. Bradley, 120–122.

5. Emmett Hoskins, 1, 6.

6. Kennan, 108–109.

7. "Reds Ask Allies to State Demands," *New York Times,* August 25, 1918, 3.

8. White, 256.

9. Unterberger, *The United States,* 285.

10. Carl Ackerman, "The Odyssey of the Czecho-Slovaks," in *Source Records of the Great War,* 151, 163.

11. The OCSNR had little choice but to go along with any and all orders of the Allied Command. Czech and Slovak officers were made aware that the legionnaires might never get home if they did not cooperate fully in this attempt to establish an anti–German Eastern Front inside Russia. Klecanda, 4.

12. Fleming, 48–51.

13. Hoyt, 160.

14. *Ibid.,* 158.

15. Baerlein, 269.

16. Military Monograph, *Siberia and Eastern Russia,* 14–15.

17. Vaněk, Holeček, and Medek, 8.

18. Dotsenko, 52.

19. Graves, 115.

20. Bradley, 110–111.

21. Later, Lieutenant Colonel Vladimír Klecanda's expertise in surveying became crucial for United States Army Intelligence during the Cold War. Klecanda submitted his own summary of the Czech and Slovak Legion's experience in the intervention period along with maps detailing locations along the fronts, village topography, and the position of the railway lines in relation to both. Later, Jerry V. Matyka of the United States Army Signal Corps translated this work, which made it invaluable to the United States government. Throughout the Cold War era all maps and physical descriptions of the Siberian terrain had been kept secret by the Soviet Union. Only a handful of detailed descriptions existed outside of Moscow's inner circle. Klecanda's early efforts to chart Siberia proved highly useful to the United States and its allies. Much of this type of documentation is only now becoming declassified. See Klecanda.

22. Manning, 52.

23. "Reds Ask Allies to State Demands," *New York Times,* August 25, 1919, 3.

24. "War Declared on United States by Bolshevik Chiefs," *San Francisco Chronicle*, August 23, 1918, 2.

25. Baerlein, 192.

26. Strakhovsky, 126.

27. "Allies Defeat Reds on Ussuri: Lenin Twice Wounded by an Assassin," *New York Times*, September 1, 1918, 5.

28. "Allies Defeat Reds on Ussuri," *New York Times*, September 3, 1918, 1 & 9.

29. "Bolsheviks Intern Entente Subjects," *New York Times*, September 4, 1918, 8.

30. "Red Press Bloodthirsty," *New York Times*, September 11, 1918, 3.

31. "Red Leaders Kill 546 More Victims," *New York Times*, September 10, 1918, 9.

32. Captain Francis Cromie had received the Distinguished Service Order for becoming one of Britain's first submarine commanders. He headed the Hong Kong submarine flotilla at the beginning of the war, and later commanded an E-19 in the Baltic Sea, where he became famous for sinking the German cruiser *Urdine*, as well as capturing ten German steamships. During the Bolshevik upheaval in Moscow, Cromie again won British Government praise for evacuating all of Britain's submarines from the Baltic Coast before the German fleet could capture them. Cromie gained recognition as a man well versed not only in Russian literature, language, and culture but for his love of the Russian people. This gained him the British Embassy position in Petrograd. See "Reds at Moscow Raid the Consulate of Great Britain," *New York Times,* September 6, 1918, 1.

33. "107 American Refugees," *New York Times,* September 8, 1918, 6.

34. Bradley, 107–109.

35. General Grave's *Aide Memoire* confused the Soviets who, though they denounced Woodrow Wilson's mandate, nonetheless continued to ask for assistance from Washington. Medical supplies, railway technical expertise, food, and clothing were rushed to both the counterrevolutionaries and to Moscow from the Wilson administration during this period. Manning, 10. See also Graves, 82.

36. Nadia Shapiro Papers. Hoover Institute, 7.

37. Bradley, 122–123.

38. On his arrival in Siberia, General Graves reported to General Otani in order to advise the Japanese commander that the United States would give the Japanese full cooperation. Under no circumstances would U.S. troops, however, be placed under Japanese command. Kennan, 108–109.

39. Harry Hoskins, *The Story of an Expedition,* 3–4.

40. White, 209.

41. *Ibid.*, 265–267.

42. *Ibid.*, 198–199.

43. *Ibid.*, 95.

44. Manning, 51.

45. Bradley, 108–110.

46. When the Legion came into close contact with White Russian contingents, Czech and Slovak troops often found themselves quickly abandoned or disregarded in the field. *Ibid.*, 133–135.

47. White, 278–279.

48. "The Association," as it became known, had been organized into five separate departments to streamline work efforts. They were the: (1) Civilian Work Department, (2) Railway Employees Department, (3) Army and Navy Department, (4) Rural Community Work, and (5) Prisoner of War Aid. For further information see Edward T. Heald, "Enroute Novo-Nikolayevsk to Krasnoyarsk," in *Witness to Revolution: Letters from Russia, 1916–1919* (Kent, OH: Kent State University Press, 1972), 314–315. See "YMCA Praised in Army Report," *San Francisco Chronicle*, May 29, 1919, 5.

49. YMCA Papers. "The YMCA With the A.E.F., Siberia," Box #57, 1, George S. Phelps Collection, Hoover Institute.

50. Much of what we know about winter conditions for both the Czech and Slovak units in the field and the populations under their care are provided by records, letters, photographs and diaries kept by the YMCA field representatives who traveled with the Czech and Slovak contingents throughout the winter of 1918 and all of 1919. William Duncan, "Uncle Duncan," as the legionnaires called him, traveled with the Sixth Regiment, observing the soldiers in battle and befriending peasants along the way. Duncan worked with the Omsk Legion where he made meticulous notes of his activities. Representative Riley worked in Tomsk and Vladivostok with the Czechs and Slovaks, Ken Miller in Irkutsk, and a Mr. Bunker in Krasnoyarsk and Novo-Nikolayevsk. Their letters describe the cruelty and horror of the conditions under which the Legion and the peasantry were left to fend for themselves. Neither the Legion nor the YMCA secretaries traveling with them felt enough was being done to help Russian or Siberian noncombatants. Steuer, 465–470.

51. Graves, 115.

52. Baerlein, 187.

53. *Ibid.*, 190.

54. Lengyel, 231.

55. *Ibid.*, 230.

56. *Ibid.*, 231.

Chapter Nine

1. Berk, 186.

2. Hoyt, 67. See also Bradley, 133–135.

3. Ernest Lloyd Harris, "The Truth about the Czechoslovak Legions in Siberia" *The Central European Observer,* vol. 11, no. 8 (April 14, 1933): 132–133.

4. "Austrian Czechs are Growing Bolder," *New York Times,* September 14, 1918, 3.

5. J.V. Polišenský, *History of Czechoslovakia in Outline* (Praha: Bohemia International, 1991), 110.

6. Hoyt, 67.

7. William Duncan, Letters home, 1918.

8. The United States chose to remain in Siberia partly to keep an eye on its ally, Japan, and to help with relief for victims of the growing chaos throughout the countryside. See Kennan, 110–111.

9. Hoyt, 190–194.

10. Fleming, 100.

11. Hoyt, 177.

12. Fleming, 95.

13. White, 112.

14. Baerlein, 207–208.

15. Fleming, 100.

16. The British always maintained that Kolchak had only their limited support and never officially backed him in his endeavors. Bradley, 125.

17. Varneck and Fisher, 165.

18. Kelley, 29.

19. *Ibid.,* 29.

20. Varneck and Fisher, 165.

21. Lengyel, 239.

22. Bobrick, 402.

23. Hoyt, 190–194.

24. Vaněk, Holeček, and Medek, 11–12.

25. Bobrick, 399.

26. Kolchak often stated that he meant for Minister Boldrev to fill the post. Kolchak remembered being astounded by the unanimous vote for him to become ruler. Fleming, 112.

27. George A. Brinkley, *The Volunteer Army and Allied Intervention in South Russia, 1917–1921* (South Bend, IN: University of Notre Dame, 1966), 190.

28. Berk, 476.

29. The manner in which the coup d'état was handled has long been a controversy. Did Kolchak act under British orders to have the Directory of Five arrested? Corroboration for this view has not been found. Kolchak always maintained, even when threatened with execution, that he never wanted the power placed in his hands. Fleming, 114.

30. Dotsenko, 74–75.

31. Manning, 160.

32. Edward T. Heald, "En Route to Chelyabinsk, December 9, 1918," *Witness to Revolution: Letters from Russia, 1916–1919* (Kent, OH: Kent State University Press, 1972) 264–265.

33. Bradley, 113–114.

34. Though he never explains where the information comes from, Bradley alleges that Gajda married Kolchak's daughter to gain even closer ties to the ex-admiral. It is known that Radola Gajda married while in Siberia even though he was reportedly already married in his homeland. Bradley, 114–115.

35. Later, the Czechs and Slovaks accused Kolchak's officers of cowardice. The Legion believed that White army officers hid out in Omsk as staff members to remain safe behind the lines while their troops continued to fight on at the front. Bečvář, 199.

36. Fleming, 118.

37. Bobrick, 403.

38. Baerlein, 225.

39. Geoffrey Hudson, "The Far East at the End of the First World War," *Contemporary History Journal* vol. 4, no. 2 (April 1969):177.

40. Bobrick, 401.

41. *Ibid.,* 403.

Chapter Ten

1. Baerlein, 268–269.

2. Heald, "Enroute to Omsk," *Witness to Revolution,* 313.

3. Description by William Duncan from a letter home written on November 26, 1919, from Chita, William Duncan Collection.

4. Fleming, 133.

5. Graves, 82–83.

6. Shapiro, 6.

7. Emmett Hoskins, 4.

8. William Duncan Collection, May 19, 1918.

9. Dotsenko, 43, 48.

10. Lengyel, 237–238.

11. Emmett Hoskins, 20.

12. *Ibid.,* 17.

13. Bobrick, 402.

14. Letter from G.S. Phelps, Sr., national secretary for Russia in Vladivostok to Dr. John R. Mott, YMCA, New York, July 15, 1919, 5–7, Hoover Institute Archives.

15. Letters Home from Edward Heald, Petersen Library.

16. George S. Phelps Collection, Hoover Institute, 3–4.

17. Steuer, 137–140.

18. Clifford C. Hatfield, "Y.M.C.A. Rural Department, September Report," Krasnoyarsk Regional Office Records, October 3, 1919, 1–3. Kautz Family YMCA Archives.

19. Hoover Institute, Box #57, 2–3.

20. Walter Grayson Collection. Gail Berg Reitzel, "Shifting Scenes in Siberia" (unpublished diaries), Siberia, 1918/1919, 296, 317, Hoover Institute.

21. White, 138.

22. Vaněk, Holeček, and Medek, 12.
23. Roland Morris, "A Railway Three Nations Want," Hoover Institute.
24. Fleming, 102.
25. Ray S. Baker, ed, *Woodrow Wilson, Life and Letters,* (New York: Doubleday, Doran and Co., Inc. 1939), 2:392.
26. Baerlein, 274–275.
27. Department of State. "Foreign Relations of the United States, 1919," 277–278.
28. Mary Andreyka, oral interview with author, Oct 1996. Mary's father left Siberia for Czechoslovakia walking with others in just such a manner. His travels home took him years. Later, he moved his family to the United States to begin life again as Czech-Americans.
29. Hoyt, 187–188.
30. Bradley, 117.
31. Berk, 466–468.
32. "Admiral Kolchak," *Saturday Evening Post,* July 31, 1920, 8.
33. Fleming, 104.
34. Klecanda, 18.
35. Imrey, 333.
36. Baerlein, 223.
37. *Ibid.,* 223.
38. Lengyel, 227–228.
39. Joseph Skelnička's memories of cooperation between the counterrevolutionary troops under Semenov and Kolchak do not always agree with official documents and primary source information of the Siberian intervention. Most of the literature from the period points to a consistent pattern of harassment on the part of Russian and especially Cossack troops when dealing with the Legion. To a great degree, Central European troops and prisoners of war were seen as interlopers in Siberian affairs. But they had been expected to take the brunt of fighting on the newly established Ussuri and Volga fronts. The Czechs and Slovaks felt that they were due at least a "thank you" from the Russians. When this did not occur, legionnaires grew hostile to Kolchak in particular. Perhaps Mr. Skelnička's memory changed with time or perhaps serving under Captain Kadlec, a much-admired White Russian officer, gave Skelnička's unit a uniquely cooperative view of the counterrevolution. Interview with Mr. Joseph Skelnička 29 Apr 1977.
40. Hoyt, 232.
41. Many, like Dr. Raše, had not been home in years. Raše's daughter had been only two years old when he last saw her. She was nine when he returned. Baerlein, 277.
42. One of a handful of unanimous decisions on Russian policy made by Allied representatives in Versailles was the recognition of the Kolchak regime in Omsk. Unfortunately, leaders in Versailles had not been informed about Kolchak's wildly swinging bouts of depression. They did receive reports, however, that Kolchak's administration continued to grow ever more top-heavy and nonresponsive. The supreme ruler had begun to hear more and more criticism by the Allied Command in France. Potach, 33–34.
43. Fleming, 142.
44. Baerlein, 218–219.
45. Lengyel, 240–244.
46. Baerlein, 219.
47. *Ibid.,* 218.
48. Fleming, 152.
49. Varneck and Fisher, 193.
50. It was hard for anyone to believe that Admiral Kolchak remained so naive concerning the wholesale dishonesty within the White Army officer corps. Although both Radola Gajda and other ally officers complained of missing and diverted supplies, apparently Kolchak continued to believe the explanations of his staff. According to his own testimony, the supreme ruler never investigated the supply situation once his generals became involved. The Soviets knew more about the apparent lack of clothing, food, and arms in the White ranks than did Kolchak. The Bolsheviks later used this knowledge to lure men out of the White Army and into the Red Army. For further information see Varneck and Fisher, 184.
51. Baerlein, 230.
52. Graves, 201.
53. Baerlein, 231.
54. Hoyt, 189.

Chapter Eleven

1. Heald, 315.
2. Hoyt, 196.
3. Baerlein, 257.
4. United States Government, Special Staff Record #164-#212, Record #165, note #83, 41.
5. White, 263.
6. White, 264–265.
7. Meanwhile, in Pittsburgh, Pennsylvania, 100 veterans of the Legion who had been evacuated earlier were provided a heroe's welcome. Most had missing limbs but stood at attention as the train pulled into Pennsylvania Station. Though suffering physically, many mentioned the treatment of their comrades that continued in Siberia. See "Tribute Paid by Pittsburgh to Bohemians," *Pittsburgh Gazette Times,* June 8, 1919, 1, 6.
8. White, 273.
9. "Czechs Routed by Hungarians in Fierce Fight; Decisive Victory Claimed by Budapest after Two-Day Battle for Town," *Pittsburgh Gazette Times,* June 9, 1919, 5.
10. Bradley, 130–131.
11. Baerlein, 228.

12. Letter to Colton from C. Alexander, February 1919, YMCA Collection, Box #57, 7, Hoover Institute.

13. *Ibid.*, 3–5.

14. Lengyel, 236–237.

15. White, 324–327.

16. *Ibid.*, 262.

17. "Bolsheviks Facing Further Internal War; More British Reach Archangel," *San Francisco Chronicle,* May 29, 1919, 1.

18. William A. Rowan, "The Odyssey of the Czechs" *East European Quarterly,* vol. 9, no. 1, 15–38.

19. This primary source was authored by Allen Henry Wright and appears to have been submitted as an article to the San Diego newspapers but never published. Allen Henry Wright's notations are dated Friday, July 4, 1919. Reif Collection, San Diego Historical Society Archives.

20. Report from Rowen to Cordier, United States Military Intelligence, Record #165.

21. "War-Worn Heroes from Siberia Debark amid Shouts of 'Nazdar' Salutation of Native Tongue," *San Diego Union,* July 4, 1919, 1.

22. Many Czech-Americans and Slovak-Americans from Los Angeles and San Diego neighborhoods had gathered together at dockside to get a glimpse of these soldiers, whom they considered heroes for surviving their arduous trek across Siberia. *The San Diego Union,* July 4, 1919, 1.

23. Russian sable furs, coffee and wool would be transported on to San Francisco during the last leg of the voyage. "Czechs Tell of Terrible Hardship of Warfare in Snowbound Siberia," *San Diego Union,* July 4, 1919, 5.

24. The *Nanking* left Siberia on June 15, 1919, from Vladivostok. She had been in service for a long time already, and had come to San Diego earlier under the names USS *Congress* and *Emanuel Alexander.* The *Nanking* left San Diego Harbor at 1:00 P.M. that same day for San Francisco, where the ship and its crew were finally released from further Legion duties. Much later, one more ship, the *Heffron,* would be stopping in San Diego. It carried 4,000 more legionnaires. The *Nanking* was owned by the British government and later sold to the Pacific Coast Steamship Company. She kept the name *Nanking,* even while in service carrying gas bombs across the Atlantic Ocean until torpedoed and sunk during World War II. Information gathered from the Frederick Reif Collection. Allen Henry Wright notes, San Diego Historical Society.

25. *The San Diego Union,* July 4, 1919, 5.

26. "S.F. Gives Ovation to Wounded Czechs," *San Francisco Chronicle,* May 29, 1919, 7.

27. *San Diego Union,* July 4, 1919, 5.

28. Report from Rowe to Cordier, Military Intelligence, Record #165.

29. Report from Tucker to Cordier, Military Intelligence, Record #165.

30. This fourth and last train was scheduled to:

> LEAVE: Camp Kearny at 12:05 P.M. on July 28, 1919. (Along this leg of the trip, a delay occurred when a freight train ahead of the Czech troop transport derailed. The transport was halted in Arizona while the freight was righted.)
> ARRIVE: Kansas City at 6:55 P.M. on July 31, 1919.
> LEAVE: Kansas City at 8:00 P.M. on July 31, 1919.
> ARRIVE: St. Louis at 8:35 A.M. on August 1, 1919 (with a delay of three hours due to engine trouble).
> LEAVE: St. Louis at 10:05 A.M. on August 1, 1919.
> ARRIVE: Norfolk, Virginia, at 2:00 A.M. on August 5, 1919. They were housed at Norfolk Army Base.

Hines report to Cordier, Military Intelligence, Record #165.

31. *Ibid.*

32. *Ibid.*

33. Report from Ross to Cordier, Military Intelligence, Record #165.

34. Report from Hines to Cordier, Military Intelligence, Record #165.

35. "President Reviews Czechoslovak Unit," *New York Times,* July 19, 1919, 4.

36. *Ibid.*

37. Hoyt, 204.

38. *Ibid.*, 204.

Chapter Twelve

1. F. A. Puchkov, "The Icy March, 1921–1922," Hoover Institute Archives, 35.

2. Fleming, 165.

3. Emphasis is my own.

4. Hoyt, 202.

5. Lengyel, 244.

6. "Americans Held Train Against Semenoff," *New York Times,* November 19, 1919, 1.

7. William Duncan Collection, Letters home.

8. Baerlein, 235.

9. Fleming, 167.

10. *Ibid.,* 171.

11. White, 345.

12. Harmon Tupper, *To the Great Ocean* (Boston, MA: Little Brown, 1965), 380.

13. "Americans Held Train Against Semenoff," *New York Times,* November 19, 1919, 17.

14. "Election in Russia When Reds Fall, Kolchak Says," *Pittsburgh Post-Gazette,* June 8, 1919, 11.

15. Baerlein, 178–181.

16. Emphasis is mine.

17. Fleming, 52.

18. White, 324–325.

19. The American forces actually left by April 1920, whereas the final American ship to help evacuate the Czechs and Slovaks did not sail until August 27, 1920. Rowan, 15–28.

20. "Denikin Army Falls Back; Towns Given Up," *San Francisco Chronicle*, November 27, 1919, 2.

21. Fleming, 160.

22. White, 345.

23. Aberrations occurred during this last phase as well. Amidst large-scale chaos, units banded together in strict discipline and formation that caused members to feel a sense of mutual obligation to one another but denied connection to the "outsiders." This became a huge problem when thousands of fleeing White troops lost contact with their own units and were denied help by other White echelons. Puchkov, 33–34.

24. Dotsenko, 99.

25. Ernest Lloyd Harris Collection, "Admiral Kolchak," 31 Jul 1920, Box #2, 120, Hoover Institute.

26. White, 345.

27. Lengyel, 246–247, 254.

28. Fleming, 163.

29. *Ibid.*

30. Hoyt, 206.

31. *Ibid.*, 203–205.

32. Tupper, 380.

33. Puchkov, 6.

34. Reitzel, 304.

35. "Big Offer to Kolchak," *New York Times*, November 22, 1919, 15.

36. Hoyt, 219.

37. "Czechs to Guard Siberian Road," *New York Times*, January 1, 1920, 3.

38. "Battle in Irkutsk Reported by Soviet," *New York Times*, January 18, 1920, 17.

39. White, 205.

40. Puchkov reports that even the Bolshevik officers chasing after the retreating armies discovered abandoned trains filled with frozen sick and wounded troops who had been abandoned clad only in bedclothes and blankets. When these trains were discovered, the Red Army reacted in horror. Employees of the Trans-Siberian line whose job it had been to transport these travelers simply left the trains parked on sidings and fled to the east along with the rest of the swell of humanity. See Puchkov, 4.

41. Ramsey Tompkins, *A Canadian's Road to Russia: Letters from the Great War Decade* (Calgary, AB: University of Alberta Press, 1989), 1–2.

42. Tompkins, 1–2.

43. Emphasis is my own.

44. Bradley, 142.

45. This letter was an attempt to inform the world about excesses in Siberia. The Legion and

its leadership worried that murder and torture had occurred in areas under their protection. Meant to inform the Allies of the situation, information such as this letter became buried within the National Archives as classified for over 50 years. Letter from Girsa and Pavlů to American Expeditionary Forces Headquarters. Record #165. Military Intelligence.

46. Hoyt, 206.

47. "Return of the Czecho-Slovaks," *New York Times*, September 27, 1919, 12.

48. Hoyt, 200.

49. Hoyt, 206.

50. *Ibid.*, 206.

51. "Revolution Starts in Vladivostok," *New York Times*, November 19, 1919, 17.

52. "Japan Prepares to Act in Siberia," *New York Times*, November 24, 1919, 2.

53. Fleming, 171.

54. Hoyt, 207.

55. General Gajda continued to believe that the Japanese had been responsible for harbor ferries disappearing during the revolt. The lack of ferries effectively isolated Czech and Slovak forces in their barracks on the island in the harbor, making it impossible for them to intervene to help Gajda's efforts. Gajda wrote that the White Russian soldiers who revolted against Rozanov were finally forced to hand over their weapons after being surrounded in the train station. Once unarmed, Rozanov's soldiers shot them in the head. "Japan Prepares to Act in Siberia," *New York Times*, November 24, 1919, 2.

56. White, 340.

Chapter Thirteen

1. National Archives, State Department File 61.00/2692, September 13, 1918.

2. Rowan, 22.

3. Rowan, 27.

4. Rowan, 15.

5. *Ibid.*, 30.

6. Vaněk, Holeček, and Medek, 14.

7. Conversely, it would be the Czech and Slovak Legion that came under criticism for commandeering trains to use in this retreat since little was known at the time of how the Japanese held boxcars and engines in the rear in order to impede the flow of people and supplies eastward to Vladivostok. The Japanese enforced this policy so that their troops could step into the situation in order to "help." White, 154.

8. Fleming, 176.

9. Puchkov, 9–14.

10. Unfortunately, the journey eastward proved to be a terrible trek for anyone involved in this massive retreat of the White Army toward the Pacific coast. Puchkov's descriptions paint a pic-

ture of families, soldiers and medics racing ahead of the Red Army only to become bogged down in the snow and ice with a mass of humanity also in flight on the Trans-Siberian Railway. Puchkov, 36.

11. Rowan, 15–28.

12. "Russians Carry Jewels to Japan," *San Francisco Chronicle,* July 4, 1918, 6.

13. Fleming, 177.

14. Hoyt, 210.

15. Baerlein, 246–248.

16. Hoyt, 217.

17. *Ibid.,* 211.

18. *Ibid.,* 221–222.

19. Browning and FitzLyon, 9.

20. "French Roused by Kolchak Case," *The New York Times,* January 30, 1920, 2.

21. White, 344.

22. Hoyt, 224.

23. Baerlein, 252–256.

24. *Ibid.,* 216.

25. Bradley, 147.

26. "Admiral Kolchak," *Saturday Evening Post,* July 31, 1920, 120.

27. Hoyt, 228–229.

28. *Ibid.,* 229.

29. *Ibid.,* 228.

30. In a lengthy description of the movement of the supreme ruler and the Omsk government, the Irkutsk newspaper *Kielo,* December 27, 1919, identified Anna Timirev as Kolchak's wife. Reitzel, 312.

31. Fleming, 198.

32. "Revolt Flaming in Siberia; Juncture with Reds Favored," *San Francisco Chronicle,* February 20, 1920, 2.

33. "All Our Forces Quit Siberia in a Few Weeks," *New York Times,* January 13, 1920, 1.

34. Bobrick, 41.

35. After moving to Verchne-Udiinsk, the Political Center Party became the foundation for the Far Eastern Republic government, a buffer state existing between China, Japan, and Soviet Russia. A Soviet puppet government between Lake Baikal and the Pacific coast, it abolished private land ownership but allowed a radical democratic form of government instead of Bolshevism. Fleming, 231.

36. Fleming, 200.

37. Bobrick, 411.

38. "French Roused by Kolchak's Case," *New York Times,* January 30, 1920, 8.

39. Hoyt, 230–231.

40. "Revolt Flaming in Siberia; Juncture with Reds Favored," *San Francisco Chronicle,* February 20, 1920, 2.

41. Fleming. 227.

42. *Ibid.,* 225.

43. Varneck and Fisher, 213.

44. Puchkov, 26.

45. Fleming, 216.

46. [No title], *Československý deník,* February 13, 1920, 1.

47. Bobrick, 410–411.

Chapter Fourteen

1. Manning, 132.

2. *Ibid.,* 132.

3. Lengyel, 253.

4. Bobrick, 413.

5. "Kerensky Going to Prague," *New York Times,* February 5, 1920, 2.

6. Bradley, 152.

7. Fleming, 234.

8. Baerlein, 239.

9. White, 342.

10. Baerlein, 238–239.

11. Kennan, 112.

12. One such story in February 1920 seemed to forecast the impending doom of many White Russians left behind to face the Red Guard. In the port of Novorossik, ahead of the Red Army, White Russian officers rushed to board the vessel *Karplin* with their wives and children. As the *Karplin* pushed off, three-inch guns opened up from a minor harbor nearby. More than 1,400 refugees, mostly women and children, drowned as a result. Paul Williams, "Government Officials, Women, and Children Sent to Death by Bolsheviki; Attack Made from Pier," *San Francisco Chronicle,* February 12, 1920, 1.

13. White, 387.

14. William J Ankeley, "An Unaccountable Accounting," *Proceedings: United States Naval Institute Journal, History Supplement* (1985): 44.

15. "Riots, Murder in Odessa After Red Conquests; Deniken's Men Scatter," *San Francisco Chronicle,* February 12, 1920, 2.

16. "Sources Say 16,000 Soldiers were Frozen to Death," *New York Times,* March 25, 1920, 3.

17. In January 1920, Ataman Kalmykov also fled to Manchuria, where he was later executed by the Chinese. For further information see White, 121.

18. After most of the Allies had sailed home, Nina Lebedeva and her lover attacked and massacred the Japanese garrison in Nikolayevsk. As ordered by 25-year-old Lebedeva, a vamp in red leather, every last Japanese soldier was slaughtered. When the Japanese recaptured the town, they burned Nikolayevsk to the ground and executed Lebedeva and her band of bandits. Bobrick, 411.

19. Bradley, 155–156.

20. "Story of Red Revolutionists; Capture of Vladivostok from Kolchak's Regime is Told," *San Francisco Chronicle,* February 19, 1920, 2.

21. Yurchak, 201.

22. Baerlein recorded 1,600 marriages of the

legionnaires in Siberia. Of the POWs on the *Mount Vernon*, 391 were Germans, 177 Austrians, and 131 Hungarians. National Archives, Quartermaster General File 579.3/92, *Mount Vernon* passenger list.

23. Balawyder, 188.

24. The vessel *Valencia* also transported two bears and a Siberian pony. The total cost for transporting some 9,000 legionnaires was estimated at around $35,000. See R.P. Brown to W.V. Cape. Canadian Military Headquarters, *"Repatriation from Vladivostok to Europe of Czechoslovak Troops."* (Ottawa: Public Archives of Canada), 732–739.

25. Balawyder, 183.

26. Though no other information has come to light, the Vlastnik family continues to hope that someday, somehow they will find out what happened to František "out there." The ceramic oval sits alongside the original photograph on the mantelpiece of the Vlastnik family home in Peru, Illinois.

Epilogue

1. Manning, 83.

2. "Foreigners Forced to Work for Red Army or Starve," *San Francisco Chronicle*, February 18, 1920, 1–2.

3. Bobrick, 413.

4. Shapiro, 8.

5. White, 353.

6. Letters and field reports from Association staff, 1920, Kautz Family YMCA Archives.

7. Bobrick, 412.

8. White, 354.

9. Fleming, 232.

10. Hudson, 177.

11. Lengyel, 258.

12. Michael Taylor, "The Czarist Sailors," *San Francisco Chronicle,* March 11, 1974, 4.

13. Hoskins and the other men who joined his lawsuit won their case against the United States government, which had to pay each between $50,000 and $60,000 for denied benefits. Many had died of natural causes by the time the case was settled. "Troops in from the Cold," *Daily Telegraph*, 1967, 9. See also Bob Schultz, "Vets of Russia Still at War," *Los Angeles Herald-Examiner*, April 11, 1971, A8.

14. Miller, 325–326.

15. In light of General Gajda's later actions against the government of Thomas Masaryk, accusations of opportunism have yet to be answered. Many of Gajda's activities while in Siberia have come under examination. He has been portrayed as a man who would do anything for power and glory including murdering prisoners under his care. Others have said that he returned to Czechoslovakia with a sizable amount of property pilfered while in Siberia. To a great extent, his early behavior does not fit with his later years, yet Gajda did save tens of thousands of peasants while in Siberia and became known by his men as a heroic leader who sided with them against corrupt White Russian officials. It would appear that the real story of Radola Gajda, though fascinating, might never be known. For more information see Varneck and Fisher, 240–241.

16. Miller, 448–449.

17. Andrejka oral history with the author. Joseph Halama and Marie immigrated to the Chicago area in 1921. They traveled through Bremen, Germany, as thousands had before them. See Mary Andrejka's letter to the author, June 1998, p. 1. Included are the inspection cards for the Bremen line with a manifest list from steerage, Czechoslovak army in Russia, number 41121, stating Halama's village of origin, date of birth, service induction date and full name.

18. From a letter written by Michael Egan, C.G.A., to Mary Andrejka of Chicago, Illinois, August 4, 1997. Egan asks if a list of gravesites exists for these lost legionnaires and whether anyone will come to care for these graves.

19. Bradley, 156.

20. Vlastnik, William Jerry, letter to the author (Peru, Jan 1998), 1.

Bibliography

Collections

American Expeditionary Forces Documents and Czech and Slovak Legion Papers. Hoover Institution Archives, Stanford University, Stanford, CA.

 Emmett Hoskins Collection. Memoirs and personal letters to family and friends.

 Ernest Lloyd Harris Collection. Photographs, letters, and communiqués, Box #1, June 1918.

 Evatsia Collection. Telegrams from the Czecho-Slovak Army to Other Echelons along the Trans-Siberian Railway, #106.

 F. A. Puchkov. "The Icy March, 1921–1922" (unpublished manuscript), 1922.

 George S. Phelps Collection. "The YMCA with the AEF in Siberia" (unpublished manuscript). 1918–1919. Box #57.

 Harry Hoskins Collection. "The Story of an Expedition" (unpublished manuscript). Personal notes and postcards.

 Nadia Shapiro. "Revolution in Blagoveshchensk" (unpublished manuscript).

 Railway Service Corps Booklet. November 11, 1922. Box #1.

 Roland Morris. *A Railway Three Nations Want*. Annual Reunion and Fifth Anniversary of the Associated Veterans of the Russian Railway Service Corps Booklet. November 11, 1922. Box #1.

 Siberia and Eastern Russia, Part I: "General Description and Introductory Information." Military Monograph Subsection, M.I.2.

 Stanley K. Hornbeck Papers. "American Expeditionary Forces in Siberia" (unpublished report).

 Stephen M. Berk. "The Coup D'État" (unpublished manuscript), 1919.

 Walter Grayson Collection. Gail Berg Reitzel. "Shifting Scenes in Siberia" (unpublished diaries). YMCA in Siberia, 1918/1919.

 William Duncan Collection. YMCA Associate Memoirs, association and personal letters, 1918–1920.

Carl W. Ackerman File, 1918–1981. Pulitzer Collection. School of Journalism, Columbia University, New York, NY.

Kautz Family YMCA Archives. University of Minnesota, Minneapolis, MN.

 Czech and Slovak Legion, AEF, and Siberian Troop correspondence, Siberia, 1917 to 1925.

 Letters and field reports from Association staff, 1915 to 1922.

 William Duncan Collection. YMCA Secretary Quarterly Reports.

Military Intelligence Division. Classified Documents. United States War Department. National Archives, Washington, DC.

 Girsa and Pavlů to American Expeditionary Forces Headquarters, Record #165.

 Handbook of Federal World War Agencies, 1917–1920.

 Hines to Cordier, Record #165.

 Ross to Cordier, Record #165.

 Rowen to Cordier, Record #165.

 Siberia and Eastern Russia, Part I: "General Description and Introductory Information." Military Monograph Subsection.

 Special Staff Records 1917 to 1921. #164–212.

 Tucker to Cordier, Record #165.

 United States Army Military Intelligence, 1917–1920.

National Archives, San Francisco Branch, San Francisco, CA.

 11th Naval District Records.

 14th Naval District Records.

Department of Military and Defense. Railways and Canals, Military Headquarters. Library and Archives, Canada.

 Report from R. P. Brown, chief accountant, to W. V. Cape, comptroller. Repatriation from Vladivostok to Europe of Czechoslovak troops. December 11, 1920.

San Diego Historical Society Archives, San Diego, CA.

Allen Henry Wright notes, 4 July 1919. Frederick Reif Marine Collection.

Czecho-Slovak Legion, July 4, 1919. San Diego Harbor Records.

Nanking, #7620, photographs 1–10. Photograph Collections.

United States Congress. Senate. Committee on the Judiciary. *Brewing and Liquor Interests and German and Bolshevik Propaganda.* 66th Congress, 1st sess., 1919. S. Res. 307 and 439.

United States Department of State. Washington, D.C.: Government Printing Office, various dates.

Lansing to Woodrow Wilson Communications: Russia. F. R. Lansing Papers, 1914–1920.

Papers Relating to the Foreign Relations of the United States, 1918: The World War.

Papers Relating to the Foreign Relations of the United States, 1919: Russia.

Papers Relating to the Foreign Relations of the United States, 1919 & 1920. Vols. 1, 2, and 3.

World War I Prisoners' Aid and Red Cross Correspondence. Donald Lowrie Papers, 1911, 1916–29, 1946–65. University of Illinois Archives, Champaign, IL.

Periodical Articles

Ankeley, Colonel William J. "An Unaccountable Accounting." *Proceedings: United States Naval Institute Journal, History Supplement* 1985.

Balawyder, A. "The Czecho-Slovak Legion Crosses Canada." *The East European Quarterly* 4, no. 2 (1920).

"The Czechoslovak Volunteers: History of Whiting, Indiana." *Nase rodina: Journal of the Czech and Slovak Genealogical Society International* 7, no. 1 (April 1993).

Harris, Ernest Lloyd. "The Truth about the Czechoslovak Legions in Siberia." *The Central European Observer* 11, no. 8 (1933).

Hudson, Geoffrey. "The Far East at the End of the First World War." *Contemporary History Journal* 4, no. 2 (April 1969).

Kennan, George F. "American Troops in Russia: The True Record." *Atlantic Monthly* 203 (January 1959).

Keyes, William. "We Are and We Shall Be: Puppetry and Czecho-Slovak Politics, 1860–1990." *Pittsburgh History: A Magazine of the City and Its Region* 1992 (Summer).

Lasch, Christopher. "American Intervention in Siberia: A Reinterpretation." *Political Science Quarterly* 77, no. 2 (June 1962).

Mamatey, Victor. "Dissolution of Austria-Hungary." *Journal of Central European Affairs* 1950 (October 10).

Rowan, William A. "The Odyssey of the Czechs." *East European Quarterly* 9, no. 1.

Smirnov, M. I. "Admiral Kolchak." *Slavonic and East European Review* 11 (January 1933).

Verner, Jaroslav J. "The Mail Goes Through: A Siberian Trip Report." *The Czechoslovak Specialist* 57, no. 2 (March/April 1999).

Zuberec, Vladimír. "Milan Rastislav Štefánik in the History of the Slovak Nation and Czechoslovakia." *Czech Life Magazine* 1992.

Newspapers

Československý deník (1918–1921)
Cleveland Plain Dealer (1988)
Los Angeles Herald-Examiner (1971)
New York Herald (1917–1920)
New York Times (1914–1922)
Pittsburgh Daily Dispatch (1918)
Pittsburgh Gazette Times (1918–1920)
Pittsburgh Post (1917–1921)
San Diego Union (1918–1920)
San Francisco Chronicle (1917–1921)
Times (London) (1915–1922)

Oral Histories

Andreyka, Mary. Interview by Joan McQuire Mohr. Chicago, IL. October 12, 1996.

Majaer, Stephanie. Interview by Joan McQuire Mohr. San Diego, CA. March 1985.

Skelnička, Joseph. Interview by Joseph Swoboda. Experiences on the Trans-Siberian Railroad, 1917 to 1920. March 18, 1977, and April 29, 1977. Czechoslovak Heritage Collection. Love Library Archives, Lincoln, NE.

Vlastnik, William. Interview by Joan McQuire Mohr. Peru, IL. May 1991.

Primary Sources

Andreyka, Mary. Letter to the author (includes Bremen shipping line inspection card #41121). June, 1998.

Baker, Ray S. *Woodrow Wilson: Life and Letters, March 1– November 11, 1918.* New York, NY: Doubleday, Doran, 1939.

Bohemia Hill Sokol Lodge #4 Committee, Pittsburgh, PA. "The Slovaks and the Pittsburgh Pact" [brochure]. Chicago, IL: Tykla Brothers Press, 1918.

Browder, Robert Paul, and Alexander F. Kerensky, eds. *The Russian Provincial Government, 1917, Documents.* Vols. 1 & 2. Palo Alto, CA: Hoover Institution Publications, 1961.

Eagan, Michael. Letter to Mary Andrejka. August 4, 1997.

Gajda, Radola. *Moje paměti: Československa Anabase*. 1920. Ann Arbor, MI: University Microfilms.

Graves, William Sydney. *America's Siberian Adventure*. New York: Jonathan Cape and Harrison Smith, 1931.

Harris, Ernest Lloyd. "The Truth about the Czechoslovak Legions in Siberia." *The Central European Observer* 11, no. 8 (1933).

Kennan, George F., "Can We Help Russia?" In *America Faces Russia: Russian-American Relations from Early Times to Our Day*, edited by Thomas Bailey. Ithaca, NY: Cornell University Press, 1950.

Klecanda, Vladimír. "Operations of the Czechoslovak Army in Russia During the Period 1917-1920." Translated by Jerry V. Matyka. *Journal of Military Science* 1921.

Masaryk, Thomas Garrigue. *The Making of a State: Memories and Observations, 1914-1918*. New York: Frederick Stokes, 1927.

Morris, Roland S. *A Railway Three Nations Want*. San Francisco: St. Francis Reunion Committee Booklet, 1922.

Tompkins, Ramsey. *A Canadian's Road to Russia: Letters from the Great War Decade*. Calgary, AB: University of Alberta Press, 1989.

Varneck, Elena, and H. H. Fisher. *The Testimony of Kolchak and Other Siberian Materials*. Translated by E. Varneck. Palo Alto, CA: Stanford University Press; London: Oxford University Press, 1935.

Vlastnik, William. "Uncle František Truhlář." Letter to the author. Peru, Illinois. January 1998.

Voska, Emanuel, and Will Irwin. *Spy and Counterspy*. New York: Doubleday, Doran, 1940.

Wright, Henry Allen. "Source Notes Taken as an Eyewitness Account of the Docking of the Czech Legion on the Ship *Nanking* in San Diego Harbor, July 4, 1919." San Diego, CA.

Reference Books

Ackerman, Carl A. *Source Records of the Great War*. Edited by Charles F. Horne. Vol. 7. Indianapolis, IN: The American Legion, 1931.

The Times History of the War. Vols. 2 and 20. London: The Times, 1915, 1919.

The New York Times Current History of the European War. Vol. 16. New York: New York Times, 1918.

Secondary Sources

Baerlein, Henry. *The March of the Seventy Thousand*. London: Leonard Parsons, 1926.

Bečvář, Gustav. *The Lost Legion*. London: Standley Paul, 1939.

Berenger, Jean. *A History of the Habsburg Empire, 1273-1700*. Translated by C. A. Simpson. New York, NY: Longman, 1994.

Bobrick, Benson. *East of the Sun*. New York: Poseidon Press, 1992.

Bradley, John. *The Czechoslovak Legion in Russia, 1914-1920*. New York: Columbia University Press, 1991.

Brinkley, George A. *The Volunteer Army and Allied Intervention in South Russia, 1917-1921*. [Notre Dame]: University of Notre Dame, 1966.

Brook-Shepherd, Gordon. *Archduke of Sarajevo: The Romance and Tragedy of Franz Ferdinand of Austria*. Boston: Little, Brown, 1989.

Browning, Tatiana, and Kyril FitzLyon. *Before the Revolution*. Woodstock, NY: The Overlook Press, 1978.

Bunyan, James. *Intervention, Civil War, and Communism in Russia, April-December, 1918: Documents and Materials*. Baltimore, MD: John Hopkins University Press, 1976.

Čápek, Karel. *Talks with T.G. Masaryk*. Edited by Michael Henry Heim. Translated by Dora Round. North Haven, CT: Catbird Press, 1995.

Conolly, Violet. *Siberia Today and Tomorrow*. New York: Taplinger, 1976.

Cremonesi, Gordon. *The Russian Army in World War I*. London: Gordon Cremonesi, 1975.

Dedijer, Vladimír. *The Road to Sarajevo*. New York: Simon and Schuster, 1966.

Dotsenko, Paul. *The Struggle for a Democracy in Siberia, 1917-1920*. Palo Alto, CA: Hoover Institution Press, 1983.

Dvornik, Francis. *The Slavs in European History and Civilization*. New Brunswick, NJ: Rutgers University Press, 1962.

Ferrell, Robert H. *Woodrow Wilson and World War I, 1917-1921*. New York: Harper & Row, 1985.

Fic, Victor M. *The Collapse of American Policy in Russia and Siberia, 1918*. Boulder, CO: East European Monographs, 1995.

Fleming, Peter. *The Fate of Admiral Kolchak*. New York: Harcourt Brace and World, 1963.

Goldhurst, Richard. *The Midnight War*. New York: McGraw-Hill, 1978.

Heald, Edward T. *Witness to Revolution: Letters from Russia, 1916-1919*. Kent, OH: Kent State University Press, 1972.

Hoyt, Edwin P. *The Army without a Country*. New York: Macmillan, 1967.

Imrey, Ference. *Through Blood and Ice*. New York: E. P. Dutton, 1930.

Kahn, Robert A. *Dynasty, Politics, and Culture, Selected Essays*. Edited by Stanley B. Winters. Boulder, CO: Social Science Monographs, 1991.

Kelley, David. *The Czech Fascist Movement,*

1922–1942. Boulder, CO: East European Monographs, 1995.

Kennan, George F. *Russia and the West under Lenin and Stalin*. Boston: Little Brown, 1961.

Kolko, Gabriel. *Main Currents in Modern American History*. New York: Harper & Row, 1976.

Kuranov, V. *The Trans-Siberian Express*. Translated by Anatol Kagan. New York: Sphinx Press, 1980.

La Feber, Walter. *The New Empire: An Interpretation of American Expansion, 1860–1898*. Ithaca, NY: Cornell University Press, 1963.

Lengyel, Emil. *Siberia*. Garden City, NY: Garden City Publishing, 1943.

Macartney, C. A. *The Habsburg Empire, 1790–1918*. New York: Macmillan, 1969.

Mamatey, Victor S. *The Rise of the Habsburg Empire, 1526–1815*. New York: Holt, Rinehart and Winston, 1971.

Manning, Clarence A. *The Siberian Fiasco*. New York: Library Publishers, 1952.

Martínek, Josef. *One Hundred Years of the CSA: The History of the Czechoslovak Society of America, 1854–1954*. Translated by R. A. Gorman. Cicero, IL: Cicero-Berwyn, 1985.

Miller, Kenneth D. *The Czecho-Slovaks in America*. New York: George H. Doran, 1922.

Morley, James William. *The Japanese Thrust into Siberia, 1918*. New York: Columbia University Press, 1957.

Nekrasov, George. *North of Galipoli: The Black Sea Fleet at War, 1914–1917*. Boulder, CO: East European Monographs, 1992.

Palmer, Alan. *The Lands Between*. New York: Macmillan, 1969.

Poche, Emanuel. *Portrait of Prague*. London: Hamlyn, 1969.

Polišenský, J. V. *History of Czechoslovakia in Outline*. Prague: Bohemia International, 1991.

Rutherford, Ward. *The Russian Army in World War I*. London: Gordon Cremonesi, 1975.

Steinberg, Mark, and Vladimír M. Khrustalev. *The Fall of the Romanovs: Political Dreams and Personal Struggles in a Time of Revolution*. New Haven, CT: Yale University Press, 1995.

Strakhovsky, Leonid I. *The Origins of American Intervention in North Russia, 1918*. Princeton, NJ: Princeton University Press, 1937.

Svidine, Nicholas. *Cossack Gold: The Secret of the White Army Treasure*. Translated by Leonard Mayhew. Boston: Little, Brown, 1973.

Taylor, A. J. P. *The Hapsburg Monarchy, 1809–1918*. London: Hamish Hamilton, 1951.

Tupper, Harmon. *To the Great Ocean*. Boston: Little Brown, 1965.

Unterberger, Betty. *America's Siberian Expedition, 1918–1920*. Durham, NC: Duke University Press, 1956.

_____. *The United States, Revolutionary Russia, and the Rise of Czechoslovakia*. Chapel Hill, NC: University of North Carolina, 1989.

Vaněk, Otakar, Volta Holeček, and Rudolf Medek. *Za svobodu: obrázkova kronika československého revolučního hnutí na Rusi, 1914–1920*. Prague: Nakladem Pamatniku odboje, 1929.

Warth, Robert D. *Nicholas II: The Life and Reign of Russia's Last Monarch*. London: Praeger, 1997.

Washburn, Stanley. *On the Russian Front in World War I: Memoirs of an American War Correspondent*. New York: Robert Speller and Sons, 1982.

White, John Albert. *The Siberian Intervention*. Princeton, NJ: Princeton University Press, 1950.

Wickham Steed, Henry. *Through Thirty Years*. Garden City, NY: Doubleday, 1925.

Williams, William Appleton. *The Tragedy of American Diplomacy*. New York: Dell, 1959.

Winter, Jay, and Blaine Baggett. *The Great War and the Shaping of the 20th Century*. New York: Penguin, 1996.

Wiskemann, Elizabeth. *Czechs and Germans: A Study of the Historic Provinces of Bohemia and Moravia*. Oxford: Oxford University Press, 1938.

Wolfe, Bertram D. *Three Who Made a Revolution: A Biographical History*. New York: Stein and Day, 1984.

Wright, George Frederick. *Asiatic Russia*. Vol. 2. New York: McClure, Phillips, 1902.

Yurchak, Peter. *The Slovaks: Their History and Traditions*. Whiting, IN: Obrana Press Inc. 1947.

Zeman, Zbyněk. *The Masaryks: The Making of Czechoslovakia*. London: Weidenfeld and Nicholson, 1976.

Unpublished Manuscripts

Miller, Daniel Edward. "Antonín Švehla and the Czechoslovak Republican Party, 1918–1933." Thesis, History Department, University of Pittsburgh, 1989.

Potach, Steven. "The Role of the Czechoslovak Legion in Allied Policy Toward Russia, 1918." Graduate seminar paper, History Department, University of Minnesota, 1975.

Steuer, Kenneth Andrew. "The Pursuit of an 'Unparalleled Opportunity': The American YMCA and Prisoner-of-War Diplomacy Among the Central Power Nations During World War I, 1914–1923." PhD diss., University of Minnesota, 1998.

Index

Numbers in **_bold italics_** indicate pages with photographs.

CPSIA information can be obtained
at www.ICGtesting.com
Printed in the USA
BVHW040624130223
658289BV00009B/1187